AMERICAN EAGLES

Second Edition

Boeing bombers from different eras overfly the NMUSAF: B-17s in 2016 and B-52s in 2022.

AMERICAN EAGLES
Second Edition

A History of the United States Air Force

Featuring the Collection of the National Museum of the U.S. Air Force

Dan Patterson, Clinton Terry

Based on Original Text by Air-Vice Marshal Ron Dick, RAF

Foreword by Colonel Eileen M. Collins,
USAF, Retired, NASA Astronaut and Space Shuttle Commander

LYONS
PRESS

Essex, Connecticut

LYONS PRESS

An imprint of The Globe Pequot Publishing Group, Inc.
64 South Main Street
Essex, CT 06426
www.GlobePequot.com

Distributed by NATIONAL BOOK NETWORK

Photographs copyright © 2023 by Dan Patterson
Text copyright © 1997, 2023 by Ron Dick and Clinton Terry
First Lyons Press paperback edition 2025

British Library Cataloguing in Publication Information available

Library of Congress Cataloging-in-Publication Data

Names: Patterson, Dan, 1953– author. | Terry, Clinton, author. | Dick, Ron, 1931– author.
Title: American eagles : a history of the United States Air Force featuring the collection of the National Museum of the U.S. Air Force / Dan Patterson, Clinton Terry, Ron Dick.
Other titles: History of the United States Air Force featuring the collection of the National Museum of the U.S. Air Force
Description: Second edition. | Lanham, MD : Lyons Press, [2023] | "Based on Original Text by Air-Vice Marshal Ron Dick, RAF." | Includes bibliographical references and index.
Identifiers: LCCN 2023046259 (print) | LCCN 2023046260 (ebook) | ISBN 9781493072958 (hardcover) | ISBN 9781493092499 (paperback) | ISBN 9781493085491 (epub)
Subjects: LCSH: United States. Air Force—History. | United States. Army Air Forces—History. | Aeronautics, Military—United States—History. | National Museum of the United States Air Force.
Classification: LCC UG633 .D532 2023 (print) | LCC UG633 (ebook) | DDC 358.400973—dc23/ eng/20231006
LC record available at https://lccn.loc.gov/2023046259
LC ebook record available at https://lccn.loc.gov/2023046260

Cover: *The Boeing B-17 Memphis Belle, restored after a 10 year effort, commands the World War II Gallery.*

Facing page:
North American B-1 cockpit.

Facing page, Table of Contents:
Boeing P-12, restored in 1982

Printed in India

Contents

Foreword

Colonel Eileen M. Collins, USAF, Retired
NASA Astronaut and Space Shuttle Commander

Father, Faster, Higher

My connection to aviation began when I was a young child, in Elmira, NY. I attended summer camp at Harris Hill, which today is the site of the National Soaring Museum. During camp activities, I looked skyward at the tow planes which carried gliders to a high altitude where they were released, allowing them to turn and "dance" among the afternoon thermals. I wanted to be part of it, but flying lessons were out of the question, as my family skimped by on a tight budget. Fortunately, my Irish American parents had a sense of adventure. My father took the four of us children to the glider field, as well as the local Elmira-Corning Regional Airport, for some no-cost entertainment: watching gliders and airliners take off and land.

My mother routinely took us to the Elmira Steele-Memorial library, where I would always leave with a stack of books. At some point, I found the section on flying. As I became a teenager, I read books with exciting titles like: Fate is the Hunter (Ernest Gann), God is my Copilot (Robert Scott), and The Stars at Noon (Jackie Cochran). My aviator heroes were men like Eddie Rickenbacker, Billy Mitchell, Robin Olds, Pappy Boyington, Iven Kincheloe, Chuck Yeager, and Lance Sijan. And the Women Airforce Service Pilots (WASPs) most certainly made me realize there was a path for young women to serve.

I learned about the Gemini astronauts at about age nine, while reading a Junior Scholastic magazine in my 4th grade class. I wanted to be just like them! Although it was obvious to me that all the astronauts were men, I remembered the WASPs and their incredible service, and thought: "I will become be a lady astronaut!"

I came to admire pilots and astronauts, of all backgrounds, and like them, I wanted to go farther, faster, and higher!

The first time I sat in an airplane was at age 19 at my Air Force ROTC summer camp basic training. The cadets took turns strapping into the cockpit of an A-7. The climb up the ladder, the dirty switches, the instruments, smell of JP-4 fuel, the noise of the flightline, and the feel of being part of the action, made me realize that this was going to be the life for me!

As I read more and more aviation history, I was fascinated by the F-100 series of aircraft, and how their development showed the progress of the Air Force's operational needs, the evolution of aerospace engineering designs, and the ability of aircraft to fly farther, faster, and higher.

I imagined myself in each of those aircraft, above the clouds, high up and far away from the problems on planet Earth, looking down upon cities or seeing distant oceans or polar ice caps. I knew the sky would be a very dark blue at such high altitudes. The air would be cold and thin, and the horizon hundreds of miles away. In a single seat jet fighter, I would be alone in the world, like a Greek god flying over a planet, or an angel playing in the clouds. All while serving and defending the United States of America, a country which gave me opportunities that no other country in the world could offer.

In 1976, the Air Force began a test program at Williams AFB, AZ, by selecting 10 active duty women as the first to attend Undergraduate Pilot Training (UPT). Then, my dream came true in 1978, when the Air Force decided to continue the program, based on the successful progress of these women. I was selected as one of 10 college seniors, who would be the first women to attend UPT immediately after college. In addition, four of us would be the first women at Vance AFB, in Enid, OK. Upon completion, I stayed at Vance for another 3 ½ years, as the first (and at the time, the only) T-38 women instructor. Eventually, the Air Force successfully completed the test program, and fully integrated the women into the flight schools, and all non-combatant aircraft. It was not until 1993 that women were allowed to qualify in combat aircraft.

While living in northwestern Oklahoma, I bought a small house on the edge of town. With no city lights nearby, the sky was so dark that I could see the Milky Way galaxy. I enjoyed the view of the night sky so much, that I bought a few telescopes and memorized the stars and constellations. I later learned that no matter where I was in the world, the sky was familiar, and made me feel close to the explorers of centuries ago, who looked at the same patterns in the night sky. I became curious about the origin, nature, and destination of our universe.

Perhaps many generations from now, pilots will be training to go places in the Milky Way galaxy, flying in ships yet to be imagined. How could I, an Air Force pilot in the age of Star Wars, be a part of that future?

Fifteen years after my wonderous encounters with the clear night sky, I had the honor of flying my first mission to Earth orbit, as a United States NASA astronaut, and Air Force test pilot. The goal of STS-63 (Feb 1995) was to perform the first rendezvous with the Russian MIR Space Station, and test the shuttle's flying, communication, and navigation techniques. We were setting the stage for the following flight which would dock with MIR, as part of the United States goal of eventually building an international space station. Our other objectives included performing a spacewalk, deploying an astronomy satellite, and performing dozens of smaller scientific experiments.

My dream of flying in space had come true, with the excitement of a space shuttle launch, the challenge of a mission, the satisfaction of successful teamwork among our flight crew, and the hard work and dedication of the support crews on the ground. I believe spaceflight will be more and more common, partly due to the remarkable human sensation of just "being" in space. The human experience is presented in both the nature of microgravity and its effect on the human body, as well as the visual beauty of looking back at the Earth from space. (Note: The international space station is about 250 miles above earth, orbits with a 51 degree inclination to the equator, speeds over the surface at 18,500 mph, and circles the earth once every 90 minutes). Over my four flights to Earth orbit, I have learned what a beautiful unique planet we live on, but also how alone we are in the universe. As I looked out at the curved horizon of earth, I realized that the giant sphere below us is an oasis in the middle of nowhere. I could not help but reflect on the many civilizations that existed on the surface below me. I thought about Earth's history: the wars, the migration of peoples, the rise and fall of rulers and kingdoms, the early explorers that sailed the Mediterranean, the great explorers of the Middle Ages, who were taking great risks while looking for new lands or new trade. I realized I had flown over top of billions of people, each person with their own plans, problems, and daily concerns.

I believe that the greatest, most inspirational mission of tomorrow, is that of space exploration and human spaceflight. I feel very fortunate to have lived on what seems like a "bridge" in aviation history. On one side, I was able to personally learn from people involved in the early development of aircraft and spacecraft, and on the other side, I can pass along my life lessons to future aircraft and spacecraft designers. With the advent of automation and artificial intelligence, the future is looking remarkably different. Regardless, the lessons from our past are still applicable to our future, and we should never forget those.

I hope many people, young and old, will enjoy this beautiful photographic collection of airplanes, art, and memorabilia, and therefore live the story of our daring and brave aviators who took immense risks while serving our great United States of America. I know readers will draw inspiration from generations of fearless fighters and adventure seekers, those with a competitive spirit and a mission they believed in, and a passion for flight. I also hope that many young people will read this collection will be inspired to follow the example of our aerospace designers, engineers, mechanics, pilots, navigators, weapons system officers, and all those who work in the air and space community, and set their sights on flying farther, faster, and higher!

Eileen Collins, May 2023

Foreword
Original from American Eagles, 1st Edition, by General Robin Olds, USAF

How I loved and admired that father of mine. Back in the 1920s and '30s he and his Air Corps friends, all WWI vet erans - Andrews, Spaatz, McNarney, Kenney, Knerr, Eubank, George - men of steel in planes of wood - would gather at one another's homes on a Saturday night at Langley Field. Their merriment drifted to the top of the stairs, where this little boy sat entranced by songs of "Mademoiselle from Armentieres" and the sad fate of people called Kiwis, whoever they were. "Tooey" Spaatz strummed the guitar and my Dad played the piano, both with a degree of un certainty, but with great gusto. They sang and talked - talked of flying in the early days, of today, and of their hopes and dreams for the future.

As I matured and my perceptions deepened, I began to understand the mean ing of those dreams. The memories of WWI underlay their determination to change things. No more would there be the horrors of the trenches, of stalemate, of attack and counterattack with thousands of casualties and no discernible gain. They would carry the war to the enemy, attack his industrial base and his lines of communication. They would destroy his transportation system, and they would erode his will to fight - all from the air, and with aircraft not yet built.

When publicly revealed, those ambitions garnered the thinkers scorn and downright resentment. My Dad and his Air Corps contemporaries were looked upon as lightweight "flyboys," whose limited capabilities were of no consequence in the grand scheme of land and sea warfare. Airmen could not occupy territory, nor rule the sea-lanes. Therefore what good were they, except to provide eyes for the real forces, and to try to deny those same eyes to the enemy. As for bombing, it was laughingly admitted that the Air Corps could probably penetrate enemy territory, but not much farther than good artillery, and certainly not as accurately nor as devastatingly. The Navy brass hadn't been impressed when Billy Mitchell sank the Ostfriesland. They claimed the test had been set up. There was no opposition, the target was anchored close to shore, and the release altitude un realistically low. In a practical sense, the Navy was right. But it had proved possible to sink a dreadnought with explosives from the air, and that lesson was not entirely lost on the admirals.

And so it went throughout the decade of the 1920s and into the mid-'30s. Aviation and aviators were viewed with awed amusement, particularly by those who occupied the hallowed seats of government. On reviewing the Air Corps segment of the Army's annual budget request, President Coolidge is said to have asked why the service didn't buy just one airplane and let the aviators take turns flying it. At one point those same visionaries had even attempted to enforce a caveat that the Air Corps should not acquire any airplane having a flight range in excess of one day's march by the infantry. Failing in that, the combined ef forts of the armchair generals and the battle

ship admirals managed for a while to re strict the airmen to operating no more than 100 miles from the coasts of the United States. General Billy Mitchell was court martialed for his outspoken belief in the future of air power and for his criticism of those who would deny that potential. The trial outraged his followers and encouraged them to greater effort. Progress was painstakingly slow. Technology could not yet provide the airframes and engines to match the dream.

All that time the threat to world peace became ever more evident. Germany reacted to the harsh terms of the Treaty of Versailles, let Hitler take power, began re arming and, with scarcely any opposition from her former enemies, marched troops into the Rhineland. The die was cast.

When Hitler struck Poland, per haps no nation was more shocked than America. Our Army and Navy were seen to be living in the past. Horse cavalry? Coast artillery? Battleships with great towers so that the lookout could see farther than the admiral on the bridge? A handful of aircraft carriers as a concession to the Navy's flyboys? In the Air Corps, our pilots still flew in open cockpits. But there was encouragement, however little and however late. By 1937 we had B-l 7s, all thirteen of them. They flew faster and higher than our so-called pursuit planes, and that suggested another problem. As a result we were blessed with the P-40, which was the best we could do at the time.

While Britain gallantly went it alone, America had time to build. Yet we were not fully ready when Japan struck Pearl Harbor. It took another two years to reach the point where America's air power could be said to have a meaningful impact on the campaigns being waged over Europe and Asia, and in the Pacific. Then vast fleets of bombers, escorted by hundreds of long range fighters, struck the enemy heartlands. Men dropped from the sky into battle. Remote forces were supplied by trains of cargo aircraft. The giant stirred and the old dreams became reality. Eventually Ger many crumbled and it was admitted that Allied air power had done much to bring about the defeat. In the Pacific a combined onslaught by sea, land, and air moved us inexorably towards the Japanese homeland. Then came Hiroshima and Nagasaki, and the world could never be the same.

Nuclear capability suddenly dominated all military thinking. The Air Force created Strategic Air Command and thought of itself as all-powerful. New docOls Forward trinal battles raged in Congress and the halls of the Pentagon. The Oval Office became directly involved. President Eisenhower theorized that a large, strategic nuclear force could provide for the common defense of the nation and its allies. Such a defensive deterrent plan was thought to be cost-effective, permitting the downsizing of the Army and Navy, and those Air Force commands other than SAC. A few dissenting voices, wise as they were, went unheeded. In short order, the main thrust of the Air Force was nuclear. It was proclaimed by none other than the Chief of Army Air Force Plans that the _atomic bomb made conventional warfare-and tactical air power "as old-fashioned as the Maginot Line."

We thought we had gained a lasting global peace, but the world divided to West and East. By 1949, the Soviets had the atomic bomb and the game was on in earnest. Each side strove to outdo the other in the arena of nuclear bragging rights:
"We have more missiles than you."
"No, you don't."
"We can make ours intercontinental."
"So can we."
"But ours are more accurate." "

Maybe, but we have ten warheads on each missile -   try to top that." "Yeah -well, we have nuclear armed submarines and you can't find them. And we have nuclear armed air craft surrounding you.

So there!"

On it went, to the point where the whole game was to out-shout the other fel ow, make him fear your capability, recog nize your readiness, and respect your determination. At the same time, each side had to make sure the other knew it was not in tending to use the destructive forces being flaunted. "Peace is our Profession" was the SAC motto. Admittedly, all of this worked, far better than the well-intended efforts of the anti-nuke soapbox orators. Unbridled nuclear warfare did not, has not, and will not occur. If one nuclear missile had ever been launched in anger, the whole system would have failed in its single role, which was NEVER TO BE USED.

Meanwhile, in spite of lessons learned (and quickly forgotten) in Korea, planning for an effective conventional air power ca-pability in the USAF languished. The emphasis was unasham-edly nuclear. The bulk of the annual Air Force budget was dedicated to the provision and deploy ment of nuclear-capable men and machines. The world lived in the shadow of interna tional suicide under apocalyptic labels devised by angry men on the thrones of power
- massive retaliation, assured second strike, preemptive strike, graduated response - spine-tingling, knee-jerking terms affect-ing every facet of civilization and every human life.

Tactical Air Command, dominated and commanded by bomb-er adherents, embraced the nuclear strike role to survive. The F-100 was not as capable in its intended air combat role as was the F-86H it replaced. It even proved to be a mediocre per-former in the ground support role. The next in line, the F-105, was de signed as a nuclear strike fighter, complete with bomb bay. Pressed into a conventional role by circumstance, it was to_ prove in valuable over North Vietnam. There it was joined by the F-4, a Navy fleet interceptor hurriedly purchased by the USAF because no Air Force aircraft matched its capability. A ghost from the 1930s, that grand old lady, the C-47 "Gooney

Bird," was resurrected to join the fighting in South Vietnam, as was another Naval aircraft, the huge propeller-driven A-1. That these diverse air craft were so successfully employed in Southeast Asia is more to the credit of the air and ground crews than to the vision of the planners in the Pentagon.

Vietnam, ghastly as it was, can be credited with forcing a re-evaluation of the role and mission of air power. Nuclear armed B-52s were given a piece of the conventional action, and carpet bombing jungle-clad mountains became the rage. Practicing a policy of limited response, America's leaders denied our forces decisive action. Instead of cutting off the head of the snake, the Air Force was relegated to chopping away at the tail, which only grew longer and longer as time passed. Our departure from Vietnam was not a military defeat, but one of political policy.
Over the past fifty years and more what we have learned, sometimes slowly, often reluctantly, is that the greater and more massive the nuclear threat and counter-threat, the less likely its use, and the more likely the advent of conventional wars and confrontations. Nuclear power, rather than deterring all conflict, serves only to deter itself No missile has ever been fired, and no nuclear bomb has been dropped, thanks to the dedication and personal sacrifice of men and women in uni-form on both sides of the East- West divide. Though we must maintain a nuclear posture for the foreseeable future, the prov-en likelihood of conflict is that of iron bombs and bullets, and, in the 1990s, for the first time since I 945, America became truly ready to face that challenge. Just ask Saddam.

Let the faces and actions of the people in this book tell the story in full. Think of the security guard walking his lonely vigil in the sub-zero cold of Minot AFB, of the maintenance, supply, and armament people working to keep the force instantly ready, of the cooks and clerks and administrative troops who make it all work. Put yourself in the cockpit of a B-52 or a KC-135 that flew the Arctic Circle on Look ing Glass alert, facing a grim, direct threat; there because world tension had reached a point of near explosion and the words fly ing between Washington and Moscow needed the force of reality. Think of the men and women who, even today, spend half of each year deployed somewhere far away. Consider their families who wait, knowing their loved ones are there to make America's presence felt, to preserve the peace, but ready to fight if need be. Re member the fighter pilots who have flown hundreds of hours in combat in the battles we could not call wars. Recall with agony those who languished in the dank cells of Hanoi for endless years. These men and women, in their own way, served their country with steadfast loyalty, with uncomplaining devotion, and with pride. We owe them an immeasurable debt of gratitude.

Robin Olds
Steamboat Springs, Colorado May 1997

Introduction

Twenty-five years ago, my colleague Dan Patterson and retired Air Vice-Marshal of the RAF, Ron Dick, collaborated to produce the first edition of American Eagles, a single-volume illustrated history of the United States Air Force (USAF), to celebrate the fiftieth anniversary of its founding. Ron's text and Dan's photographs told the story of American military aviation from the first Wright Flyer to the end of the 20th century. The second edition of American Eagles revisits some of the topics featured in the first edition but condenses and adds to the narrative while looking at some of the dramatic changes that the 21st century has forced the USAF to address as it defends the United States and wages its military conflicts in the air.

Ron Dick passed away in 2008. Prior to his retirement in 1988, Ron served as Head of the British Defence Staff stationed in Washington, DC. In that retirement, he and Dan got together to combine Dan's aircraft photography with Ron's encyclopedic knowledge of aviation and its history. The original book remains available, a testament to the enduring quality of both the text and the photographs.

In the second edition, I join Dan by updating the text of the first edition. As the reader will quickly see, I have drawn heavily on Ron's original text, condensing it somewhat to accommodate a stronger emphasis on the aircraft and the people who are and have been responsible for what the USAF was and has become. I have tried to retain Ron's narrative style as much as possible given the differences in time, place, and background.

Dan and I began as professional colleagues some thirty-five years ago and quickly became friends. In the interim, I moved on from the world of business to pursue an advanced degree in history, well into middle age. I come to this enterprise from that world of academic history instead of military service. I am, at this writing, professor of history and liberal studies at Mercer University in Macon, GA, where I have taught for the last twenty-one years. Two of my teaching fields and fields of study are the history of technology and the history of war, both of which contribute heavily to this study. Technologies, of course, are much more than inventions, things, gadgets, or innovations. Technologies are ultimately cultural systems that change the way humans live in their world and interact with each other. War, I argue to my students, has a similar function. It is its own agent of change, change through violence. In a long career of studying war as an agent of change I often wonder why humans are so ready to use war as a means of conflict resolution when it has such a poor record of actually resolving conflict. Technology and war have gone hand in hand since prehistory, and this volume, in its emphasis on the ongoing innovation of military aviators, attests to the importance of addressing the next imagined dilemma.

One of the important backstories to the narrative is the need to keep military preparedness and political considerations independent of each other to the extent that is possible. In the wake of the World War, the United States chose a path toward isolation at the exact time the lessons of the war might have been directed toward investigating solutions to the problem of integrating air power into the American way of prosecuting war. At the end of World War II, with the political, economic, and ideological threat of a bipolar world upon the nation, it took the nation five years to arrive at the realization reflected by NSC-68: that US no longer had the luxury of enjoying the isolation two vast oceans provided. In the wake of the September 11, 2001 attacks, the United States received a shocking reminder that enemies might not be nation-states, and countering their aggression might call for new inventive responses.

This book represents, then, an updated tribute to the men and women who defend and fight for the United States of America on the 75th Anniversary of the founding of the USAF as a separate branch of the nation's military. It is the story of people who dedicated themselves to something more important than themselves.

Clinton Terry
North Bend, Ohio
March 30, 2023

Preface

This new book proves that you never know what's going to happen when the phone rings, and has been an unexpected opportunity to renew and update the first large book that Ron Dick and I undertook and published in 1997.

When the phone rang in 1994 it was Ron calling about the opportunity to bid on the official book for the U.S. Air Force's 50th in 1997. We made the bid and were awarded a contract. Then the reality set in: actually creating what became a 464 page full color book.

Twenty-five plus years later I must once again say thanks to Ross Howell of the now gone Howell Press for believing in the book and in our work. I must also give a shout out to some other colleagues who helped make the journey from an idea to the first edition of American Eagles. Canadian author Donald Nijboer was a great sounding board. And thanks to my late Dad Bill Patterson, who taught me design and typography and how to stay focused when working toward an ambitious goal.

I must say here that working with Ron Dick, retired Air-Vice Marshal with the RAF was a privilege and a completely wonderful experience. Together we published 17 books over 16 years. Ron died in 2008 and that left a large void in the lives of all who knew him. A good friend told me later in 2008, "what you guys did would be considered an entire career, I don't imagine you're gonna quit." I certainly did not quit.

Now almost thirty years since we started down the road of the first edition, producing this second edition has been another wonderful experience. Rick Rinehart, our publisher gave me a few guidelines and a very ambitious timeline: a slightly smaller book, fewer pages, more photos, and and an updated history of the Air

Force, once again illustrating it with the collection at the National Museum of the United States Air Force. He encouraged me to use as many of the original photos and weave the project together with new images made at the Museum.

The new images made at the Museum have been another wonderful experience. The collaboration with Museum photographer, Ty Greenlees, has been a partnership of professionals demonstrating our passion for making excellent photographs of these "sculptures that fly." The book is a seamless combination of images made twenty-five years ago and images made just yesterday.

The guidelines were actually pretty open and we collectively decided to include many more portraits of the people who made the U.S.A.F., and the Army Air Forces before, come to life. Ron and I talked often that these flying machines did not spring out of the ground. Human beings invented them, engineered them, built them, flew them, and many died in them. The stories of human achievement surpass the hardware that is left behind.

Dan Patterson, April 1st 2023.

13

"The Wrights were well aware that flying machines would likely drop explosives on their journey to the millennium, and they were not pacifists enough to let that prospect keep them from selling the machine to soldiers,"

James Tobin, To Conquer the Air: The Wright Brothers and the Great Race for Flight.

Still, the first client for their would-be instrument for peace was none other than the U.S. Army. Under contract in 1909, the Wrights built the two-seat, 735-pound Wright Military Flyer, the world's first military airplane. It was designated Signal Corps Airplane No. 1 and cost the Army $30,000.

Johnathon E. Briggs, Baltimore Sun

"On July 20, 1969, when Neil Armstrong, another American born and raised in western Ohio, stepped onto the moon, he carried with him, in tribute to the Wright brothers, a small swatch of the muslin from a wing of their 1903 Flyer."

David McCullough, The Wright Brothers

The dream of flying like birds had been a part of the human quest to expand its ability to understand and dominate the natural environment from the advent of civilization. Greek, Roman, Hindu, and Chinese religion and mythology all included flight as a natural extension of the human experience. The Roman poet, Ovid, predicted human flight as a natural extension of mankind's

But it would be well into the 18th century before lighter than air flight became possible and heavier than air flight remained practically impossible, even unpowered flight, for most of the 19th century. But the second and third waves of the industrial revolution, the advent of inexpensive high-quality steel and electrical technologies, opened the world to exciting new possibilities. The idea

Orville Wright's Korona V Field Camera and lens projected the image of the first flight in 1903 onto the camera's ground glass.

practical understanding of the world around it. Leonardo da Vinci studied the anatomy of birds, making drawings of how humans might duplicate avian flight with wings of wood and fabric.

of a drivable land vehicle, the automobile, attracted hundreds who tried to capitalize on the opportunity.

Powered flight attracted only a few visionaries. Clement Ader managed to get a steam-engine powered airplane off the ground without controls in 1890 and Hiram

16

Maxim, designed an enormous piece of machinery that barely got off the ground in 1894. Samuel Langley was in the active stages of creating a workable airplane when the brothers Wright completed their first flight at Kitty Hawk, North Carolina. Otto Lilienthal and Octave Chanute added much to the study of flight and aerodynamics, Chanute publishing a comprehensive volume on

the history and technical of aviation in 1894.

Wilbur and Orville Wright joined the quest to fly in the 1890s. Unlike the others, at least to that point, the Wrights concentrated on controlling flight. Noticing how buzzards changed wing shape as they glided the

brothers became convinced that what became known as wing-warping would allow them to control the aircraft in flight. By 1902, they had worked out that a vertical stabilizer, the rudder, allowed them to control the glider in banked turns as the pilot deflected the wing shape through a cable and pulley system. Having a practical and predicable airframe, the brothers turned their attention to the powerplant.

Two specific problems had to be addressed; powered flight required an internal combustion engine light enough for the glider frame and a propeller or propellers to turn engine power into effective forward propulsion. Charlie Taylor, who served as mechanic for the Wright's bicycle shop, invented a suitable engine, using cast iron cylinders meshed with an aluminum block to save weight. The engine proved to be a true innovation, the first to combine a lightweight block with the strength of iron cylinders. Water cooled, the finished engine produced twelve horsepower at 1090 rpm. If the engine was an engineering marvel, the propellers were works of art. Using boat propellers as their model, the brothers came to view propellers, as Ron Dick said in the first volume of American Eagles, "as wings moving through the air along a helical path in the vertical plane." Set behind the wing to avoid spoiling the airflow, the propellers completed the aircraft.

The story of December 17, 1903 has been told any number of times, but was relatively poorly documented at the time. No press accompanied the Wrights to Kitty Hawk and while there, the brother spent little time and effort into recording their accomplishments. Nevertheless, by the end of day, they had completed four successful flights, the last a full 59 seconds in duration. Powered flight in a heavier than air aircraft had become a reality. The original flyer never flew again. Flipped over by a strong gust of wind, the flyer could not be repaired in the field.

Once back in Dayton, the Wrights improved their invention with a more powerful engine and aeronautical improvements. At Huffman Prairie, an eighty-acre field east of Dayton and now part of Wright Patterson AFB, the Wrights build a second flyer in 1904 and a third in 1905. By the end of the year they could fly precise patterns and stay aloft as long as the onboard fuel supply held out, some 38 minutes in early October. Flyer III, in the words of Ron Dick, "was the first practical flying machine," at a time when no other would-be aviator had achieved even the most rudimentary success.

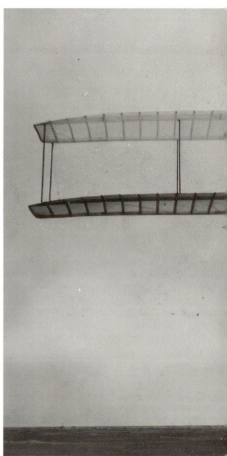

This page: *The Museum's replica of the Wrights' wind tunnel. Their experiments with this first aeronautical method of exact observations provided them with the first principles of successful manned flight.*

Below left: *The Wrights' patent drawing for their 1902 flying machine.*
Above: *The Wright 1902 glider proved their airfoil theories to be correct. They flew this glider more than 1,000 times as they learned to fly.*

These multiple exposures of the Museum's 1909 Military Flyer illustrate the Wrights' solutions to three-axis control of a flying machine.

Top right: *The canard moved up and down to provide pitch control*
Center: *The wings warp to provide roll control*
Bottom right: *The rudder moves to the left and right to provide yaw control.*

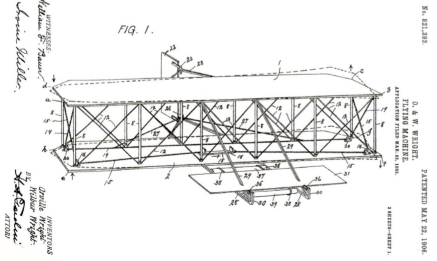

FIG. 1.

No. 821,393.

O. & W. WRIGHT.
FLYING MACHINE.
APPLICATION FILED MAR. 23, 1903.

PATENTED MAY 22, 1906.

2 SHEETS—SHEET 1.

WITNESSES

INVENTORS
Orville Wright
Wilbur Wright
BY
ATTOR.

18

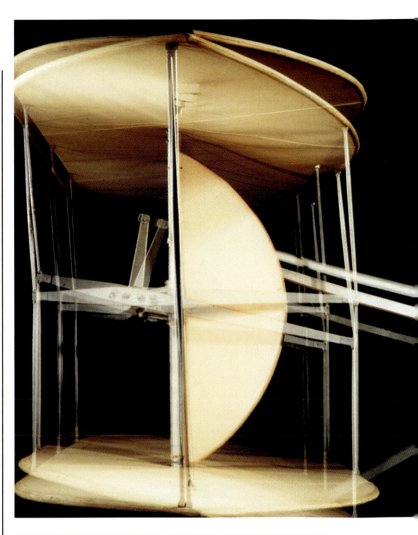

Eager to protect their invention and earn some return on their considerable investment, the brothers applied for patents and offered to sell machines to the American and British governments. Neither responded enthusiastically and the Wrights spend more than two years out of the public eye, improving the engine and building aircraft, but not flying.

The brothers had focused on building their powered aircraft as an extension of their gliders which used cables and pulleys to deflect the trailing edges of the wing, allow the pilot to control the aircraft aloft. They came to this concept, which became known as wing warping, by observing how birds glided. Wing warping had its limitations however. The structural framework of the wing had to be controllably flexible, which limited its overall strength and required the pilot to constantly "fly" the airplane.

As their ability to control the flyers improved at Huffman Prairie, the Wrights sought to protect their invention with a patent. They hired Ohio attorney, Henry Toulmin, to seek a patent for "a flying machine," which was ultimately granted in May, 1906. The patent acknowledged the new and unique method of controlling flight in a heavier than air machine, powered or not, which applied to both the Wrights' concept of wing-warping and its derivative, ailerons, which would

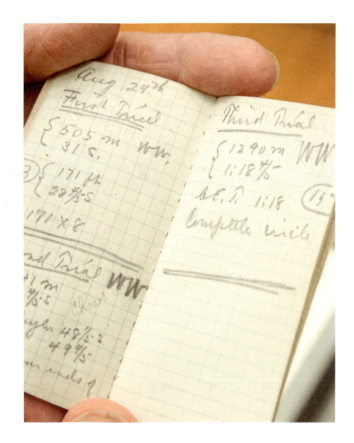

The Library of Congress holds the original Wright documents and artifacts related to their invention of the aeroplane. This notebook from 1905 notes on August 24 that Wilbur (WW) flew a complete circle.

This page: The Museum's replica of Signal Corps Number One features the Wrights' inspired invention of the aerial propeller, a rotating airfoil. These propellers are originals donated to the Museum by the Wright family.

Facing Page: *The Wrights wrote to the industry of motorcars to inquire about a lightweight 4 - stroke gasoline motor. After being refused, they designed their own. Built by their mechanician Charlie Taylor, the Wright motor, the first to have a cast-aluminun block, weighed less than 200 pounds and produced 12 horsepower. This surviving of the original three is on display at the Dayton Engineers Club, where Orville Wright was a member.*

soon become the standard method of lateral control. The Wrights had argued, and the patent office had accepted, that their method of controlling the aircraft extended to variations of the wing structure and control surfaces. They had invented the method and were owed royalties from all who used it.

The resulting patent litigation has often been described as a war. The brothers filed no less than a dozen separate major lawsuits were filed and litigated, each one validating the patent. One of the challengers, Glenn Curtiss, who, like the Wrights, had owned a bicycle shop. Curtiss moved on to motorcycles, building and racing single cylinder motorcycles. As an aviator, Curtiss joined forces with Alexander Graham Bell and the Aero Club of America, making considerable progress with aileron control system, entering and winning the Scientific American Cup and its $25,000 prize in July, 1908, for a recorded flight longer than one kilometer. The Wrights had been invited but declined to participate, citing contract negotiations with the United States. The brothers had already logged flights of more than twenty miles but were still using a

Gil Cohen's painting, The Wrights at Huffman Prairie-1905.

The Museum's collections include this wrench, which was used by Charlie Taylor.

21

Above: *The Museum's exact replica of the 1909 Military Flyer features several original items, including the 1908 Wright Upright 4 aeroplane motor. Also original are the chains, sprockets, and propellers. These originals were donated to the Museum by the Wright family.*

Top Center: *the Wright system of chain-driven propellers. The chain crosses over itself through tubing to create opposite-turning propellers, creating a torque-free propulsion.*

Right: *Seen here is the Wright-designed method of lubricating the propeller shaft.*

Facing page: *Looking straight down the center of the 1909 Wright Military Flyer, the Wright open design can be seen.*

The Museum's 1909 Wright Military Flyer as seen on exhibit. In the lower right corner is bust of Charlie Taylor, the mechanician who built the first aeroplane motors which were designed by the Wrights.

WRIGHT
1909
Military Flyer

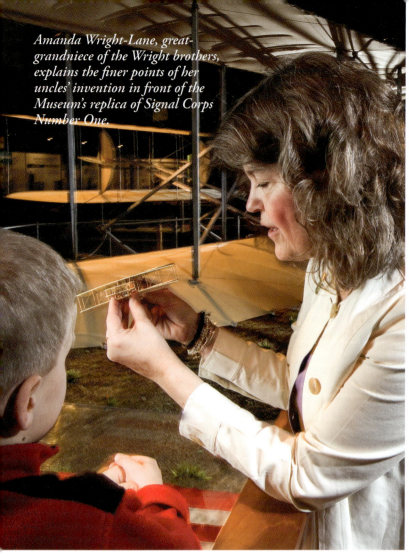

Amanda Wright-Lane, great-grandniece of the Wright brothers, explains the finer points of her uncles' invention in front of the Museum's replica of Signal Corps Number One.

catapult system for takeoff, which was contrary to the rules. In response, the Wrights warned Curtiss that he had flown using technology covered by their patent with a pointed letter which appears to have been ignored.

Ultimately, the Wrights won the patent battles, in court at least, but it was the aileron flight control system that won the technological war. Ten years after Kitty Hawk, enterprising aviators, daredevils even, were violating the Wrights patent, in America and Europe. Having the law squarely on their side proved to be insufficient. Ultimately, the Great War and the possibility of using airplanes for observation, combat, and bombing.

Their defense of the patent corresponded with the attempt to find a way to sell the flyer and turn aviation into a profit producing business. The approached both the British and American governments entertained proposals regarding the sale of the flyer, but the governments lack of foresight and the Wrights reluctance to make a public demonstration with a contract in place. In October 1905, the Board of Ordinance and Fortification, flatly rejected the Flyer, stating unequivocally, "The Board does not care to…take any further action until a machine is produced which by actual operation is shown to be able to produce horizontal flight and to carry an operator."

Discouraged, the Wrights stopped flying for more than a year, concerned that to do so might allow others to see the flyer in operation and duplicate it. They did not, however, waver from their determination to make flying both practical and profitable. New improvement were made to the engine and they continued to build aircraft. Interest in the Flyer from France prompted them to crate and ship one to France in 1907 but it was more than a year before Wilbur could travel to France to demonstrate what the Flyer could do.

Would-be French aviators had been struggling with the problems the Wrights had solved, but lack the insight needed to make substantial progress despite the fact that Octave Chanute had delivered a lecture in Paris back in 1903 that reveal many of the Wrights' discoveries. Likewise, the publication of the patent in 1906

Ivonette Wright Miller and Horace Wright, niece and nephew of the Wright brothers. Author and photographer Dan Patterson made this portrait at the Museum in 1984.

proved not to be enough to jump start a program to produce a working airplane. But the limited success of the French convinced the Wrights to renew their efforts, in the United States and France, to convince both governments to purchase the plane.

A new proposal sent to the Board of Ordinance and Fortification found new interest. President Theodore Roosevelt had heard of the Wright's experimentation had prompted the Board and the Army Signal Corps to look at the possible uses of the Wright Flyer. On August 1, 1907, the Signal Corp established an Aeronautical Division under Captain Charles Chandler to investigate how aircraft, balloons and flying machines, might be adapted to military use. For the first time, the military

Glenn Curtiss of Hammondsport, NY, was one of the leading builders of 4-stroke gasoline powered motors in the early 1900s. His company began building competing aircraft to the Wright Company and took advantage of his extensive engine knowledge. He challenged the Wright patent for aircraft control using ailerons as opposed to wing warping. He was supported by the Aerial Experiment Association, founded by Dr. Alexander Graham Bell.

Greg Cone of the Wright Experience, the world's leading expert on Wright aeroplane motors, examines some of the Musuem's Wright collection. Seen here are forms made for castings and forgings.

The photograph above illustrates the breadth of the Museum's experience for visitors. Here the very earliest days of flight are represented by the Wright 1909 Military Flyer, a license-built, (in Ohio) Bleriot, identical to the aeroplane Louis Bleriot flew across the English Channel in July of 1909. Suspended is the Museum's replica Curtiss Pusher. Behind these are the aircraft of World War I. The lavender Fokker D VII and the rudders of the Caproni Ca. 36 bomber.

The Bleriot XI is the version of the aeroplane which was flown across the English Channel by the French aviation pioneer Louis Bleriot. The aeroplane was powered by a 3-cylinder Azani motorcycle engine, which had a nasty tendency to explode after around 20 minutes. Bleriot flew through a rain shower halfway across the Channel to cool the engine.

had taken an active step toward creating a United States Air Force. The new Aeronautical Division soon issued Signal Corps Specification No. 486, inviting bidders to supply the Corps with "…flying machine supported entirely by the dynamic reaction of the atmosphere…." The specification closely adhered to the Wright's estimates their Flyer could achieve. A suitable plane would be able to take two persons aloft, weighing 350 lbs., reach a speed of 40mph, and fly for 125 miles, and land on an unprepared field with damage, gliding safely without damage should the power-plant fail.

With the prospect of contracts to manufacture airplanes in both France and the United States, the Wrights decided, finally, to display to the public what their Flyer could do. In France, Wilbur demonstrated the Flyer at LeMans in early August 1908, impressing both prospective buyers and the public with the planes easy maneuverability and ability to climb and descend at the will of the pilot. Any doubts that the Wrights' had mastered powered flight were put to rest, while showing erstwhile French aviators just how high a mountain they had to climb.

In America, at Fort Myer, outside Washington D. C., Orville began demonstrating the new Type A Military Flyer, duplicating Wilbur's success in France. For two weeks Orville made demonstration flights, reaching an altitude of 310 feet, carrying military observers along side

he very simple cockpit of the Bleriot XI.

Orville Wright demonstrates the Military Flyer over Fort Myer, Virginia.

The aftermath of the fatal crash at Fort Myer.

on several of the flights. On the last day, disaster struck. Carrying Military advisor, Lt. Thomas Selfridge, as his passenger, Orville circled the Ft. Myer until a crack developed in the starboard propeller, which upset the balance of the plane. The unstable propeller hit one of the guy wires stabilizing the rudder, causing Orville to lose control of the plane. From a height of about 75 ft. the plane descended rapidly, landing nose first, seriously injuring Orville and killing Lt. Selfridge, who earning the morbid distinction of being powered flight aviation's first fatality.

The accident did not offset the success of the previous two weeks so far as the U. S. Army was concerned. Recovered from his injuries,

Orville returned to Ft. Myer the following summer, with a new Flyer that met the requirements of Specification No. 486. On July, 30, with Lt. Benjamin Foulois as his passenger, Orville completed a cross-county flight from Ft. Myer to Alexandria, Virginia at a measured speed of 42.593 mph, securing a contract to supply the Flyer to the United States Army. On August 2, 1909, the Army accepted delivery of the Flyer, the world's first military airplane.

The new United States Aerial Fleet got off to an inauspicious start. With almost no budget, one airplane and two pilots who had received about three hours of instruction from Wilbur Wright after he returned from Europe, the "aerial fleet" began experimental flights on October 26, 1909. Ten days later, on November 5, the pilots damaged the aircraft bad enough that it had to be sent away for repair. The two pilots, with no airplane to fly, were sent back to their regular units. The Aerial Fleet, officially, had no plane nor pilots to its name.

The repaired Flyer was sent to Fort Sam Houston in Texas to avoid winter weather around Washington and Lt. Benjamin Foulois, who had taken three brief flying lessons with the Wrights, was assigned to oversee the transfer and learn how to fly the aircraft. After some correspondence with the Wright on "how to avoid basic disasters," Foulois began to fly the plane and investigate what could be done with it. Into the summer of 1910 Foulois struggled to learn how make the Flyer into a safe and workable representation of the Aeronautical Division. With a budget of only $150, often supplemented by his own private funds, Foulois braved gusty winds, a temperamental engine, and forced landings to keep the fleet of one in the air. By the end of 1910, the Flyer worn out for all practical purposes, the Aeronautical Division

was perilously close to being grounded. Congress had rejected a $200,000 appropriation simply because no enough of the membership could imagine the importance of flight to the military.

Publishing magnate Robert Collier came to the short-term rescue, purchasing a new Wright Type B Flyer and leasing it to the Army for one dollar a month. Several months later, perhaps being shamed by Collier's generosity, Congress approved an appropriation of $125,000 specifically for military aeronautics as part of a larger War Department bill. While hardly extravagant, the appropriation meant that the Army would continue to investigate what possible use it might make of this new-fangled machine.

Europeans, on the other hand, quickly took to investigating the possibilities of flight. Faced with a constant threat of war, minor or major, England, France, and Germany saw some the possibility that airplanes might prove useful. English pilot, Louis Bleriot flew across the English Channel in 1909. The French received Wilbur's demonstrations enthusiastically. Glen Curtiss' Model D, which became the second airplane added to the American "fleet" won the first place trophy at the world's first air meet near Reims. All in all, between 1908 and 1913, European governments spent heavily on developing military uses for powered flight. Germany and France both invested more than $20 million dollars. Russia, noted for being behind the curve militarily, invested $12 million. Belgium, a minor power by any measure, added $2 million to the total. By comparison, the United States spent a paltry $500 thousand. To be sure, many of the older officers dismissed the use of aircraft in military operation, but enough of the officer corps, especially the younger officers saw that aircraft would somehow be integrated into military operations should war break out in the foreseeable future.

Work progressed slowly in the American service. Congress finally made specific appropriations for military aeronautics in 1911, which represented both progress and shortsightedness given what was being done in Europe. The Aeronautical Division promptly ordered five new airplanes, two Curtiss Model D and three Wright Type B Flyers. The Curtiss Model D, like the Wright Flyer, had the propellers and engine behind the pilot, but used ailerons for lateral control instead of wing-warping. The invention of the aileron, a hinged "little wing" on the trailing side of the wing, allowed for the main wing to be fixed in place while the hinged surfaces controlled movement around the longitudinal axis. The idea of aile-

The Wright Company School of Aviation was opened at Huffman Prairie, where over 100 early aviators received flight training. As the clouds of war gathered several of the students were destined for military flying.

Top: *Norman Prince wearing the white skimmer hat got his flight instruction at the Wright school. He went on to volunteer to fly and fight for France in World War One and is one of the founders of the Lafayette Escadrille.*

Center: *US Army Lt. Henry "Hap" Arnold also learned to fly at the Wright School. Arnold went on to be US Army Air Forces Chief of Staff during World War II.*

Bottom: *Canadian Arthur Roy Brown learned to fly at Huffman Prairie along with a cadre of Canadian aviation cadets. In 1918 while flying a Sopwith Camel, Brown has been credited with shooting down Manfred von Richtoffen, the German "Red Baron."*

The students at the Wright Company School of Aviation seen here using the 1910 version of the flight simulator. Flying a Wright aeroplane required a keen sense of balance. Here a student must demonstrate the ability to balance on a plank across a two-wheeled cart while shouldering a pole with weights at either end.

A few of the Wright treasures from the collections Division. A wooden mallet used for aeroplane maintenance; encased in Plexiglass and certified by Orville Wright are a piece of the original wing covering and a part of the wooden structure from the 1903 Wright Flyer. A photograph of Lt. Benny Foluois, talking with Orville Wright, who was tasked with teaching himself to fly the army's newest and only aeroplane. Charlie Taylor's wrench and a wing fitting are resting on a piece of the 1903 wing fabric which Astronaut Neil Armstrong carried to the surface of the moon in July of 1969.

ron itself preceded the Wrights' success by full 35 years. British inventor Matthew Piers Watt Boulton received a patent for the device first described in a paper written in 1864, which he expected to allow pilots to control gliders. It would become the standard for lateral control rather quickly as more powerful engines made the strength of a fixed wing increasingly important.

With no clear understanding of how the Army would use aircraft and no real mission, the Aeronautical Division, which had airplanes and a rudimentary flying school, had a difficult time finding its place. For reconnaissance, it lacked radio. For warfare, it lacked weaponry. For transport, it lacked capacity and range. Pilots and officers experimented with firing rifles and dropping small bombs by hand but no real program of adapting aircraft to military operations came of it short term. In September 1911, Henry "Hap" Arnold, who went on to hold the rank of General of the Air Force, flew the first plane to carry the mail from the Nassau Boulevard airfield to

Hempstead, Long Island. Shortly thereafter, Arnold and fellow Lieutenant Thomas Milling successfully experimented with adapting radio to air-to-ground communication, instantly improving the ability of the Division to use planes for reconnaissance. Other technological improvements followed regularly, but when war began in Europe in the summer of 1914, the Aeronautical Division remained a service unit in search of a mission.

One of the ongoing challenges in these early years, never quite solved, was that flying was horribly dangerous. From the death of Thomas Selfridge in September, 1908 until February 1914, Army aviators suffered eleven deaths. Signal Corps flight records show that in 1911 alone, one pilot or passenger died in an accident for ever 65 hours long in the air. Crash landing were commonplace, so much so that many pilots suffered multiple incidents. Technological improvement came slowly and few new innovations made a significant difference. By 1912, when Wilbur Wright passed away from typhoid

Russell Smith's painting, **Black Jack's Air Force.**

fever in May, the Wright Flyer were little more than an updated version of the Flyer that made the first flight in 1903. It was still a pusher biplane, using wing-warping for lateral control, with no cockpit to keep the pilot out of the windstream. Flight technology had passed the Wright design by.

Prior to the entry of the United States into the war in Europe, the Aeronautical Division had one opportunity to demonstrate just how unprepared the U. S. was for using aircraft to support military operations. In 1916, the Mexican Revolution spilled into New Mexico when Pancho Villa attacked Columbus, New Mexico angry at being denied America supplies to support his troop. In response, President Woodrow Wilson sent 15,000 troops under General John Pershing to end the threat and capture or kill Villa if possible. The 1st Aero Squadron war ordered to accompany the expedition. Arriving six days after Villa had left, the planes arriving by rail due to the absence of landing fields, the aviators soon found out how ill-equipped they were. Tasked with supporting assisting ground operations, the 1st Squadron soon found that it could not deal with the extremes of temperature and wind nor climb high enough to clear the area's ten thousand feet mountain ranges. A sim-

ple attempt to deliver dispatched to Chihuahua City by Lt. Benny Foulois and Lt. Herbert Dargue proved disastrous, the pilots barely able to return to Columbus with heavily damaged aircraft. The limited capabilities of the Aeronautical Division were clear to anyone who wanted to examine it performance. But by this time, the warring nations of Europe were beginning to use aircraft effectively. When the U. S. began to contemplate entry into the war, it was understood that effective air support of troops in the field would be required. Still, despite a new $13 million appropriation for military aeronautics passed in August 1916, the Armay Air Service had only one functioning front-line squadron with an additional one being readied. The United States contemplated war in Europe as no better than 14th ranking world aviation power, an inauspicious situation, by any measure.

Chapter 2
The Crucible of War, 1917-1918

This photo made in April 1916 is of the original members of the Lafayette Escadrille. These men volunteered to fly and fight for France, believing in the cause "Liberté, Egalité, Fraternité." Left to right: Elliot Cowdin, Kiffin Rockwell, Captain Georges Thenault, Norman Prince, Victor Chapman. By the end of 1916, only the commander, Captain Thenault, was still alive.

The Dying Airman

A handsome young airman lay dying,
And as on the aerodrome he lay,
To the mechanics who round him came sighing,
These last dying words he did say:
'Take the cylinders out of my kidneys,
The connecting-rod out of my brain,
Take the cam-shaft out of my backbone,
And assemble the engine again.'

Anonymous

Facing Page: The Museum's SPAD VII, with the red cowling, is in the colors of the Lafayette Escadrille, and is the pursuit airplane that opens the Great War exhibit. The Museum's AVRO 504 is suspended above the Thomas-Morse Scout, and behind that is the Fokker Dr.1.

The outbreak of War in Europe in the summer of 1914 turned the idea of using airplanes to support warfare from the theoretical to the practical. So far, airplanes had not been used to support military operations in the field. For the most part, senior officers looked at aeronautics as perhaps a tool to assist with reconnaissance, but certainly not as a weapon to wage war on the enemy. It did not take long, however, for both the Allies and Central Forces to see that cavalry could no longer provide accurate and real time information to field commanders and that aircraft could pick up at least some of the slack. Pilots could quickly scan the scene below to determine where troops might be massed and where an assault might be direct. Even in the opening weeks of the war, observation aircraft provided critical intelligence that proved crucial to field commanders, for both sides.

The use of airplanes to attack the enemy developed as quickly as technologies could be adapted to flight. Small, simple bombs, dropped without benefit of a bombsight, were ineffective for the most part but the idea showed promise. Pilots used handguns and single shot rifles with similar results, but again, the possibility of more effective use of firearms could easily be imagined. The Wright brother's concept of locating the engine and propellers behind the wings would allow for mounting a machine gun forward of the wing. But "pusher" airplanes proved to be significantly slower than

Above: Victor Chapman while serving in the French Foreign Legion, before joining the Escadrille.
Below: Victor Chapman was the first American airman to be killed in combat, his grave at the Meuse-Argonne American Cemetery in France.

Rockwell asked that if he were shot down, to be buried where he fell. His initial grave near Roderen, France. Shot down on September 23, 1916.

Kiffin Rockwell wearing protection against the bitter cold conditions of aerial combat in an open-cockpit pursuit airplane.

planes with forward mounted engines. Using a machine gun to fire directly forward through the propeller required the development of synchronized firing mechanisms. In a relatively short period of time all the Western Front combatants had synchronized firing systems even though the Germans had to copy a French design, albeit unsynchronized, taken from a downed airplane.

Both sides regularly improved their airplanes so that any advantage one side gained was soon countered by the other. The talent of the individual pilots mattered almost as much as their equipment. Over the course of the war, more than 1800 pilots accumulated more than five confirmed victories, earning the title "ace." The Germans, English, and French each had their ace of aces, who became legendary heroes for their success in aerial combat. Manfred von Richthofen, William Avery Bishop, Rene Fonck, and Edward Rickenbacker, among others, earned a celebrated status few soldiers achieved. Richthofen, of the famed Flying Circus, would be killed in combat in April 1918, had 80 confirmed victories. Fonck, France's most prolific aviator, avoided dogfights, preferring to descend rapidly from a high altitude on unsuspecting targets, is credited with at least 75 downed German airplanes may have downed as many as 100. Bishop, a Canadian flying for Britain, recorded 72 victories although some historians claim his totals might be inflated. Rickenbacker, the American ace of aces, who only recorded his first kill on April 29, 1918, ended the war with 26 confirmed victories.

For the Americans, President Wilson formally pro-

The contents of Rockwell's pockets when he was shot down and killed: his engraved cigarette case, his watch, a photo of his fallen friend Victor Chapman, and wrapped in string a piece of the propeller from his Nieuport 11, embedded with the soil of France, his bloodstained handkerchief on top. (Rockwell Family Collection).

claimed the United States as neutral on August 4, 1914, days after the war began. American neutrality, despite the claim, favored the Allied cause and many American young men joined the Allied war effort by crossing into Canada and sailing to England or France to volunteer for service. Americans who went to Europe in support of the Allied war effort often joined the French Foreign Legion. The idea of forming an aerial squadron of American volunteers began as an idea from Norman Prince and William Thaw, who first proposed that volunteer pilots enlist in the French Air Service in January, 1915. It took a year before enough American and French support could be raised to support such a unit. Once Jarousse de Silac, undersecretary of Foreign Affairs, saw that having American pilots serve with the French would pay untold propaganda benefits, the unit began to take shape. Originally named the Escadrille Americaine, a name that troubled some leaders since the United States remained neutral, the squadron was eventually named the Lafayette Escadrille (LE) in honor of the French hero of the American Revolution.

The LE began operations of 20 April 1916 and took to the air for the first time on 13 May. Over the course of

the next twenty months, thirty-eight American pilots flew with the squadron, nine of whom died in combat. The American pilots were known for their aggressive flying and distain for flying in formation. The squadron served in every combat area in France and was credited with 57 downed enemy aircraft, including sixteen by the LE "ace of aces, Raoul Lufbery. Their unique style soon attracted attention in the United States and beyond, which brought additional Americans to Europe to join the French and British flying corps. These new pilots, more that 200 in all, were generally assigned singly or in small numbers to existing French units rather than the LE. The LE disbanded in February 1918 to be absorbed into the greater American effort. LE pilots became instrumental in the success of the of the new squadrons, flying mission and training pilots on how to fly in combat. The small number of LE pilots meant that

A hangar full of Nieuports ready for action.

The solution to the problem of cooling early aircraft
engines was to keep the crankshaft still and spin the
finned cylinders around it. The le Rhone rotary weighed
308 pounds and gave 110 hp.

The Nieuport 28 kept the le Rhone engine very closely cowled. Sections along the outer rim of the cowl were open to allow the spinning motor's oil to be flung into the slipstream. World War I pilot's were covered with oil when they retuned from a mission.

Above: *The cockpit of the Camel is noticeably different from the Nieuport 28, seen on page 54.*

Below: *The Museum acquired the Halberstadt CL IV on display in 1984. Badly deteriorated at the time, its restoration was a joint international cooperative venture by the Museum fur Verkehr und Technik in Berlin, Germany, the Smithsonian Institution's National Air and Space Museum, and the National Museum of the United States Air Force. It is marked as the CL IV of the squadron leader of the Schlachtstaffel 21, which is known to have engaged elements of the US Army's 94th and 95th Aero Squadrons in mid-July 1918, during the Chateau-Thierry battle.*

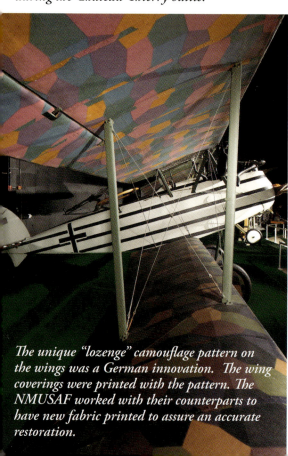

The unique "lozenge" camouflage pattern on the wings was a German innovation. The wing coverings were printed with the pattern. The NMUSAF worked with their counterparts to have new fabric printed to assure an accurate restoration.

The ubiquitous Curtiss OX-5 aircraft motor. Curtiss pioneered the V-shaped motor, which dominated liquid-cooled engine designs.

Eugene Bullard was the first African American fighter pilot. He served with the Lafayette Escadrille. His autobiography is titled, "All Blood Runs Red". He signed and gave this document to the Air Force Museum in 1961.

The enameled pins were worn by Bullard.

the over the course of its existence the impact the LE had on the overall air war was relatively light. But the unit's service at the forefront of American combat aviation helped bridge the gap between an experimental and largely disjointed flying service attached to the Signal Corps at home and the very purposeful development of air power to wage war in Europe.

Many other Americans joined the ranks of the flying expatriates before the Army could organize the Expeditionary Force. Prior to the declaration of war, the flow of Americans into Europe was small, but expanded dramatically immediately thereafter, for both air and ground personnel. In France, beyond the LE, American volunteers applied to join the Lafayette Flying Corps, an um-

brella organization which functioned as the processing and training unit for Americans in France, sending those who successfully completed their training to the LE and other French combat units. Similar arrangements existed between the Royal Flying Corps (RFC) and the Ameri-

can volunteers, although never as large as the French program. LE pilots did much of the training of AEF pilots, especially regarding air combat. Raoul Lufberry and James Norman Hall personally trained the American "ace of aces, Eddie Rickenbacker.

An even smaller scale operation, never more than 400 Americans, trained pilots in Italy. Frustrated by language difficulties, limited flight time, and old Farmans aircraft, a relatively small number of pilots, who learned as much from each other as their instructors, completed the Italian program. Those who moved on to advanced training found themselves flying the Caproni heavy bombers. The Capronis were among the first aircraft expected to attack strategic targets well beyond the battlefield. With a wingspan of seventy feet and three engines, a fully loaded Caproni could carry almost 2,000 lbs. of bombs with a range of 400 miles. For the few Americans who ultimately flew the Caproni on bombing missions, they received some of the earliest experience in strategic bombing.

Perhaps the most important officer of the American air war and by any account the most important going forward was William (Billy) Mitchell. Mitchell arrived in France only a few days after the declaration of war and quickly found himself serving at the headquarters of General John Pershing. On his own initiative Mitchell, a major at this point in his career, familiarized himself with all aspects of the French air service, including headquarters, airfields, supply depots, even mechanics sheds. He borrowed French airplanes to fly his own reconnaissance missions over the battle front. He summarized his activity with a set of reports to Washington commenting on whatever he had seen and making recommendations about what the Air Service should do when it arrived.

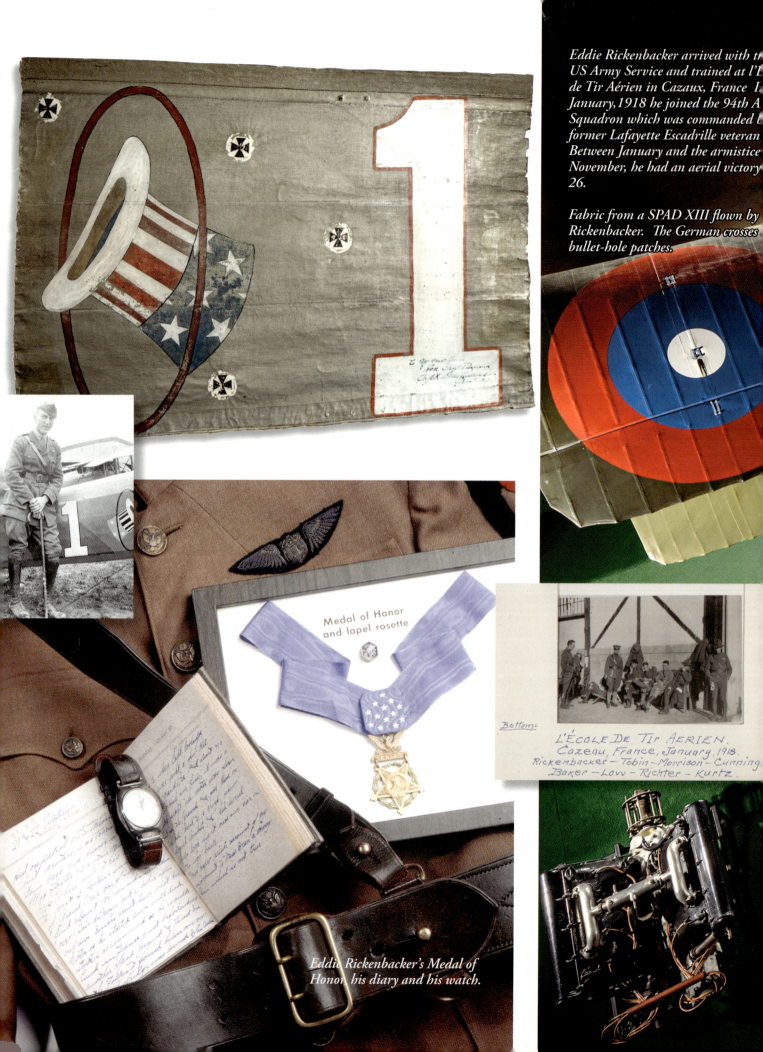

Eddie Rickenbacker arrived with the
US Army Service and trained at l'É...
de Tir Aérien in Cazaux, France I...
January,1918 he joined the 94th A...
Squadron which was commanded b...
former Lafayette Escadrille veteran...
Between January and the armistice...
November, he had an aerial victory...
26.

Fabric from a SPAD XIII flown by
Rickenbacker. The German crosses
bullet-hole patches.

Medal of Honor
and lapel rosette

Bottom:
L'ÉCOLE DE TIR AERIEN.
Cazeau, France, January, 1918.
Rickenbacker - Tobin - Morrison - Cunning...
Baker - Lovv - Richter - Kurtz.

*Eddie Rickenbacker's Medal of
Honor, his diary and his watch.*

The Museum's SPAD XIII. Favored by the Army Air Service, the SPAD was fast and maneuverable. In the lower left corner the powerplant for the SPAD, a 220 hp Hispano Suiza motor. It is painted like the fighter that Eddie Rickenbacker flew.

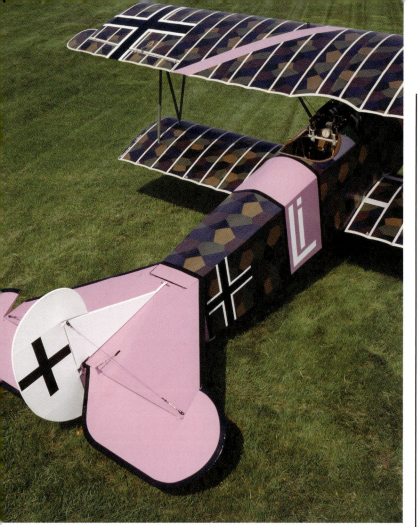

The Fokker D VIIs were often painted in exotic color schemes. This lavender finish was favored by Lt. Rudolph Stark of Jasta 35b in October 1918. The cockpit was typically uncluttered, the two Spandau machine guns just above.

Mitchell, the son of a United States Senator from Wisconsin had served in the Army since the Spanish-American War and came to aviation through a posting in the Signal Corps. He had seen Orville Wright demonstrate the Flyer at Ft. Myer in 1908 and learned to fly at he Curtiss School at Newport News. Mitchell's career had been on the fast track and his assignment in the Air Service only accelerated the curve. He became the Signal Corps representative of the General Staff in 1912, at the age of thirty-two, and temporary head of the Aviation Section of the Signal Corps in 1916, then to become permanent assistant to Lt. Col. George Squier. He was on his way to France, at the rank of major, when Congress declared war.

Although Mitchell spent most of his time in France, at or near the front, he worked closely with Major General Hugh Trenchard of the RFC. Trenchard, who would later serve as Chief of Staff of the Royal Air Force (RAF), was one of the first and strongest advocates of the offensive and strategic use of air power. Aircraft should be used aggressively to penetrate deep into enemy territory to take the war beyond the combat front. Operation of air services should be under a unified command. Mitchell quickly accepted Trenchard's ideas and made them the centerpiece of his own ideas for the development of American air power.

The original organization and deployment of the Air Service under the American Expeditionary Force (AEF) did not go particularly smooth. General Pershing looked for how to adopt and adapt the best of the British and French methods into what would work for the Americans. As might be expected, such uncertainty often provoke serious disagreements and animosity and Mitchell was never far from any of the controversy. Pershing, for his part, found Mitchell to be particularly good at what he did and promoted him to the rank of Lt. Col. And Aviation Officer on the General's staff in June 1917. More promotions followed; Air Commander, Zone of Advance (front lines), Chief of Air Service for 1st Corps, 1st Army and then Army Group. Along with the increased responsibilities came a promotion to Brigadier General.

Mitchell's prickly temperament irritated superiors and subordinates along the way. General Benjamin Foulois, head of operations, production, and maintenance for the Air Service, who was, at this moment, Mitchell's superior, and had served as his subordinate and equal over the years, asked General Pershing in June, 1918 that, Mitchell "be immediately relieved of duty…," and sent home. Pershing declined, more than willing to tolerate two headstrong, independent minded military thinkers, even when they clashed.

The cockpit of the SPAD XIII, while still simple was more complex than its predecessors. The pilot's field of view could not have been helped by the framing of the small windscreen.

Lt. Col. William Thaw, a veteran of the Lafayette Escadrille. At the end of the war he was a flying ace and a decorated member of the French Legion of Honor. A piece of SPAD XIII fabric cut by William Thaw, his personal pocket altimeter.

Caproni Ca. 36: During World War I, Italian aeronautical engineer Gianni Caproni developed a series of multi-engine heavy bombers that played a key role in the Allied strategic bombing campaign. His bomberswere produced not only in Italy, but also in France and the United States.

In late 1914 Caproni designed the Ca. 31, powered by three Gnome rotary engines. The following year, Caproni produced a new version, the Ca. 32. Very similar to the Ca. 31, it had three FIAT 100-hp water-cooled in-line engines. Three months after Italy's entry into World War I, the first Ca. 32s attacked an Austrian air base at Aisovizza, and by the end of the year, regular raids were being mounted against other Austrian targets.

Caproni continued to refine his successful design with the introduction of the Isotta-Fraschini -powered Ca. 33. Toward the end of the war the definitive version, the Ca. 36, went into production. Changes from the Ca. 33 were small but included five-section wings that made disassembly and surface transportation easy. Ca. 36s remained in Italian air force service as late as 1929.

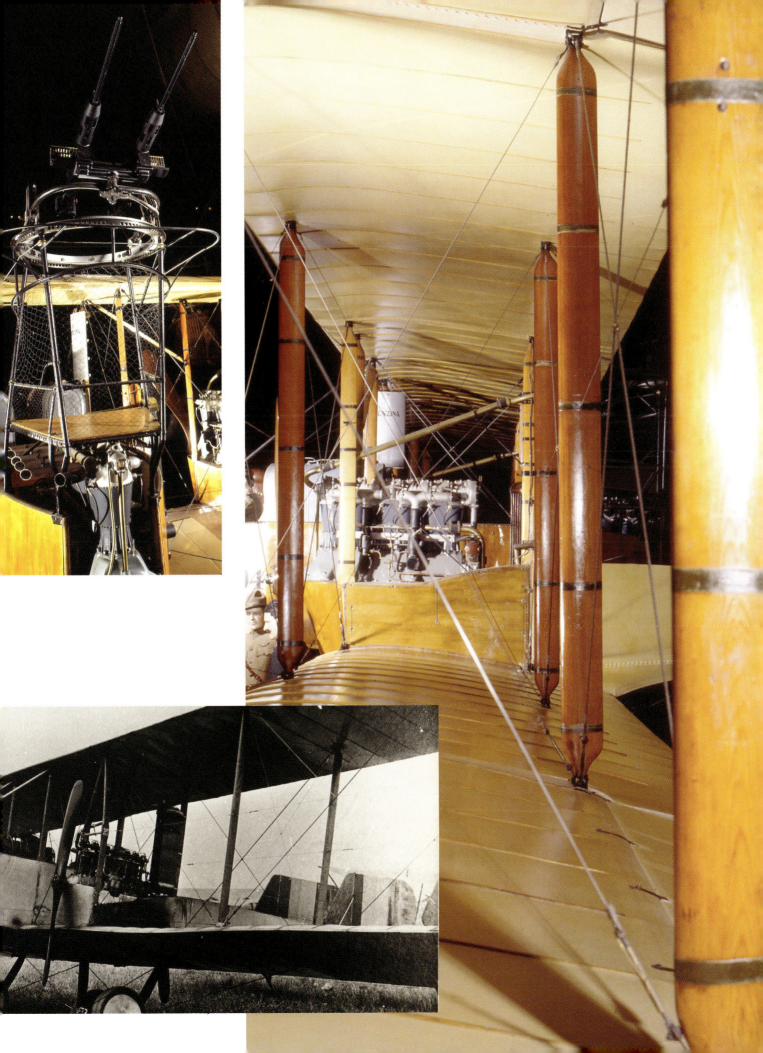

American strategic bombing was first flown in Italian Caproni bombers. In his painting artist Bill Marsalko illustrates an American-flown mission over the Alps.

Restored by Museum specialists, the museum obtained the
Ca. 36 on display from the Museo Aeronautica Caproni
di Taliedo in Italy in 1987.

The NMUSAF Musuem's fully restored Caproni Ca. 36.
The nearly 75-foot wingspan dwarfs the crew stations in
the center. The rear gunner's position seen here on top
of one of the three Isotta Fraschini V.4B 150-hp water-
cooled, 6-cylinder motors.

Raoul Lufbery was the ace of the Lafayette Escadrille, scoring almost half of the squadron's aerial victories. The signed photo is of Major Lufbery alongside his Nieuport 28 after the USA entered the war and the volunteers to France were transferred to the American Air Service.

President Theodore Roosevelt's sons saw combat in both world wars. Quentin became a pursuit pilot and was sent to the combat zone. He flew with the 103rd Squadron, flying the Nieuport 28. After just a few missions he was shot down and killed on July 14, 1918. The Germans recovered his body and made this simple grave marker from ash tree branches, bound with wires cut from his crashed Nieuport 28, to note his burial.

Quentin's brother Theodore became an infantry leader and was in the first wave with the 4th Division when it assaulted the French coast at Utah Beach on June 6, 1944. Six weeks later he died of a heart attack and was later awarded the Medal of Honor for his actions. The two brothers are buried next to each other in the American cemetery overlooking Omaha Beach.

Far left: *The cockpit of the Nieuport 28 is a very spare sight. There are very few instruments. The pilot's seat is constructed from basketwork to save weight. The silver switch at the left is the only engine control; the "blip" switch was used to control the engine by turning the engine on and off.*

This page: *Standard armament for the Nieuport 28 was two Vickers .303 machine guns, offset to the left, firing through the propeller.*

General Billy Mitchell (center) and his staff in the later stages of World War I. Billy Mitchell wore this uniform tunic when he commanded the US Army Air Service in France during the US involvement in The Great War.

The Americans had little effect on the air war until 1918. With essentially no preparation until the declaration of war and little production capacity, the Air Service delivered planes and equipment slowly, frustratingly so, over the course of 1917. This delayed American participation in air combat as an independent service until the spring of 1918. The first airmen took flight on April 14, a year after the U. S. declared war. Lts. Winslow and Campbell of the 94th Squadron answered an alarm and immediately jumped in their Nieuports to take to the air. No sooner had they cleared the airfield when they almost collided with two German aircraft flying toward them through the heavy mist. The American pilots quickly dispatched the surprised Germans, shooting both aircraft down literally in sight of their cheering colleagues on the ground. As starts go, this was nothing short of spectacular, a great boost for morale and a tough act to follow.

The problem, of course, was not just a matter of building aircraft and moving materiel. With allies and enemies working tirelessly to gain advantage over each other, the newest technology could be obsolete in a matter of months. The Americans flew planes of British and French design if not manufacture for the most part. The American ace of aces, Eddie Rickenbacker flew a Nieuport 28, new to the fleet in 1918, for the most part, a plane which replaced the N.17 (1916), which replaced the N.11 (1915), which replaced the pre-war N.10. Others flew the British Sopwith F.1, nicknamed the Camel. The Camel, a single-seat fighter, single-engined with two machine guns synchronized to fire through the rotating propeller. When it entered service it was as maneuverable as nearly every other plane flying, so much so, that the RFC did its best to supply Camels to as many squadrons as it could. But by the summer of 1918, the newest German planes had relegated the Camel to no better than second place.

Billy Mitchell proved to be the combat leader that made the American Air Service a better than respectable fighting corps. In the early stages of the summer campaign of 1918, Mitchell made his mark as commander and tactician. On July 15, in a borrowed SPAD, he went off on a lone reconnaissance flight along the Marne. Near the town of Dormans, he came across five pontoon bridges carrying German soldiers to the front. The bridges were under constant attack by Allied aircraft and strongly defended by German planes and anti-aircraft fire. Rather than join the fray, Mitchell decided to shift the attack away from the bridges toward a German supply base close by. If successful, such a mission would destroy badly needed supplies, forcing the Germans to divert its efforts away from the bridges and front line toward defending their rear. The plan worked as planned, and as Mitchell would say later, it was "the first case on record where we, with an inferior air force, were able to put the superior air force on the defensive and attach whenever we pleased…."

With the Germans forced to regroup, the Air Service became available to assign General Pershing's attempt to remove the Germans from the St. Mihiel salient in preparation for a general offensive. Mitchell, now Chief of Air Service, First Army, argued for a great concentration of air power, the largest ever to that point. American, French, British, and Italian units concentrated 1,481 aircraft on 14 separate airfields. All told, 701 fighters, 366 observation planes, 323 day bombers and 91 night bombers were prepared to face a German force estimated somewhere between 200 and 300 aircraft. Mitchell planned to use this disparity in force to simply overwhelm the Germans. One-third of the combined force would support the ground attack, and the other two-thirds would be split to attack targets of opportunity on the flanks and behind the lines. If all went well, the Germans would not just find themselves defending just one more frontal assault, they would be defending every aspect of their military operation in the salient.

As it has often been noted, the plan of attack did not survive contact with the enemy, but it worked more than well enough. Pouring rain and low clouds acted as a ceiling, keeping Mitchell's attacking force at a very low altitude to the point of the pilots being eyewitnesses to the damage they were inflicting. Eddie Rickenbacker, the American ace, who attacked a column of German troops head on described the carnage. "Dipping down at the head of the column I sprinkled a few bullets over the leading teams. Horses fell right and left. One driver leaped from his seat and started running for the ditch. Half way across the road he threw up his arms and rolled over on his face…."

The weather proved to be a double-edged blade, keeping the air assault close to the ground but also limited what Mitchell's combined forces could do. But their efforts kept the Germans on the defensive throughout the battle and the vast majority of the fighting occurred on the German side of the front. Losses on both sides were high. In some cases, losses force some units from the field. But in the end, Mitchell's combined air attack helped the Allies win the day. Pershing, in congratulating Mitchell, commented, "The organization and control of the tremendous concentration of air forces…is as fine a tribute to you personally as it the courage an nerve shown by your officers, a signal proof of the high morale which permeates the service under your command."

The Americans continued to support the Allied war effort, but only two more months of combat yet to come, nothing quite so dramatic followed. By the Armistice

Dayton inventor Charles F. Kettering developed during the war the earliest idea of an unmanned air vehicle. The war ended before the Kettering Bug *could be deployed. A simple concept of a bomb, with a small engine, wings, and tail, it was launched from a carriage that ran on rails and pointed toward the enemy. When the fuel ran out, the* Bug *hopefully glided to the target.*

of November 11, the American Air Service could claim that it had performed well. In seven months of active combat, its pilots claimed 781 enemy aircraft and 73 balloons shot down. They had participated in more than 150 bombing missions and delivered at least 250,000 pounds of bombs. American flying casualties were surprising light. In all, the flying corps suffered 569 combat casualties (164 killed, 103 wounded, 102 captured, 200 missing). Another 654 men lost their lives from other causes; 319 in accidents and 335 died of others causes, a number of those due to influenza. The flying related deaths could have been reduced had the service required the pilots to have parachutes at the ready.

The limiting factor to American performance was not related to skill, courage, or audacity but rather due to inability of American industry to supply the Army with materiel. Had the war continued into 1919, a fully

The Museum's Eberhard SE-5E seen here before the full restoration in 1984. Exhibiting woodworking craftsmanship and a very simple flying control system. The reader should contrast this open view of a fighter from 1918 with the uncovered F-86 from the early 1950s, on page 192.

armed and staffed Air Service would have made an even stronger contribution to the Allied war effort on the Western Front. That said, the importance of air power in the World War was far from decisive. The importance of the arrival of the airplane as a weapon of war was much more tied to the future than the present day. It had become apparent, even to some of the harshest early critics, that the use of air power had permanently changed the nature of warfare and that much had been learned about how to use aircraft to the advantage of ground commanders. By the end of hostilities on 11 November 1918, it could be said that air power alone could not secure victory, but that the absence of air power could ensure defeat. Reconnaissance alone made much of the difference. Even at the strategic level there was enough evidence, though thin, that with improved technologies and new tactics commanders could destroy an enemy's ability to wage war well beyond the front lines.

By the end of the war, the Air Service had found its mission going forward. The post-war contraction of the Air Service as the United States disarmed, could not reverse what had been learned. Air power had officially become an important part of war and warfare. Aviation commanders like Mitchell and Spaatz, who themselves had flown in combat, would have much to contribute about how the U. S. would use airplanes in the future. American manufacturers sought to compete with Europe and began to see beyond the military use of aircraft and look toward civilian applications. The World War had let the genie out of the bottle.

A recent restoration from the Museum's collection which represents the era of World War I. The Thomas-Morse Scout became the favorite single-seat training airplane for US pilots during World War I. The Scout first appeared with an order for 100 S4Bs in the summer of 1917. The US Army Air Service later purchased nearly 500 of a slightly modified version, the S4C. Dubbed the Tommy by its pilots, the plane had a long and varied career.

The Tommy on display was donated to the museum in March 1965 by Capt. R. W. Duff, Miami, Florida. The Museum's restoration team spent about two years restoring this aircraft, which is now on display in the Early Years Gallery.

Left: General Billy Mitchell's uniform, medals, spectacles, and the red pennant which he flew from his aircraft during the bombing trials off the east coast of the USA.

During World War I, the Air Service began making test flights at high altitude. On September 18, 1918, Capt. Rudolph W. "Shorty" Schroeder set a world record of 28,900 feet in a Bristol airplane from McCook Field. In 1919 he established three more world altitude records, and on February 27, 1920, in a LePere airplane fitted with a General Electric turbo-supercharger, he reached a world-record height of 33,114 feet. When he removed his goggles to change oxygen flasks in order to continue breathing in the rarefied atmosphere, the minus-63 degree-air temperature immediately froze his eyeballs.

Schroeder passed out from the lack of oxygen and carbon monoxide poisoning and the LePere plummeted nearly 6 miles in two minutes; at the very last moment, he regained consciousness and

Chapter 3
The 1920s: Debates and Derring Do

"We crashed not because we ran out of gas, but because we ran out of knowledge."

Inscription on a cup awarded to survivors of accidents, McCook Flight Test Section, 1920s

pulled the plane from its dive. Although he was almost totally blind, Schroeder was able to locate McCook Field and land safely.

He was awarded this silver cup.

The Armistice of November 11, 1918 ended the fighting in Europe, but what would come was yet to be decided. The Allies would unilaterally dictate a treaty at Versailles, holding Germany primarily accountable for the carnage of the last four years. Much had been destroyed and the Allies could not agree on many of the pressing issues. The American President, Woodrow Wilson, took an active role in writing the treaty, but his desire to create a workable peace ran headlong into the British and French desire for revenge. Four great empires, the German, Austro-Hungarian, Russian, and Ottoman, fell to revolution, creating power vacuums throughout much of Europe and the Middle East. No plan existed for replacing what had been destroyed. Wilson's idea of the self-determination of peoples ran hard against the practical realities that ethnic peoples did not divide themselves neatly geographically. For the United States, truly the last nations standing in 1919, a retreat into isolationism meant that it would try as best it could to stay away from European political and diplomatic trouble. For the military, and by extension, the Air Service, this meant cut budgets, reduced staff, and a cutback in technological development, all at the time when the Service was beginning to hit its stride.

For the Air Service, the war ended with its mission only partially fulfilled. Starting with very little, American airmen had learned to fight well and had made important contributions to Allied aerial success by the end of 1918. The future might have appeared promising, but the Americans were a long way from matching what the English and French had accomplished. Hearing and investigations found indecision, disorganization, and poor judgement in any number of places, but most of the problems were rooted in the old problem of trying to do too much in too short a period of time. The U. S. had been behind the curve on airplane design, acquiring raw materials, manufacturing capacity and expertise, but lacked a definite plan for creating a combat ready air force.

The DH-4 was an ever-present element of the US Army Air Service during and after World War I.
With inadequate funding to buy new aircraft, the newly created U.S. Army Air Service continued to use the DH-4 in a number of roles during the lean years following the war. By the time it was finally retired from service in 1932, the DH-4 had been developed into over sixty variants.

Below: The cockpit of the Museum's DH-4.

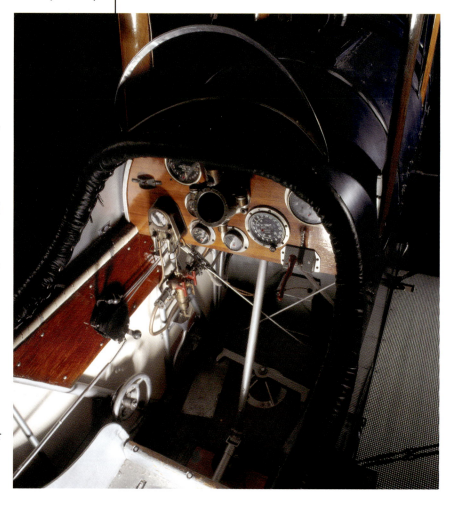

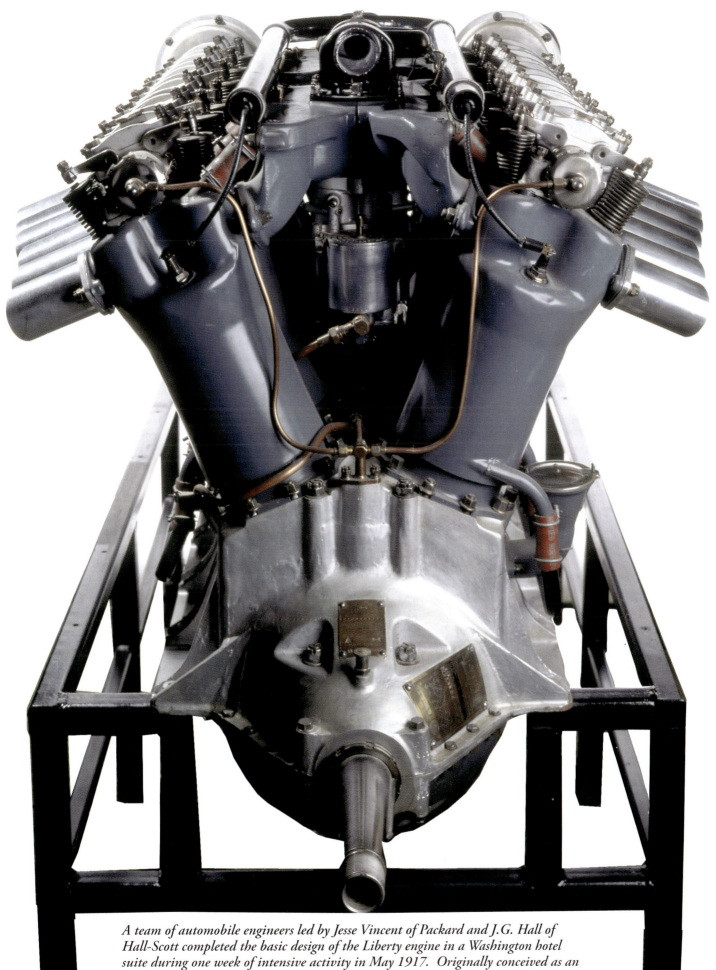

A team of automobile engineers led by Jesse Vincent of Packard and J.G. Hall of Hall-Scott completed the basic design of the Liberty engine in a Washington hotel suite during one week of intensive activity in May 1917. Originally conceived as an eight-cylinder engine it went into production as a V-twelve producing 400 hp. 20, 478 Libertys were built, and became the backbone of American military aviation until the late 1920s.

General Electric F-1 turbosupercharger. Developed by General Electric engineer Dr. Sanford Moss, the experimental concept was to collect the exhaust from the Liberty engine and cycle those gases through a compressor and an intercooler to bring the air pressure to a match of that at sea-level and feed that back into the engine for sea-level performance. The concept worked, and a GE-equipped Le Pere Lusac was flown to altitudes as high as 40,000 feet from McCook Field in Dayton, Ohio. These experiments led to the Army Air Forces' aerial abilities in World War II. Compare this unit with the GE unit on page 116.

Above: *The propeller attached to the Liberty clearly stamped with the information from McCook Field.*

Left: *The prototype compressor rotors and high-temperature welding.*

Below: *Test pilot John Maccready at left and Dr. Sanford Moss on the right.*

This painting from the Museum's collection depicts John Macready's record setting flight in a supercharged Le Pere Lusac to over 40,000 feet, signed by the pilot.

John Macready and the high altitude Le Pere Lusac.

The high altitude flight mask and goggles worn by Macready on his high-altitude flights.

solved many of the major problems. By the end of the war, American manufacturers had turned out 13,574 Liberty engines and were producing 150 per day. The Liberty engine continued to be used in American aircraft for more than a decade.

But how was the Air Service to continue the considerable and incomplete progress of building a new combat corps based on rapidly developing technologies in a world of a deescalating Army? That air power was going to be an integral part of warfare going forward was a given. The experience of combat had been difficult to learn and

came with disaster and tragedy, but the Service had every reason that with the appropriate resources, the United States would soon compete with the British and French. That optimistic expectation ran headlong into the reality that the United States military was going to deescalate as quickly as it had built itself up to fight. For the Air Service and its leaders, the problem was how to convince Congress to fund what the Service knew would be essential going forward. As Benjamin Foulois would put it, "The General Staff of the Army—either through lack of vision, lack of practical knowledge, or deliberate intention to subordinate the Air Service need to the of other combat arms—has utterly failed to appreciate the full military value of the new weapon, and, in my opinion, has failed to accord it its just place in our military family." Billy Mitchell, often at odds with Foulois, heartily agreed.

These problems were partially overcome by using European designs, such as the SPAD single-seat fighter, the Bristol two-seat fighter, the DH4 reconnaissance/light bomber and the Caproni, tri-plane heavy bomber. Trying to adapt European aircraft to American engines proved to be more difficult than originally imagined, although the eight cylinder Liberty engine

The problem of the future had multiple parts to it, money, military philosophy, organization, technology, and vision. There was no clear answer to any of the questions. Reductions is size and budget were a given. A Service of

O-247-109N-23) (1-4-29-1:05 P.M.) (12-4000) Refueling The "P" over Burbank.

1200 had quickly become 200,000 and then cut to less than 10,000 by the mid-1920s. Ninety percent of the aircraft and engine orders were cancelled leaving manufacturers high and dry without government contracts. Congress cut the budget from $460 million in 1919 to $25 million a year later, reasoning, it seems, that if the

McCook Field developed aircrew flight clothing designed to ensure survival and ability to perform their tasks in the harsh conditions at high altitudes.

U. S. had fought "the war to end all wars," how much money needed to be spent on adding a new flying corps to the American armed forces?

Many looked at the issues of military philosophy and organization as two sides of the same coin. How would the next war be fought, and what would the role of air power be in the fighting? The answer to those questions led straight to the problem of organization. The airmen argued that the war, going forward, would require that nations use air power to support and augment ground troops. The best way to do that was to have a separate and independent branch of the armed service dedicated to aviation in support of all other units. Both the Senate and House of Representatives entertained such proposals but took no action on creating a United States Air Force.

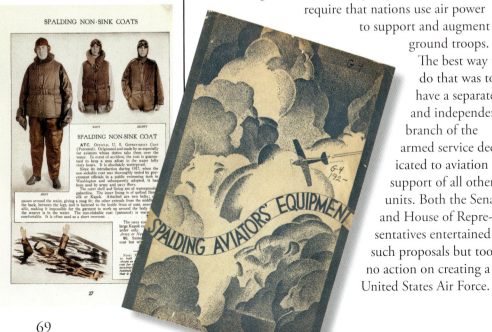

Blunder Trophies:
A blunder trophy was created for presentation to a pilot who had made some kind of ridiculous or inexcusable mistake while flying, such as taxiing into a parked airplane or taking off without sufficient fuel and being forced down "out-of-gas."

Photo: April 6, 1926. McCook Field, Ohio. Pilots of Flight Test Branch, Engineering Division.
L-R Front: R.G. Lockwood, Lt. George P. Tourtellot, Lt. James H. Doolittle, Lt. William H. Amis,
2nd row: Lt. Harry A. Johnson, Lt. E.H. Barksdale, Lt. J.A, Macready, Lt. James T. Hutchinson, Lt.
R.C. Moffat, L.G. Meister - (shown with "Flying Jackass" & Quacking Duck" Trophies).

Opposition from members of the Army and Secretary of War Newton Baker convinced Congress to keep the Air Service as a combat arm of the Army with no more than 1,500 officers and 16,000 enlisted personnel. Congress raised the rank of the Chief of the Air Service to major general and gave the Service full control of its own research, development, training, and procurement. Tactical units would be commanded by flyers. Advocates for an independent Air Force, such as Mitchell and Foulois, were disappointed, but given that most senior army officers could not see that the Air Service could do more than provide close tactical support on the battlefield.

At the center of the reorganization of the Air Service and most of the controversies surrounding it stood Billy Mitchell. Many expected Mitchell to be appointed Director of the Air Service, but found himself third in command, in charge of Training and Operations, behind Major General, Charles T. Menoher, who had been an artillery officer. As a member of the General Staff, Mitchell made his ideas well known to anyone who might be listening. He believed that an independent Air Force was critical to future of the military, that there would be future wars, and that air power would play a central role in any future war. Air warfare would be strategic as well as tactical, and would, by extension, involve the attack on areas that brought war to civilian populations. Future wars would prove Mitchell correct on that account, but in the wake of the World War, the idea of total war he expected horrified many in civilian and military society. Mitchell went so far as to argue that as air power developed, naval power would be far less important, inviting the wrath of the Naval command as well as that of his opponents in the Army.

General Menoher ran interference for Mitchell to the extent he could, but keeping Mitchell in check proved to be more than he could accept. He resigned in September 1921 to be replaced by General Mason Patrick, who came from the old army establishment and had some experience dealing with Billy Mitchell. Patrick agreed with Mitchell's insistence on building a strong air corps, but even strong agreement was not enough to keep Mitchell in check. When his appointment as Assistant Chief of Air Service expired in 1925, Mitchell was not reappointed, reverting to his permanent rank of colonel and being set to Texas as a form of exile. There, when the Navy lost two aircraft in a matter of days and the Secretary of the Navy said it proved the United States had nothing to fear from an airborne invasion. Mitchell, unable to contain himself, went directly to the press, attacking the "incompetency, criminal negligence, and almost

Among the many aviation engineering aspects performed at McCook Field, aircrew survival was one of the areas of innovation and invention. Parachutes were tested with pioneering flights and actual emergency rescues.

Brigadier General William Mitchell (1879-1936). Returning from World War I covered in glory, Billy Mitchell was thought by many (including himself) to be the ideal man for appointment as Chief of the Air Service.

71

The Museum features an exact replica of the Martin MB-2 bombers which were flown under the command of General Billy Mitchell to prove that large naval combat ships could be attacked and sunk by air forces.

treasonable administration of our defense…" by the Navy and War Department. Convicted at a court martial for "conduct of a nature to bring discredit upon the military service," Mitchell's only option was to resign the service. It would take the nation another two decades to realize how advanced Mitchell's understanding of the possibilities of air power, when President Harry Truman posthumously awarded him a special Medal of Honor.

Tight budgets and the overall national attitude toward involvement with Europe kept experimental activity at a bare minimum. The Engineering Division, headquartered at McCook Field outside Dayton produced real advancements on experimental aircraft, including bombers, and any number of important ancillary technologies, engines, propellers, cannon, bombsights, etc. Experimental activity lessened in the face of budget cuts after 1923 and new designs simply met Air Service specifications rather than explored new technologies. Consequently, many of the 1920s American aircraft continued to look remarkably similar to the aircraft being used in Europe at the end of the war. The Keystone Bomber, for example, an open-cockpit twin-engined biplane, became a mainstay of the fleet. Engines were improved and the ceiling increased, but the basic design was not changed. Likewise, for fighter technology, Boeing and Curtiss produces some agile single-seater planes capable of reaching nearly 200 mph and 25,000 ft, but the basic design remained the open-cockpit biplane with a machine gun firing through the propeller arc. Boeing and Curtiss competed with each other for contracts rather than compete based on new technological advancements.

Technology may have lagged, but that did not impede the adventurous airmen from finding the limits to what could be done in the aircraft

73

Keystone B-3 of the 9th Bombardment Squadron, March Field, California.

The open cockpit and bombardiers' positions in the MB-2. The bombardier who successfully targeted and sank the battleship was Staff Sergeant Ulysses Nero.

General Billy Mitchell's famous series of airplane-versus-battleship tests from 1921-1923, when his Martin MB-2 bombers proved the vulnerability of warships to air attack by sinking the captured German battleship Ostfriesland.

The US Army undertook the first organized around-the-world flights in 1924. fBuilt for this mission the four Douglas World Cruisers set out from Seattle in April and concluded the mission by the end of September 1924. The aircraft could be outfitted with traditional wheeled undercarriages or with pontoons for the overwater flights.

Resurrection Bay Stopover, *(from an oil painting by Chris French FGAvA © Chris French 2023).*

The Douglas World Cruiser Chicago arrives at Teterboro Field, New Jersey.

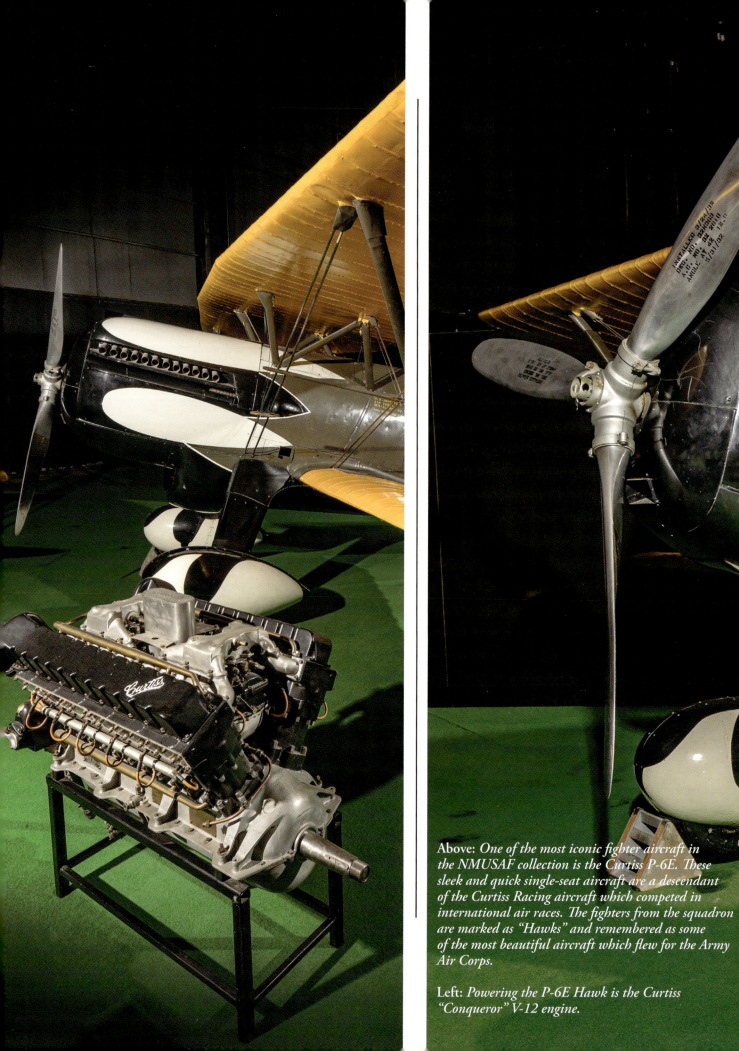

Above: *One of the most iconic fighter aircraft in the NMUSAF collection is the Curtiss P-6E. These sleek and quick single-seat aircraft are a descendant of the Curtiss Racing aircraft which competed in international air races. The fighters from the squadron are marked as "Hawks" and remembered as some of the most beautiful aircraft which flew for the Army Air Corps.*

Left: *Powering the P-6E Hawk is the Curtiss "Conqueror" V-12 engine.*

they had. Army pilots in Army aircraft participated in any number of racing and distance competitions, largely supported by senior officers because success in these events would help them make a stronger argument for air power. Some efforts touched on the dramatic, even the comic. In 1921,

Henry H. (Hap) Arnold managed to win a race between

Some of the pilots took every advantage to demonstrate their ability with an aircraft and amaze anyone who might be paying attention. One of theses pilots, Lt. James H. Doolittle, who is most known for his WWII accomplishments, in New York for the 1925 Pulitzer competition, took the opportunity to promote the event by flying down the streets of Manhattan between the skyscrapers, right side up and inverted. He later found himself in hot water for taking (and winning) a five-dollar bet for sitting on the axle of the landing wheels while another pilot landed the plane. He survived, unharmed, and was instantly grounded for a month for his trouble. Doolittle proved himself to be much more than a daredevil, earning a master's degree and doctor of science at Massachusetts Institute of Technology in two short years. He went on to develop redesign a cockpit layout to include an accurate altimeter, a directional gyro, and an artificial horizon. With the help of an extant radio that could be homed onto a runway, Doolittle became the first to fly a set course and land the plane on instruments alone.

The 1920s ended with the United States still not committed to making air power an integrated part of the American military. Billy Mitchell's advocacy, appreciated by most who served with him, often alienated those whose support was critical to achieving the goal. American isolationists, who had no stomach for another war nor keeping the nation ready to fight one, stood strongly opposite those who understood that the importance of aircraft and the tactics and strategy of aeronautics when the next war inevitably would come. The Great Depression, a real test of the American capitalistic economic system added to the complicating factors. With little in the way of resource to do what the advocates of air power knew needed to be done, the Service stagnated as much as moved forward. From July 1927 to June 1932, a plan to fill the Corps with 1,650 officers, 15,000 men, and 1,800 serviceable aircraft remained well out of reach. But economic hard times, isolationism, and pacifism were yet to be tested by a Germany beat down by an oppressive treaty and economic hardship and a nationalistic and militaristic Japan just beginning to assert itself in the Far East.

his Curtiss DH-4 and a flock of homing pigeons from Portland, Oregon to San Francisco despite having spotted the pigeons a forty-five minute head start because he could not get the engine to start. Army aircraft, sometimes specially built, regularly participated he air racing events, particularly the Pulitzer Trophy event, winning in 1920, 1922, 1924 and 1925. After the 1922 victory, Billy Mitchell flew the winning Curtiss R-6 of Lt. Russell Maughan to a new air speed record of 222.97 mph.

Top left: *Jimmy Doolittle was one of the United States Army's most seasoned test pilots. He flew some of the earliest pioneering flights which tested flying on instruments, long-distance endurance flights, and set transcontinental speed records proving the military's goals to be able to react to long-distance threats.*

Above: *Flying for the USA in the international Schneider Trophy races Doolittle defeated all others in 1925 when the races were held on Chesapeake Bay.*

Top right: *In a photograph made by author/photographer Dan Patterson in 1967 one of the surviving Curtiss racing floatplanes, in a Museum storage facility,*

Left: *A surviving wing from one of the Curtiss RC-3 racing planes flown by Jimmy Doolittle.*

Bottom right: *The Schneider Trophy, named the* Flying Flirt *on display at the London Science Museum after the United Kingdom won the trophy outright in 1932.*

PART NO. G101A-6
A.C. NO. 36-1755
INDEX SET AT 27
MAX. 26.0 42°,
MIN. 19.5 42°,

HAMILTON STANDARD PROPELLER COMPANY

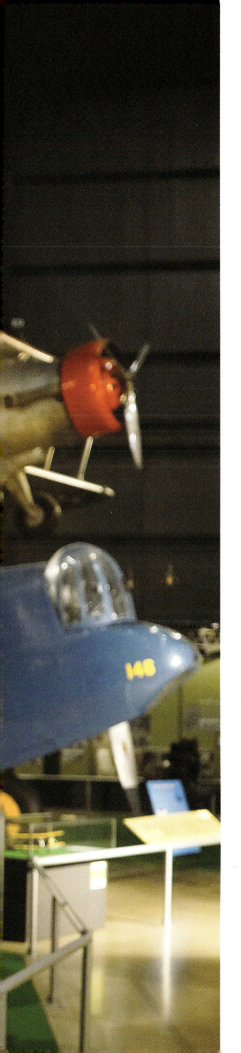

Chapter 4
The 1930s: Changes and Constraints

"Air power is as vital a requirement to the military efficiency of a great nation as land power or sea power, and there is no hope for victory in war for a nation in which it is lacking."
(Major General Frank Andrews, 1938)

Classic American aircraft from the period between the world wars on show at the National Museum of the United States Air Force.

The 1930's began as a continuation of the 1920s for the Air Corps. A worldwide economic panic could now be added to the ongoing spirit of pacifism, isolationism, and governmental frugality. The threat of Japanese militarism and Hitler's reconstituted German Empire had yet to fully occupy the minds of American military thinkers and the civilian government, leaving the Air Corps to deal with rapidly developing technologies, and old school thinking of senior army commanders who remained fully prepared to fight the last war. In 1931, General Benny Foulois became Chief of the Air Corps, succeeding General James Fechet, who had served as Chief since 1927. Foulois began his career in military aeronautics in the Aeronautical Division of the Signal Corp in 1908 and had for a time served as the only pilot in the Army. A long been a strong advocate for an independent air force, Foulois found himself trying to find a way to balance the needs of creating an effective Air Corps within the Army. The general staff, always looking out for its interests as well as the army's, slowly came to accept the idea of a GHQ Air Force, under the auspices of the General Headquarters, separate from other lines of command. It took time for the idea to gain a foothold and once implemented in 1935, the newly founded GHQ Air-force separated air combat units from the rest of the Air Corps, while proved far less than ideal.

One of the ongoing problems regarding military aviation had been the relationship of the Army and Navy to military aviation and each other. In January 1931, newly appointed Army Chief of Staff, Douglas MacArthur and Chief of Naval Operations, Admiral William Pratt reached an agreement that divided the duties and responsibilities of the two service. The Navy would be based on the fleet and

General Benny Foulois's uniform jacket when he was the Army Air Corps Chief of Staff.

support naval activities afloat. The Army would be land based, defending the coasts, at home and overseas. When Pratt retired in 1933, his successor, Admiral William Standley, had the Navy develop its own land based planes to defend the coasts, essentially duplicating the Air Corps responsibility. The Army General Staff continued its own efforts to provide for coastal defense, extending it to conducting long-range reconnaissance missions over water, with the ability to intercept and attack enemy shipping if the need arose. Such long-range reconnaissance aircraft might, of course, serve double-duty as strategic bombers if properly equipped, adding a long-wanted capabiliy to the Corps arsenal.

Air power theory and technological reality had been at odds with each other in the 1920s but that began to change over time. Newer aircraft could fly higher, faster, further, and carry heavier cargo. The Boeing B-9, an all-metal, stressed skin monoplane with a retractable undercarriage, was introduced in 1931, reflected some of the best design and manufacturing improvements being developed. Months later, Martin introduced the B-10, which completely overshadowed the B-9. A cantilevered monoplane with all-metal stressed-skin, the B-10 featured retractable landing gear, an enclosed cockpit, variable pitched propellers, a glazed gun-turret, full engine cowling, and an internal, powered-door bomb bay. The future of American air power had arrived, for long-ranged reconnaissance and maybe, just maybe, strategic bombing.

The Air Corps understood what the B-10 added to its capabilities and immediately set about demon-

Top: *Shortly after Wright Field opened in 1927 Charles Lindbergh* (second from right) *was a visitor after his return from his epic solo crossing of the Atlantic. He was met by army officers and Orville Wright* (third from left).

Center: *Army Curtiss Hawk pursuit aircraft in a tactical formation.*

Bottom: *Martin B-10 crewmen dressed for cold-weather operations, inspecting skis attached to the undercarriage.*

Another bomber which led the way into the future of air power is the Martin B-10, the world's first all-metal bomber which had a retractable undercarriage, a fully enclosed bomb bay and enclosed gunners' positions. It was powered by an early version of the Wright Cyclone R-1820, which would power tens of thousands B-17s a decade later.

The authors were able to find some rare 8mm color film of US Army aircraft deployed to the Philippines in the 1930s. Luckily, 21st century scanning technology makes it possible to recover and enjoy these images. Special thanks to colleague Donald Nijboer in Toronto, Canada, for these rare images.
Here, a Martin B-10 in flight.

The Museum spent years searching worldwide for an example of the Martin B-10 for its collection. A wonderful example of the rich heritage of the USAF, the B-10 holds a key place in American aviation history.

When Museum staff learned that the only known surviving B-10 was in Argentina, discussions began with Argentine officials to obtain this historic American aircraft for the Museum. As a magnificent gesture of friendship between Argentina and the United States, the Argentine navy presented this aircraft as a gift to the United States on behalf of Argentina on August 21, 1970.

A flight of Martin B-10s was commanded on a long-distance mission to Alaska by Colonel Henry "Hap" Arnold (center, with sunglasses) in 1934. The mission was designed to demonstrate the flexibility of air power and the ability to deploy over great distances quickly.

Left: A piece of fabric from one of the mission B-10s.

The Museum's B-10 might appear ungainly while on the ground, but with the undercarriage retracted and trimmed for flight, the B-10 was faster than the pursuit aircraft the Army Air Corps was operating at the time. Seen here, the all metal fuselage is paired with two 775-hp Cyclone R-1820 engines.

The Wright Aeronautical Corp. introduced the 9-cylinder, air-cooled, R-1820 radial engine in 1931. Developed from earlier "Cyclone" engines of the late 1920s, the larger and more powerful R-1820 produced 575 hp; however, engineers dramatically improved its performance over many years of production, with several later versions being rated at 1,525 hp.

Developed by the Boeing Aircraft Co. at its own expense, the P-12 became one of the most successful American fighters produced between the World Wars. This capable single-seat aircraft is powered by a Pratt & Whitney "Wasp" 500-hp radial engine. The cockpit being very elegant and direct, the essential flying instruments displayed in the center. The P-12E on display served with the 6th Pursuit Squadron in Hawaii during the 1930s, and the army retired it in 1940. Marcellus Foose and Glen Courtwright of Oaklawn, Illinois., donated it to the Museum in 1973, and museum specialists completed restoration in 1983.

Straight on till morning, *by Russell Smith, © 2023*

The US Army Air Corps flew the country's air mail for several months in 1934 when the US Post Office and the government were unable to fulfill the job. That short period of time was fraught with terrible weather and a series of tragic accidents. The venerable DH-4s, many built to see action in World War I, was the aircraft most of them flew.

Right: *Aviation routing beacons were placed every few miles along the air mail routes.*

Top left: *Air-mail pilots wings from the Museum's collections.*

Left: *A piece of aircraft fabric from an army aircraft which flew the mail.*

Far left: *At the National Postal Museum in Washington, D.C. a Dayton-built DH-4. The fabric fuselage was covered with plywood to strengthen the aircraft and to hold the heavy mail bags.*

strating what it could do. In June 1934, Colonel Henry (Hap) Arnold led a squadron of B-10s on an expedition from Washington, D. C. to Fairbanks, Alaska. Over the course of six days the squadron flew 4,000 miles in just more than twenty-five hours, without incident. While in Alaska, the squadron completed a 20,000 square mile photographic survey of the territory. The return flight to D. C. included an over water leg from Juneau to Seattle, avoiding, for the first time, a stop on foreign soil.

The problem of the usefulness of a corps that supported land warfare three thousand miles from the most imaginable battlefield continued to dog the Air Corps and spilled over into the political realm. When President Roosevelt cancelled the airmail contracts with commercial airlines in February 1934, the Air Corps was pressed into service on short notice. After all, flying is flying. General Foulois was given ten days to organize the operation, put the men and equipment in position, prepare the aircraft to carry cargo, and begin training pilots on the routes. Unable to say no, Foulois did what he could with what he had, dividing the nation into three separate zones, headquartered in New York, Chicago, and Salt Lake City.

The audaciousness of the assignment and short time allowed to implement it prompted any number of observers to warn the President and aviator of what might occur. Particularly vocal in his criticism was none other that Eddie Rickenbacker, the World War ace, now Vice-President of North American Aviation, who warned that commercial airlines flew exact routes with aircraft

The Boeing B-9 escorted here by a P-26.

specifically designed for the task and pilots with extensive training. Rickenbacker's concerns were quickly confirmed. On the very first day of flying, two aircraft crashed killing three pilots, prompting Rickenbacker to call the operation 'legalized murder."

Things did not approve and thankfully, for the pilots and crew, the experiment lasted only a few months. By the time the Air Corps ended their service on June 1, 1934, sixty-six planes had crashed on mail delivery flights, killing twelve. Six more died in training or ferrying flights. Fifteen others remained hospitalized from crash-related injuries.

But the failure of the Air Corps to succeed at what can only be called an inappropriate mission brought the problems of an inadequately funded air force into clear focus. President Roosevelt summoned both Foulois and General McArthur to a White House dressing down. Other recriminations followed, ultimately leading to Foulois' resignation in December 1935. The follow up did more than just assign blame. When more objective investigators looked at the details of what had been required of the service

Future general in the Army Air Forces, Ralph Royce (third from left), and a P-26.

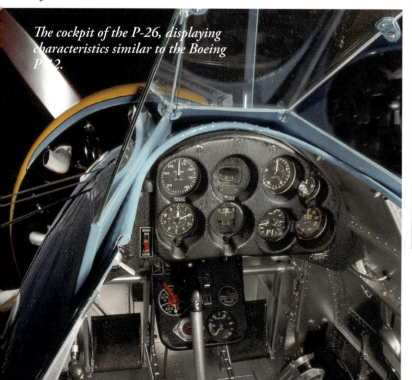

The cockpit of the P-26, displaying characteristics similar to the Boeing P-12.

The P-26A marked a significant step in the evolution of fighter aircraft, becoming the US Army Air Corps' first all-metal monoplane fighter in regular service. Affectionately nicknamed the "Peashooter" by its pilots, the P-26A could fly much faster in level flight than the Air Corps' older wood-and-fabric biplane fighters. The P-26A also had a higher landing speed. Although not initially delivered with wing flaps, P-26As were later fitted with them to reduce landing speeds.

Even with its monoplane design and all-metal construction, the Peashooter retained some traditional features, such as an open cockpit, fixed landing gear, and external wing bracing. The P-26A became the last Air Corps fighter to have these obsolete characteristics.

This P-26A reproduction is painted to represent the commander's aircraft of the 19th Pursuit Squadron, 18th Pursuit Group, stationed at Wheeler Field, Hawaii, in 1938.

Also in the 8mm films from the Philippines, seen here are actual in-flight and operational photos of the P-26 "Peashooter."

Boeing's XB-15 became a one-of-a-kind experiment. The accompanying P-26 accentuates the fact that the XB-15 was a very large aircraft, with a wingspan of 149 feet.

The XB-15 proved to be too large for the available engines of the 1930s and was a lumbering performer, but became invaluable in paving the way for soon-to be-built Boeing Clippers, and for the later B-29.

and what resources had been available, both the President and Congress were forced to concede that the service and its pilots had as well as could be expected under the circumstances. An internal Army investigation led by Deputy Army Chief of Staff General Hugh Drum recommended that the GHQ Air Force proposal be adopted and the War Department Special Committee on the Army Air Corps, more commonly known as the Baker Board, after its chair former Secretary of War Newton Baker, concurred with the Drum Report although it tied Air Corps reforms, badly needed it acknowledged, especially with regard to training and communication technologies, to the Army at large.

The P-35, a forerunner of the Republic P-47, was the Us Army Air Corps' (USAAC) first production single-seat, all-metal pursuit plane with retractable landing gear and an enclosed cockpit. The USAAC accepted 76 P-35s in 1937-1938, and assigned all but one of them to the 1st Pursuit Group at Selfridge Field, Michigan.

Despite confirming that a majority of the investigative boards remained suspicious on the importance of air power in peacetime and in whatever war might be on the horizon, the GHQ Air Force began operations on March 1, 1935. Separate from the Air Corps, the GHQ Air Force controlled combat units, leaving training and logistics to the Air Corps. Although the heads of the two service reported to the General Staff, the separation produced any number of questions and disagreements over responsibilities and chain of command. The separation of units only lasted four years, until March 1949, but it had been a step in the right direction and helped prepare the Air Corps for the now rising dangers coming from Germany and Japan.

The color image from 8mm film made in the Philippines of a P-35, between the world wars.

Beyond the problems of organization and appeasing politicians who were not quite sure what to do with a new combat unit in peacetime, the Air Corps faced the problem of what airplanes they would need going forward. Pursuit and reconnaissance aircraft were a given and the airmen themselves always insisted that a strategic bomber force needed to be part of the mix. This ran afoul of those who saw American war preparation as unimportant in the era of a world safe for democracy or those who could not accept a weapon system that, by design, could wage war on civilian populations.

For a time, the Air Corps considered a number of solutions to the problem of newer bombers having enough firepower and carrying enough speed to fly, many believed, without fighter escort. General Oscar Westover, who had replaced Benny Foulois in December 1935, reported that bombers could operate without support and doubted that pursuit aircraft could intercept and engage at high speed. Attempts were made to use multi-seat fighter aircraft that carried much heavier cannon and had the ability to drop bombs on the enemy, but none of these experiments produced a workable solution.

For most of the 1930s the Air Corps accepted the Boeing P-26 as its standard fighter. Much improved over the old wood and fabric fighters of the 1920s, the P-26 was the first all metal, single wing pursuit and fighter aircraft, but

The aircraft on display, the only known surviving P-35, served with the 94th Pursuit Squadron, 1st Pursuit Group. The aircraft was restored by the 133rd Tactical Airlift Wing, Minnesota Air National Guard, with assistance from students of the Minneapolis Vocational Institute. It is marked as the P-35A flown by the 17th Pursuit Squadron commander, 1st Lt. Buzz Wagner, in the Philippines in the spring of 1941.

The enclosed cockpit of the Seversky P-35.

ROMA·CHICAGO·NEW YORK·ROMA

CROCIERA AEREA DEL DECENNALE 1933·XI

IDROVOLANTI S.55X-SAVOIA MARCHETTI - MOTORI ASSO DA 750 HP.
ISOTTA FRASCHINI - MAGNETI, CANDELE E BATTERIE DELLA MAGNETI MARELLI -
CARBURANTE PER AVIAZIONE STANAVO DELLA SOC.ITALO·AMERICANA PEL PETROLIO·GENOVA

ESENTE DA BOLLO   GRAFICHE I.G.A.P. ROMA·MILANO

Italian aviator General Italo Balbo led an entire squadron of Italian Air Force flying boats, the SM-55, on a long distance deployment, appearing at the Chicago Worlds Fair in 1933. The twenty-four Italian military aircraft arrived at 5:00 p.m. over the Chicago waterfront, alighted on Lake Michigan, and anchored in formation next to Navy Pier. The Italians were given a heroes' welcome..

The intercontinental mission from Rome to the heart of the USA was a fact not lost on American military airmen.

still had a fixed undercarriage and open cockpit. It could hold 235 mph in level flight, acceptable a first but soon to be eclipsed by Boeing's newest bomber, the B-17, and the newest designs from Mitsubishi and Heinkel. Newer fighters from Seversky and Curtiss, radial-engined, single

seat, single wing, closed cockpit and retractable landing gear soon extended the speed to nearly 300 mph, but that did not match the performance of planes being built in Europe.

Much of the development of new aircraft focused on building a heavy bomber to replace the Martin B-10. In 1934, the War Department approved the Air Corps request to build an aircraft capable of reinforcing either coast of the United States or its overseas possessions without refueling. The design would be such that the plane could also be easily adapted to strategic bombing duty. General MacArthur encouraged the project, noting that a heavy bomber, "makes it possible to inflict damage on an enemy in the rear areas of his armies and his zone of interior…." The concern that the Air Corps would have a purely offensive heavy bomber at its disposal had finally been decided in its favor.

The experimental aircraft built by Boeing, designated the XB-15, exceeded all expectations. The plane took some three and a half years to build, with a wingspan of 149 ft and a gross weight of 70,000 lbs. Much of it was invented on the fly as engineers tackled problem after problems as they encountered them. Ultimately design outran technology and the XB-15 became a one-off experiment, the plane proved to be too much for the available engines. But the lessons learned in building the XB-15 were soon in building two additional Boeing bombers that would leave an indelible mark on WWII aviation history.

Even while building the XB-15, Boeing entered the competition in August 1934, to build another bomber the replace the only recently acquired Martin B-10. Specifications expected the new bomber to carry at least one ton of bombs at 200 mph over no less than 1.020 miles without refueling. Ideally, the bomber would have a range of 2,500 miles and a top speed of 250 mph. A working prototype was expected to take part in a flying competition at Wright Field in August 1935, one year hence. Three companies produced aircraft in time for the competition; Martin updated the B-10 with the B-12, Douglas brought an updated version of the successful DC-2 airliner designated the DB-1. Boeing's offering, the Model 299, stole the show. The completed new four-engined plane had been flown in from Seattle, nonstop, at and average speed of 232 mph. By the end of two months of exhaustive tests, the 299 had proven itself superior to the competition. Then, on the final test flight, the 299 reared, stalled, and crashed. The pilot had left the controls locks engaged, leaving him unable to lower the nose once the plane took off. By default, the crash handed the competition to Douglas and the DB-1, now redesignated the B-18. Douglas was immediately awarded a contract for 133 aircraft. That might have been the end of it, but the officers of the GHQ Air Force had been so impressed with the 299 that they ordered thirteen for flying evaluation. Now the Y1B-17, it had already taken on the moniker by which it would always be recognized, the "Flying Fortress." A Seattle reporter, amazed by the five gun positions and overall size of the aircraft, gave it the nickname and so it remained.

As tensions rose in Europe with Germany rearming and

When America's leading World War I ace Eddie Rickenbacker visited Berlin in 1935, Ernst Udet presented Rickenbacker with these two plates as a token of his 1935 visit. Udet painted them himself, with one plate featuring a caricature of Rickenbacker, and the other a caricature of Udet. The plate featuring Udet reads "To Eddy: Berlin 12-12-35." It is signed by Rickenbacker, Udet, and a handful of other German officials.

aggressively pursuing policies aimed at reasserting its place among the nations of Europe after the humiliation of the Versailles treaty, the Air Corps prepared for the possibility of war. Many thought that Germany's annexation of the Sudetenland and Austria only delayed an inevitable war against Nazi aggression. At the very time the nations of Europe tried to negotiate a settlement that would avoid war, the Air Corps lost its leader. General Oscar Westover, flying an A-17 on an inspection tour of western facilities, crashed on approach to the Lockheed airfield at Burbank, California. Westover had been a

Curtis P-36A Hawk
The P-36, developed from the Curtiss Hawk Model 75 originally designed for France, was first produced for the US Army Air Corps in 1938.

The airplane on display is the first P-36A delivered to the Air Corps. It is painted to represent the P-36A flown by Lt. Philip Rasmussen during the Japanese attack on Pearl Harbor, December 7, 1941.

strong advocate of an independent air force, but had often had problems with the dual nature of the command structure of the Air Corps and the GHQ Air Force. His successor, Maj. Gen. Hap Arnold, inherited an air force still saddled with restrictions associated with being subordinate to the traditional army's thinking and command structure, yet with great promise.

President Roosevelt, who had always been a strong advocate for the Navy, was in the process of adjusting his attitude toward air power even as Arnold took command. As Harry Hopkins, Roosevelt's advisor and Secretary of Commerce would remark after the Munich crisis, "The President was sure then that we were going to get into a war and he believed that air power would win it." Arnold's tenure would begin with a new attitude toward the importance of air power in a war that, more and more, appeared to be a certainty. Roosevelt asked Congress for 20,000 military aircraft and facilities to support building 24,000 each year. Congress, balked on the full request, but did authorize a force of 6,000 planes and the capacity to build an additional 3,251 new aircraft over a two-year period.

Despite the disparity of the request and Congress' ap-

proval, this represented clear progress. Taking what they could get for the moment, Air Corps planners designated 3,300 of the aircraft as combat planes and that was to include a number of new models; thirty-nine B-17B four-engined bombers, seven Consolidated B-24 bombers still in the prototype stage, 524 Curtiss P-40 fighters, thirteen Lockheed P-38 fighters, twelve Bell P-39 fighters, thirteen Republic P-43 fighters, and 186 Douglas A-20 attack bombers which filled a long-standing gap in the Corps arsenal. North American and Martin would contribute new medium bombers, the B-25 and B-26 when completed.

The expanded Air Corps reorganized when General Frank Andrews left his command of the GHQ Air Force, the unit lost its equal but tenuous status with the Air Corps. Rather than maintain the difficult arrangement of co-equal but uncertain command structure the GHQAF was placed under the Chief of the Air Corps, General Hap Arnold. No one could fathom at this early juncture just how much responsibility would be placed on the shoulders on this single officer. He would preside over the greatest expansion of military power ever undertaken

Left: Boeing Model 299 being rolled out in Seattle.

Above: Model 299 over Wright Field.

Right: The crash of Model 299 was just a few yards from the current location of the National Museum of the USAF.

to that point and later serve as commanding general of the Army Air Forces after the United States entered the war. With the President defining the mission, that the Air Corps would no longer be tied to defending coastlines, Arnold had the luxury, if it could be called that, of building the Corps rather than fighting for it. All the pieces needed to make the United States a major player in aviation warfare would be provided and it was Arnold's job to create the air force capable of using the pieces effectively.

When Germany attacked Poland on September 1, 1939, the reorganization had barely begun. The Air Corps had just 26,000 officers and men, only 2,000 of whom were pilots. Compare that to the German Luftwaffe, founded in February 1935, which included nearly half a million men and more than 50,000 aircrew. By one account the U. S. had approximately 400 operational aircraft to the Luftwaffe's 4,000.

Fortunately for the U. S., it would not be called on to fight for another two years, but few doubted the U. S. would be brought in at some point. Arnold and his colleagues understood that all estimates of the size and power of the force required to take on Germany and a militarized Japan already at war in China were inadequate by any measure. The possibility of two enemies meant that the United States needed to create, build, and be ready to deploy the greatest air combat force yet seen.

Boeing YB-17s in formation over New York City, October 1939, photographed by Paul Fedelchak.

Paul Fedelchak was born in Brownsville PA, on June 22, 1917, and served as an aerial photographer in the US Army Air Corps.

A formation of Douglas B-18A Bolo medium bombers flying over Miami, Florida, on Army Day, April 1940.

The Douglas Aircraft Co. developed the B-18 to replace the Martin B-10 as the US Army Air Corps' standard bomber. Based on the Douglas DC-2 commercial transport, the prototype B-18 competed with the Martin 146 (an improved B-10) and the four-engine Boeing 299, forerunner of the B-17, at the Air Corps bombing trials at Wright Field in 1935. Although many Air Corps officers judged the Boeing design superior, the Army General Staff preferred the less costly Bolo (along with thirteen operational test YB-17s).

The Air Corps later ordered 217 more as B-18As with the bombardier's position extended forward over the nose gunner's station. Stationed at Wright Field from 1939 to 1942, the B-18A on display was acquired and restored by the Museum in 1971. It is painted as a B-18A serving with the 38th Reconnaissance Squadron in 1939.

Ladies in Waiting *Photographed in 2010 in the Museum's restoration hanger, two of the most renowned B-17s. On the right is the only B-17D in existence. Now undergoing restoration in 2023, the* Swoose *has a colorful past and military flying history. On the left is the now-completed B-17F* Memphis Belle. *These two bombers represent a complete history of the famous* Flying Fortress. *The B-17D exhibits the characteristics of the original design, which was a defensive aircraft tasked to defend the shores of the USA.*

The B-17 was rethought as the USA moved toward involvement in a global war. The B-17F emerged as an offensive weapon, a bomber designed to take the war to the enemy and defend itself - a theory about to be sorely tested in the skies over Hitler's Europe.

Chapter 5
Air Power Unleashed: World War II

From the Museum's vast collections, this still life represents the American airman's experiences in the air while flying, fighting, and dying in the USAAF's aerial offensives. The "short snorter", which is a banknote inscribed by people traveling together on an aircraft; signed by Jimmy Doolittle.

Don Gentile's RAF Eagle Squadron uniform jacket and hat. In the foreground is the wingtip of a Bf 109 he shot down.

Don Gentile (Dominic Salvatore Gentile) was born near the Museum in Piqua, Ohio, on December 6, 1920. He learned to fly in high school, and in 1941, he enlisted in the RAF. He was assigned to combat in 1942 as a member of No. 133 Eagle Squadron. In 1942 when the three Eagle Squadrons were transferred to the AAF as the 4th Fighter Group, Gentile was commissioned a second lieutenant and began a fabulous combat career flying Spitfires, P-47s, and lastly P-51s.

Less than a week before the Germans launched their Blitzkrieg on Poland in the early hours of September 1, 1939, the Soviet Union and Germany agreed, publicly, not to go to war with each other for a decade and, secretly, mutually divide Poland and Eastern Europe. With their ideological opposite officially in agreement, the German military launched its combined arms invasion of Poland; infantry, artillery, mobile armor, and air support. In less than a month, Polish resistance collapsed, giving way to a well organized and technologically superior force. Germany and the USSR divided the spoils. Britain and France, as promised, declared war on Germany in a matter of days but neither was in a position to mount a serious attack against Germany from the west. Caught unprepared, the French and British stood by, unable to offer Poland anything that would help them hold off the blitzkrieg.

The instantaneous success of the combined arms cam-

paign masked some shortcomings in the performance of the Luftwaffe, which might have been seen as a harbinger of the future if anyone had been paying attention. It would have been too much to expect that the Luftwaffe perform flawlessly, after all it had only been an official part of the German military for four years, but not all went according to plan. To be sure, it performed well fighting tactical battles in support of troops and columns in the field, especially against a weaker enemy. But the Luftwaffe outnumbered the Polish Air Force by almost four to one and the experienced and well-trained German aircrews flew technologically superior planes. Its success should have been expected.

Despite the success, there were important concerns, largely invisible to the British and French at this early date, that should have given the Germans pause. In one month, the Luftwaffe lost 285 aircraft and ran low on both spare parts and armaments. All well and good for a short campaign against a weaker enemy, but how would the Luftwaffe hold up against French and British once they were ready to fight? And what about the Americans, who to this point had really not made a serious attempt to be an air power?

In retrospect, the ability to replace lost planes should have been worrisome; even more troubling, the problem of spares and armament. But the quick way the German combined arms assault dispatched the Polish military left the British and French stunned, so much so that, despite declaring war in a matter of days, the two Western powers took no action until Germany attacked through Belgium and the Netherlands in May, 1940, ending what some had called derisively, the "phony war." The Germans were nearly as effective in the West as they had been in Poland. By June 4, they had driven the British off the mainland at Dunkirk and by June 22, they had forced the French to surrender. Only Britain remained, off the coast awaiting whatever assault the Germans might direct its way.

But as with Poland, success over weaker and less pre-pared enemies masked serious deficiencies in the Nazi air war. The Luftwaffe had lost some 1,500 aircraft, more than 1,000 of them in combat. The British and French losses, in comparison, numbered 1,800 aircraft but many of those losses had been from planes abandoned on airfields overrun by the German assault. But taking the war to the British was going to be a difficult venture. The British had evacuated their army mostly intact at Dunkirk and any cross-channel invasion of Britain required strategies and technologies that did not yet exist. Importantly, but not yet obviously so, the Germans were missing one big piece of the defeating Britain puzzle. The Luftwaffe began the war with no strategic bomber. Both the Junkers JU188 and Heinkel He 111 had been designed in the mid-1930s and had not been serious-ly redesigned. State of the art in 1935 was obsolete by 1940. With bombers slow, poorly armed and defended, the Luftwaffe was soon to find that the British had certain advantages despite their poor showing so far.

The failure of the British and French efforts to hold off the Germans stunned most Americans. That Germany could build such an effective military since it began to rearm in 1933 seemed incredible. American isolation-ism still held the upper political ground and American politicians were loathe to even suggest the U. S. get involved, despite being openly sympathetic to the British and French cause. On September 3, when Britain and France declared war, President Roosevelt announced,

"This nation will remain a neutral nation, but I cannot ask that every American remain neutral in thought as well." It was only when the Germans soundly defeated the combined alliance in France and that Britain itself faced the next Nazi threat that the U. S. began to see that Germany could defeat America's allies and what such a loss might mean to American interests in Europe and the rest of the world. Italy, a German ally, Japan, not in a position to render aid to the Germans but militarily of the same mind, possibly even Latin America, whose connections to the U. S. were often strained, together would challenge America's position to such a degree that isolation would no longer protect it. In May 1940, with France nearing collapse, President Roosevelt called for an astounding 50,000 aircraft supported by the ability to build 50,000 annually.

For the Air Corps, the problem quickly became one of having enough money but not enough time. It was expected to expand from twenty-four to fifty-four groups by April 1942 and then to eighty-four groups, 21,000 aircraft and 400,000 men by June 1941, all as a neutral power. But expanding production and training facili-ties took time and Britain needed help. The problems seemed overwhelming. Though production substantially increased over the course of the year, American factories delivered only 800 aircraft a month at the end of 1940, a long way from the nation's projected requirements.

Dayton, Ohio, area resident Nadine Nagel flew as a WASP pilot. In the collections of the Museum is her WASP uniform jacket and WASP. pilot wings. The uniform cap belonged to WASP founder Jacqueline Cochran.

From the Museum's collections a selection of WASP documents and photographs. The women pilots were featured on the cover of Life magazine. The document with Jacqueline Cochran's signature are the orders which created the unit. The small photo in the center is pilot Nadine Nagel.

Helping the British proved to be its own great obstacle. As a neutral nation, the U. S. embargoed arms sales to belligerents until November 1939, when a new "Cash and Carry Act" took effect, under which Allied nations could buy arms from the U. S. and transport them in their own ships. Further liberalization followed, culminating in the passage of the "Lend-Lease Act" of March 1941. Under Lend-Lease, the U. S. could transfer military equipment to an ally providing it be returned at the end of hostilities. President Roosevelt liked it as lending a neighbor a garden hose to "help him put out a fire." Although designed primarily to help the British, it had outstanding orders for 14,000 American aircraft in June, the Act might also be used to help the Chinese against Japan and very soon applied to the Soviet Union after the German invasion began in June. Roosevelt had characterized the U. S. as the "great arsenal of democracy," in December 1940, and the nation did its best to be that. But it was also clear that the U. S. would need a few of those weapons for itself as the months passed.

At the moment the U. S. struggled to make itself that democratic arsenal, Britain faced its greatest challenge. In July 1941, the Luftwaffe launched a campaign to overwhelm Britain's air defenses in preparation for a cross-channel invasion. The Germans expected nothing less than to subdue the British in the same way Poland and France had fallen, but immediately found that the Luftwaffe had neither the equipment nor training to fight a strategic campaign against a determined enemy. By the time the high command called off the bombing campaign in October, the Luftwaffe had lost more than 1,700 aircraft to 950 for the Royal Air Force. A German invasion of the British Isles would be postponed indefinitely, ultimately forever.

Inspired in part by the heroic British defense its homeland, American support increased dramatically. The formation of the Joint Aircraft Committee (JOC) in September balanced the needs of the three principal customers of the U. S. aircraft industry—the U. S. Army

WASP veteran pilots Betty Blake and Dawne Seymour flew all types of aircraft for the Army Air Forces. Ferrying new aircraft from manufacturers to air bases across the country, their efforts allowed male pilots to be assigned to combat roles.

Dot Swain seen here on the left was the subject of late author Ann Cooper's book about WASP pilots; Ann, on the right, wrote extensively about woman aviators.

WASP Special Delivery, *by Gil Cohen.*

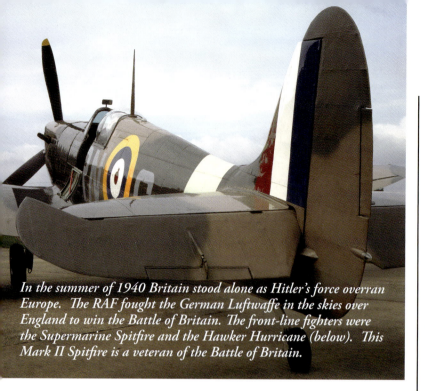

In the summer of 1940 Britain stood alone as Hitler's force overran Europe. The RAF fought the German Luftwaffe in the skies over England to win the Battle of Britain. The front-line fighters were the Supermarine Spitfire and the Hawker Hurricane (below). This Mark II Spitfire is a veteran of the Battle of Britain.

Air Corps, the U. S. Navy Bureau of Aeronautics, and the British Purchasing Committee. The JOC became an important part of the administration when Lend-Lease became law in March 1941. After the Battle of Britain, the United States, though still not an active belligerent, had thown its ever-increasing weight behind its lone ally in opposition to Nazi Germany. For better and worse, Britain and the United States were now partners against the fascists of Europe.

Going forward, British and American military services openly cooperated about how to defeat Germany. Cooperative discussion had begun as early as August 1940 and intensified in January 1941, ultimately to establish what would be known as the "Germany First" doctrine. The

final agreement, released on March 27, 1941, known as ABC-1 (American-British Coversations-1), perhaps the most important example of military cooperation between a neutral power and a belligerent, stated that the "Atlantic and European are is considered to be the decisive theater" in the global conflict and that the American Army bombardment units would "operate offensively in collaboration with the Royal Air Force, primarily against German military power at its source." A second agreement, ABC-2, recommended that both nations accelerate production of aircraft, suggesting that the U. S. built 60,000 aircraft per year.

Federal dollars built the manufacturing facilities and the auto industry redirected its efforts toward managing production. Ford Motor Company, for example, proved to any critic that the methods of mass production could be applied to building aircraft as well as Ford sedans. Construction of the manufacturing facility at Willow Run, Michigan started by July 1940. Production began in the summer of 1941, ultimately completing a B-24 Liberator every 63 minutes. Overall industry production rose to 96,000 planes in 1944 from only 900 in 1939. Air strength in 1944, taking into account combat and accidental losses, rose from 12,000 in 1941 to 80,000 in 1944.

So far as the U. S. and British military was concerned. The U. S. was active participant in the war against Germany, no matter what the isolationists at home said or thought, nor how tense relations with the Japanese might proceed. Additional organizational restructuring accompanied the Germany First agreements. Robert A. Lovett became Assistant Secretary of War for Air, giving the Air Corps a direct advocate at the highest level of the Cabinet. Charged with accelerating aircraft production and streamlining policies and procedures, Lovett led the creation of the United States Army Air Forces (AAF) to oversee all aspects of Army aviation. The Air Corps and Air Force Combat Command, which replaced the old GHQAE, now reported to the new AAF. General Hap Arnold now held two positions, Chief of the AAF and Deputy Chief of Staff to General George C. Marshall, Army Chief of Staff. As with the previous organization structures, this did not immediately solve all problems, but did make a strong step toward autonomy for the AAF. Hap Arnold accepted the arrangement, content to see it as progress although advocates for full autonomy remained dissatisfied. Arnold worked well with Marshall and fully understood that the pressing issue at that moment was being ready for the war almost certain to come. Detailed plans for implementing ABC-1 accepted that the AAF would hold an offensive role and increased previous estimates of required strength to 239 combat groups and 2.2 million personnel to support 26,416 combat and 37,051 training aircraft. The estimate included 135,000 aircrew and approximately 7,500 heavy bombers.

An air force of that size with offensive capabilities required the ability to train each and every one of those estimated 135,000 airmen. To accelerate the process, General Arnold contracted with nine of the nation's largest civilian flying schools to handle primary fight training for the USAAF. At its peak, fifty-six civilian flight schools would provide initial training to USAAF pilots. The task was daunting enough. Each pilot received approximately sixty-five hours of training in a biplane like the Boeing PT-13 or 17 or, alternately, in a monoplane like the Fairchild PT-19. After mastering the simple maneuvers and flying solo, the pilots moved on to closed cockpit aircraft such as the Vultee BT-13 (known as "The Vibrator), for another seventy-five hours of hours of aerobatics, formation, navigation, and instrument flying. Advanced training, another seventy hours of seasoning for the new pilots, included an introduction to aerial gunnery. Multi-engine pilots moved on to aircraft like the Curtiss AT-9, a twin-engined, low wing trainer. After the advanced training, cadets earned their wings and promotion to second lieutenant. To give some idea of the extent of the program, from July 1, 1939 and August 31, 1945, the USAAF trained 193,440 pilots and another 124,000 began training but failed to complete it.

After earning their wings, pilots graduated to combat aircraft, usually an older model such as the P-40 fighter or B-18 bomber. Once familiar with the new aircraft, pilots were assigned to an operational unit in the U. S. for combat training before being assigned to a unit overseas. In all, the new pilot had received no less than 400 hours of instruction and practice before facing combat. Luftwaffe pilots, by comparison, received 150 hours of pre-combat training. The Japanese made do with as little as 100 hours. By the time the Japanese attacked in December 1941, the AAF had grown to more than 350,000 men in seventy combat groups. By war's end the AAF had more than 2.25 million in uniform.

As the nation headed increasingly toward war in Europe, U. S. cooperation with Great Britain increased. Roosevelt committed the U. S. to providing fifty WWI era destroyers to the Royal Navy in exchange for ninety-nine year leases on airfields in Newfoundland, Bermuda, and

at various sites in the Caribbean. The AAF built additional bases in Greenland and Iceland. All this expansion was designated as defensive in nature, but to anyone paying attention, the U. S. had joined the Allied cause against Germany.

The focus on Europe masked the growing tensions in the Pacific and, to the extent it could given the president's focus on the threat of Nazi Germany, the AAF strengthened its presence on the islands in Pacific. Some effort had been made to reinforce existing bases in the Philippines and Hawaii and new airstrips appeared on islands such as Midway, Johnston, Palmyra, Canton, and Christmas, but not so much that it inspired confidence

Waiting for the US Army Air Forces was the battle-tested Luftwaffe and the dangerous Messerschmitt Bf 109.

that the U. S. could defend its widespread outposts. As almost an afterthought, the AAF prepared defensive bases in Alaska, but not with enough resources to deter a determined enemy.

By December 7, 1941, the United States and its AAF had made a significant commitment to defending itself and joining the Allies in Europe. But it was some ways away from being ready to join the fray or turn the tide if it did. Hindered in part by its neutrality in name only, the U. S. lent the aid it could and awaited further developments. The attack on Pearl Harbor that day proved to be that development, although not the one the U. S. expected.

The Wright-Cyclone R-1820 9-cylinder
radial engine developed 1,200 hp. It
was a rugged and reliable engine,
used extensively during World War II.
The Hamilton Standard three-bladed
propellers could drag the B-17 to well
over 30,000 feet.

Part I

The Engines That Won the War

The Wright Cyclone R-1820 served as one of the most important engines of the mid-20th century, first developed as the P-2 engine in 1925, updated in 1931 to the R-1820. A nine-cylinder, single row, air-cooled, supercharged radial engine, the R-1820 became a mainstay of bomber and commercial air fleets, producing between 600 and 1500 horsepower, depending on the model. The engine was used exclusively on the B-17 Flying Fortress and on many of the Douglas commercial airliners, from the prototype DC-1 to the DC-5. It proved to be a reliable workhorse of the American fleet that could withstand the rigors of combat, to the point of losing a cylinder or more and continue to produce power. The R-1820 used General Electric superchargers, to increase engine performance at high altitude. Mated to the Hamilton Standard constant speed, three-bladed propeller, the engine could propel the B-17 to altitudes exceeding 30,000 ft.

The Rolls-Royce Merlin engine first saw service in the RAF, powering both fighters and bombers, including the Hurricane, Spitfire, Mosquito, and Lancaster, among others. A liquid-cooled, supercharged V-12 piston engine, it provided consistent power at high altitude using a two stage superchargers. Licensed to Packard in the United States, the Merlin powered the P-51 Mustang fighter. The supercharger proved to be essential to the success of the Merlin, which allowed the engine to operate at altitudes above 30.000 feet.

The V-1710 engine, produced by the Allison division of General Motors, originally used a single stage supercharger which produced about 1,000 horsepower. Constantly updated over its usable life, a two-stage supercharger version produced 1600 horsepower. As with the Merlin, the Allison found its way into a variety of aircraft, including the Lockheed P-38, Bell P-39, Curtiss P-40 and the North American A-36. Typically, the Allison made more horsepower with less boost from the supercharger than the Merlin, was easier to service and manufacture.

Pratt & Whitney's powerful radial engine, the R-2800 Double Wasp. This engine featured twin rows of 9 cylinders each.

The supercharged engine developed over 2,000 hp. The R-2800 powered the P-47 Thunderbolt as well as the B-26 Marauder, among many other American aircraft.

Seen here attached to engine number 2 on the Museum's B-17G is a General Electric turbo-supercharger. The exhaust-driven supercharger allowed the Army Air Forces to carry out a high-altitude offensive against the Axis forces across the globe. This technology was developed by GE in conjunction with the Army Aviation Engineering HQ at McCook Field in the early 1920s. *Please see the photos of a prototype from that development on pages 66-67.*

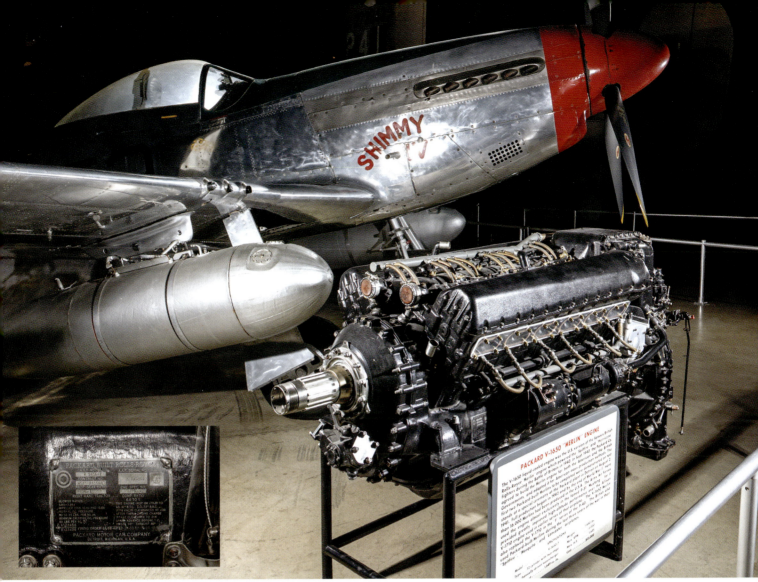

PACKARD V-1650 "MERLIN" ENGINE

The Allison V-1710 V-12 aircraft engine, seen here with a Lockheed P-38, which flew with 2 of these engines. Developed by Wright Field engineers along with Allison, the engine powered the P-40 and the P-38, and was the original engine fitted to the P-51. At the rear of the cutaway engine the single-speed turbine impeller can be seen. This supercharger did not provide sufficient power above 10,000 feet, where aerial combat was taking place, which jeopardized the uses of the P-51.

Bottom left: *The tool chest of a US Army Air Forces ground crewman. G.I. issued tools as well as the ubiquitous baseball glove and a pack of smokes.*

In 1942 Rolls-Royce test pilot Ronnie Harker was given the opportunity to test fly the Mustang I, (the Allison-powered P-51A). After landing he wrote a letter which stated that the performance with the inferior engine equaled or surpassed the current Spitfire (Mk V) below 10,000 feet, and that fitted with the current Rolls-Royce Merlin would be the fighter the Allies were seeking to win the air war over Europe.

Above: *Seen here is a Packard-built Rolls-Royce Merlin engine. Packard built under license nearly 55,000 of these engines.*
Right: *The two-speed, two-stage, gear driven Rolls-Royce supercharger proved to be the answer at combat altitudes.*

117

The Curtiss AT-9 Fledgling *(more often called the* Jeep*) was a bridge between single-engine trainers and multi-engine combat aircraft. It was not easy to fly, but it's idiosyncrasies were useful in preparing pilots to take on the challenges of high performance twins like the B-26 or the P-38. Two 295 hp Lycoming R-680-9 radials gave it a maximum speed of nearly 200 mph.*

Part II
The Airplanes That Trained an Air Force

Air Service pilots trained in in a variety of training aircraft from the radial-engined, bi-plane to the twin-engined bomber that transitioned new pilots to the aircraft they would fly in combat. At its most basic, pilots learned their craft on the Stearman-Boeing Model 75 Kaydet, designed by Stearman Aircraft which was acquired by Boeing in 1934. Over its lifetime more than 10,000 of the Model 75 were constructed, many to train Air Service pilots. The Kaydet was a straight-forward, ruggedly constructed, easy to fly open bi-plane that could stand considerable abuse. Student and training pilot sat in a fore-aft configuration with dual controls. The Kaydet also served as primary trainer for the Navy and the Royal Canadian Air Force.

The two most important monoplane training aircraft were the Ryan PT-22 Recruit and the North American T-6 Texan. Both were single engine, low wing trainers front-rear cockpit planes that combined simplicity and sturdiness. The Ryan was built as a primary flight training aircraft and was quickly retired at the end of the war. The T-6 became the advanced trainer of choice for transitioning pilots to combat aircraft. Powered by a Pratt & Whitney R-1340 engine the T-6 allowed the student pilot to see what flying combat aircraft would be like. The T-6 went on to extensive combat experience, not just in the USAAF and not just in WWII. As of the 2020s, it is still flown extensively and is a staple at airshows some 80 years after its introduction.

Multi-engined advanced training was divided into several different aircraft. Once of the most used was the Curtiss-Wright AT-9 (the Jeep), a low-winged monoplane with retractable landing gear, powered by two 295 hp Lycoming R680-9 radial engines. Pilot and student sat in a side-by-side configuration. Knows as a somewhat difficult plane to fly, it proved to be great training for the multi-engined combat bombers. Others included the Beechcraft AT-10 and Model 18. The AT-10 was used mostly as an advanced trainer, but the Model 18 went on to be one of the most popular twin-engined aircraft long after the war. In continuous production from 1937 to 1969, the AT-10 saw service as a business aircraft and small airliner in addition to its military use.

Fairchild PT-19A
Cornell Fairchild developed the PT-19 in 1938 to satisfy a military requirement for a rugged monoplane primary trainer, and it went into quantity production in 1940. In addition to those manufactured by Fairchild, the Aeronca, Howard, and St. Louis Aircraft Corps. produced Cornells. Fleet Aircraft Ltd. produced them in Canada.

Ryan PT-22 Recruit
Primary trainers represented the first of three stages of military flight training -- primary, basic, and advanced. Prior to 1939, the Air Corps relied entirely on biplanes as primary trainers, but in 1940 it ordered a small number of Ryan civilian trainers and designated them as PT-16s. They were so successful that the Air Corps then ordered large numbers of improved versions, among them the PT-22. By the time production was completed in 1942, the Air Corps accepted 1,023 PT-22s. .

Stearman PT-13D Kaydet
The United States and several Allied nations used the Kaydet as a standard primary trainer from the late 1930s to the end of World War II. Originally designed in 1933 by Lloyd Stearman for the civilian market, it received the designation PT-13 Kaydet when the US Army Air Corps adopted it in 1936. Two years later, the Boeing Airplane Co. purchased the Stearman Co. and continued producing many versions of the Kaydet using different engines.

Tuskegee students talk about flying their Stearman biplanes. At far left is Capt. Benjamin O. Davis Jr., the squadron commander.

North American AT-6 Advanced flying school prepared a cadet for the kind of single- or multi-engine airplane he was to fly in combat. Those who went to single-engine school flew AT-6s for the first 70 hours during a nine-week period, learning aerial gunnery and combat maneuvers and increasing their skills in navigation, formation, and instrument flying.

ARMY AIR FORCES
PILOTS NAVIGATION KIT
AIR CORPS
UNITED STATES ARMY

The NMUSAF Curtiss P-40E was originally a Kittyhawk, the export model produced for the RAF. It has been restored as a Warhawk and finished in the markings of Chennault's American Volunteer Group in China, the Flying Tigers.

This flag was flying when the Japanese attacked the US military bases in Hawaii. The Pacific Fleet was the primary target and suffered the greatest losses. The US Army barracks and the Army Air Force airfields were also hit by the sneak attack.

Duke Hedman in front of his AVG P-40 in China.

Colin Kelly flew his B-17D against the Japanese fleet just after the attack on Pearl Harbor and the Philippines.

Part III
The Blow Falls in the Pacific

Billy Mitchell, the staunch advocate of air power and what might likely happen within his area of expertise, predicted as early as 1924 that the United States and Japan would find themselves at war with each other. Not just that, Mitchell expected that the Japanese would attack at Pearl Harbor "on a fine, quiet Sunday morning." Mitchell did not live to see his prediction come true, but the attack of December 7, 1941 proved the visionary to be eerily correct. Launched from six aircraft carriers from two hundred miles north of their target, the Japanese delivered their attack in complete surprise. As designed, the Navy took the brunt of the strike. All eight of the battleships present suffered serious damage or were sunk. Shore installations, including the airfields, took nearly as much damage in not quite as dramatically as the ships in the harbor. Inland, aircraft had been massed in the open or stored in hangars, command being more concerned about sabotage than an aerial assault. The

In April of 1942 the USA struck back by sending a US Navy task force with USAAF B-25 bombers on board the USS Hornet to attack Japan. The first major combined operation of the war saw the navy get the bombers as close to Japan as possible.

In the cockpit of the NMUSAF B-25, Travis Hoover on the right and Tom Griffin to his left. Hoover was the pilot of the Number 2 bomber and Griffin the navigator of the Number 9 bomber.

The relatively simple cockpit of the Museum's B-25 as the aircrews would have seen their aircraft in April, 1942.

Japanese pilot took advantage of the opportunity before them. By the end of the day, only 83 of the 234 Army aircraft on Oahu remained serviceable. The only note of good fortune was that the aircraft carriers happened to be at sea that morning, avoiding destruction. The Japanese lost twenty-nine planes in combat and several more returning to the carrier, negligible given the success of their surprise.

The Japanese pressed their advantage in the Philippines. News of the Pearl Harbor attack reached General MacArthur about 3:00 a.m. local time. General Lewis Brereton immediately requested he be permitted to launch an attack on the Japanese airfields on Formosa, well within range, but was denied the opportunity to make his request directly to General MacArthur. Without approval and with a Japanese attack on Clark Field believed to be imminent, Brereton order aircraft to take to the air to avoid the problem of Pearl Harbor. MacArthur eventually approved the mission to Formosa. Brereton ordered the planes back to Clark Field to refuel and arm. While on the ground, the Japanese attacked, having delayed their departure from Formosa due to heavy fog. The delay proved fortuitous for the Japanese, who destroyed much of the Far East Air Force on the ground that first afternoon.

A small number of B-17s and a motley collection of other aircraft that survived the first day did their best to hold off the invasion of the Philippines, but proved to be little more than an annoyance to the Japanese, who forced the Americans to withdraw in May 1942. The United States had failed to define its interest and to properly assess the danger of

On the deck of the Hornet, Col. Jimmy Doolittle stands with admiral Marc Mitscher and the volunteer Army Air Forces crewmen. Just behind the Admiral's left shoulder is Tom Griffin.

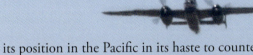

its position in the Pacific in its haste to counter the Nazis in Europe. Ultimately, it had found itself unprepared to fight against any enemy, much less a prepared enemy with surprise on its side. Lacking first rate equipment and communication facilities combined with weak defenses and almost non-existent intelligence, the U. S. mission in the Philippines had little chance of holding off the Japanese. Above all, it found, in the words of General Jonathan Wainwright, commander of ground forces, "the futility of trying to fight a war without an air force."

At first, and for a while, the Japanese air force appeared to be invincible. The Mitsubishi A6M, Type O, better known as the Zero, could outfly any Allied fighter. Powered by a 950 horsepower radial engine, the Zero was capable of 330 mph speeds, not quite as fast as some of the competition, but combined with a high rate of climb and excellent maneuverability, it proved to be more than a worthy enemy. Japanese ace, Saburo Sakai, who described the Zero as "a dream to fly," scored some sixty-four victories against enemy fighters. Extremely light, only slightly more than 5,000 lbs. without armor, the Zero had a range of nearly 2,000 miles with a drop tank. The lack of armor and self-sealing fuel tanks would eventually reveal themselves as serious design flaws, but

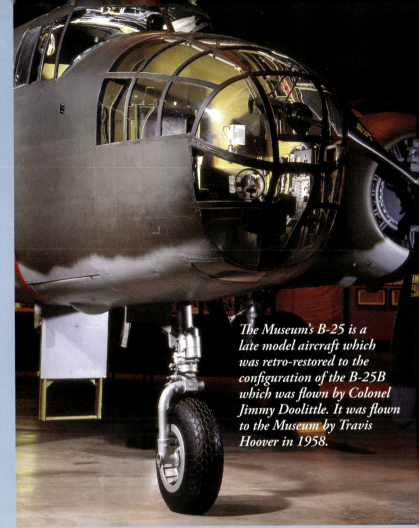

The Museum's B-25 is a late model aircraft which was retro-restored to the configuration of the B-25B which was flown by Colonel Jimmy Doolittle. It was flown to the Museum by Travis Hoover in 1958.

In this archival photo the deck of the Hornet is crowded with army bombers.

for the moment, the Zero ruled the skies. Only when American pilots figured out how to use their superior speed and diving ability to their advantage, did the playing field level.

After the mission Doolittle promised the "Raiders" that they would gather each year to celebrate their accomplishment. He persuaded the City of Tucson to create this unique set of eighty silver goblets, each engraved with names of the men who volunteered for this perilous mission. As each of the men passed away the goblet was turned upside down at the annual gathering. Included is also a bottle of Hennessy Cognac from the year of Doolittle's birth, 1896. The last man alive would then open the bottle and toast his fellow airmen.

Congress awarded the Raiders a Congressional Gold Medal in 2014.

Major Dick Cole (left) was the last man standing and toasted his mates in 2013. The last four of the Raiders gathered at the NMUSAF in 2012. A flight of sixteen B-25s, the same number as the 1942 mission, flew in salute to the men still present. Left to right, Dick Cole, David Thatcher, Tom Griffin, Edward Saylor.

Three events in the first half of 1942 came to give Americans some hope in the Pacific theater. In China, the American Volunteer Group (AVG) of the Chinese Air Force, later known as the Flying Tigers, led by Claire Chenault, helped the Chinese against the Japanese invasion. Chenault had left the Army Air Corps in 1937 when he could not resolve his disagreement with his superiors that a fighter-based air force was preferable to a bomber-based force. Hired by the Chinese to improve their performance, Chenault organized the AEG to attack the Japanese in China and Japan itself. Training in Burma, the AEG attracted pilots from the U. S. Army, Navy and Marines. Flying Curtiss P-40s as part of the Chinese Air Force, and using hit and run tactics whenever possible, the Flying Tigers quickly became a thorn in the side of the Japanese, recording a won-loss ratio of combat losses of at least two to one in favor of the American/Chinese. The Tigers disbanded in July 1942, to be absorbed into the USAAF, bringing with them the experience of being able to fight, and defeat, the Japanese in the air.

The second ray of hope came from an act of arrogant defiance. President Roosevelt wanted an attack made on the Japanese home islands to demonstrate that the United States was a force to be reckoned with, despite its early losses. The president expected such an attack would also boost morale at home, much needed at the moment. Planners decided to send B-25 twin-engined, medium bombers, each carrying a crew of five, from the aircraft carrier Hornet to drop their payload of bombs directly on Tokyo. In many ways, the plan defied all logic. Sixteen planes were to take off from a carrier with a flight roll of plus or minus five hundred feet. The planes would fly to Tokyo, drop their bombs, then continue on to designated airfield in China, not having the range to return safely to American controlled air fields.

Despite the challenges, the plan was approved and set to go for mid-April. Lt. Col. Jimmy Doolittle would lead the attack. On April 18, some 650 nautical miles east of Tokyo and two hundred miles before their expected take off, the Hornet encountered Japanese patrol boats, prompting the decision to take off immediately rather than wait to see what the Japanese might do. With little deck space available, but travelling at twenty knots into a thirty knot wind, all sixteen made it off the deck. Doolittle brought the group together, setting off

to Tokyo. On the way, they were observed by any number of Japanese vessels and drew anti-aircraft fire, but each of the bombers dropped their payloads at various points in Tokyo, Kobe, and Nagoya.

So far, so good, but the Doolittle Raiders still need to continue on to China and that part of the mission did not go so well. Fifteen of the B-25s managed to reach the Chinese coast but fading light, bad weather, low fuel, and radio silence kept all fifteen from finding Chinese airfields, the crews either bailing out or crash landing. Three died on impact, a number were injured, and eight were captured by the Japanese, three of whom were executed as war criminals. The lone sixteenth B-25 landed without damage near Vladivostok, in Russia, where it was taken by the Soviets and the crew interned, until they could be repatriated through Iran in May 1943. In many respects the raid could not be considered a success. Yet it demonstrated to the Japanese that the United States had not been cowed by its early setbacks. There was more to come, and sooner than anyone expected. The third ray of hope, indeed, a blinding bolt of lightning in comparison, came from reversing one of the parts of an extensive four-pronged attempt to expand the fringes of the Japanese empire. But the Japanese had lost face by even allowing the Americans to make an ineffective foray against the homeland and that had to be addressed. At Port Moresby in New Guinea, Guadalcanal in the Solomons, the Aleutians off Alaska, and Midway Island in the middle of the Pacific, the Japanese would try to extend their presence, saving face, yes, but also striking while the iron remained hot. American code-breaking efforts benefited immensely from the increased levels of fleet communications, allowing the United States to direct its limited resources to just where they might do the most good, ultimately thwarting the expansion effort.

But the great Japanese defeat in all of this came at Midway Island. The Americans had made enough progress breaking the Japanese Naval Code to be able to predict that Midway Island was one of the targets. Forewarned, the Navy prepared itself to defend the island. After an initial attack from the Japanese aircraft carriers inflicted significant damage on the airfield and island fortifica-

The Japanese air Force and naval Air Forces began the war with the USA with a formidable fighter, the Mitsubishi AM6 (Zero). This nimble single-seat fighter was designed by the great Japanese aircraft designer Jiro Horikoshi. The Museum's Zero was recovered from the South Pacific actions near New Guinea and restored by the Museum's talented restoration staff.

tions, but failed to deliver a knockout blow, American planes attacked the Japanese fleet with little success. While rearming with bombs to renew the attack on the island, the Japanese commander receive word that an American aircraft carrier had been spotted and reversed the rearmament from bombs to torpedoes. Before the Japanese carriers could launch their aircraft, American dive bombers attacked, wrecking three of the Japanese carriers in a matter of minutes. Later the same day, the fourth Japanese carrier met the same fate as the first three. The threat to Midway Island had been destroyed, irreplaceable aircraft carriers had been sunk, and the initiative in the Pacific air war had spun in favor of the Americans.

The AM6 had a relatively small Sakai radial engine which was offset by the lightweight construction and almost no armor protection. The "Zero" took part in every aerial combat action across the Pacific.

Part IV
The European Air War

The situation in Europe changed as quickly as it had in the Pacific, but without the immediate consequences. Only four days after the attack on Pearl Harbor, Adolf Hitler, in perhaps his worst decision of the war, declared war on the United States. Without such a declaration, President Roosevelt would have to turn away from the "Germany first" policy he preferred to dealing with the Japanese in the Pacific, which he considered to be the lesser of the two evils. While the German declaration of war committed the U. S. to war on two fronts, it also freed the President to deal with whichever threat deemed most serious at the moment.

In the short term, the U. S. was able to do little more to help the Allied cause than it was already doing. The earliest threat from Germany came from the Untersee boats, the submarines, patrolling off the Atlantic Coast. The U-boats moved into American coast waters immediately and enjoyed tremendous success against American ships, naval and commercial. Attacking at night when the outline of ships were backlit against the light from the port cities, U-boats sunk American ships faster than

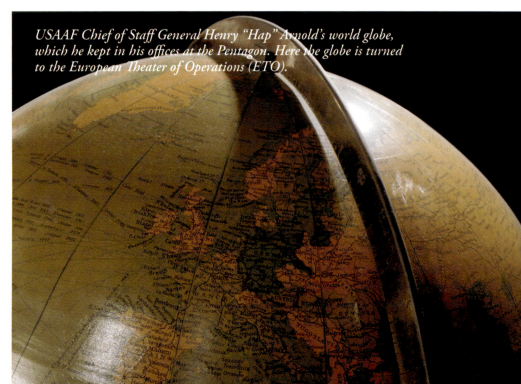

USAAF Chief of Staff General Henry "Hap" Arnold's world globe, which he kept in his offices at the Pentagon. Here the globe is turned to the European Theater of Operations (ETO).

In this photo the heart of the USAAF fighter forces is represented, here with the North American P-51D Mustang, the Lockheed P-38 Lightning, and the Republic P-47 Thunderbolt.

The NMUSAF has two Republic P-47 Thunderbolts in the collection. In this photo the early war model is the P-47D. At this angle the powerful Pratt & Whitney R-2800 engine can be seen just behind the Curtiss Electric four-bladed propeller. This supercharged engine would develop almost 2,500 hp at takeoff power.

This photo taken by the 390th BG illustrates the contrails so often developed at high altitude. The sweeping curves of incoming fighters contrasts with the straight lines of the bombers. A P-47 is silhouetted in the center.

Bill Manos flew the P-47 with the 9th Air Force, which was formed after the D-Day landings in June 1944 to support the army as it fought across France.

The NMUSAF second P-47 is restored as a 9th AF fighter.

they were being built. The Navy, busy elsewhere, was not prepared to deal with such a concentrated assault and the USAAF was requested to carry out anti-submarine patrols. Flying a collection of B-18s, B-25s, and older B-17s and aided by the Civil Air Patrol, many of them unarmed, the USAAF took some time to become an effective deterrent. Matters improved with experience and the fitting of USAAF with radar after March 1942, but it was not until July 7, 1942, that a Lockheed A-29 recorded the first confirmed sinking. Attacking from fifty feet at 220 mph, the A-29 released three depth charges on a U-boat that had submerged only twenty seconds before. All three depth charges hit close enough to cause damage and sink the submarine.

Despite the slow start, the air patrols were more effective than the rate at which U-boats were sunk.

After the invasion the forces discovered that the men in the air and the men in the tanks had radios which were incompatible. They could not receive each other's frequencies. In a hastily called conference of generals on Omaha Beach, General Patton, commander of the 3rd Army, and General Quesada, commander of the 9th Air Force, sat on empty crates and solved the problem. Aircraft radios were issued to the tank commanders, and each day a pilot from the 9th Air Force rode in the lead tank to coordinate the air cover. As the 3rd Army advanced across Europe, the tanks had close air support directly above.

A Thunderbolt receives field maintenance.

Sonobuoys, radar altimeters, and improved depth charges all contributed to the effectiveness of the patrols. Replacing older aircraft with B-24s specially fitted to the task completed the upgrades. After the war, Admiral Karl Doenitz, Supreme Commander of the Germany Navy, singled-out the radar equipped B-24 as the decisive factor in the defeat of the U-boat fleet.

Direct action to join the air war in Europe began in February 1942 with the formation of a bomber command headquarters in Britain under Brigadier General Ira Eaker. This new air force, the Eighth, after one false start, occupied a large manor house near High Wycombe, west of London. With the help of the RAF, the command set out to acquire and build the airfields and facilities needed to support the American men and aircraft soon to be on their way. Eaker's easy going manner helped smooth the transition. Originally the RAF took responsibility for much of the logistics needed to support the Eighth as it established its presence. In all, the cooperative effort worked well. Disagreements were few, but not unimportant. The RAF wanted the Eighth's fighter units to defend some sectors of Britain itself, which the Americans questioned because it meant U. S. planes would essentially be defending a foreign nation and that any such defensive activity took away from the Eighth's mission to take the war to Germany. Beyond that, the two forces disagreed on the deployment and use of heavy bomber. With experience from the Blitz and early attempts at daylight strategic bombing, the RAF preferred night bombing runs to operating in daytime. The Eighth, was committed to daylight bombing, convinced its fast, well-armed bombers could

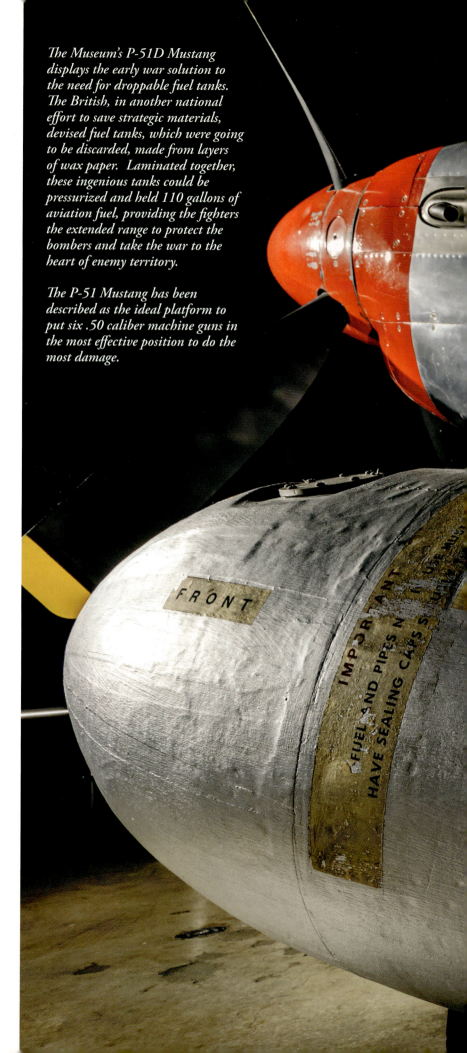

The Museum's P-51D Mustang displays the early war solution to the need for droppable fuel tanks. The British, in another national effort to save strategic materials, devised fuel tanks, which were going to be discarded, made from layers of wax paper. Laminated together, these ingenious tanks could be pressurized and held 110 gallons of aviation fuel, providing the fighters the extended range to protect the bombers and take the war to the heart of enemy territory.

The P-51 Mustang has been described as the ideal platform to put six .50 caliber machine guns in the most effective position to do the most damage.

The air war over Europe was fought by young men from across the USA and from of every part of the nations population. Clarence "Bud" Anderson flew with the 357th Fighter Group of the Eighth Air Force. He finished the war having flown 116 missions with 16 1/4 aerial victories. After the war he remained in the Air force and flew as a test pilot.

get through to their targets unescorted and bomb more accurately during daylight. Neither air force had the ability at this early date to test their competing doctrines but the disagreement was not quickly resolved. By May, American ships began to arrive with planes and equipment and on June 18, Major General Carl Spaatz assumed command of the Eighth.

The first American airmen to see combat took to the air at the end of June, 1942 and some engaged the enemy for the first time attached to RAF squadrons. It was not until August 17 that twelve B-17Es of the 97th Bomb Group flew its initial mission on Rouen against very light resistance. Similar raids produced similar results, modest success and very few losses. Beginning in October, Luftwaffe fighters began to take their toll on the B-17s and B-24s as their attacks moved further across France and the Netherlands into Germany.

The air war on the easily reached targets in Western Europe was interrupted by the need to support the Allied invasion of Northern Africa. This would be

the first amphibious assault of the war for the Americans and British, a true combined arms operation. Some 33,000 American troops under Lt. General Dwight Eisenhower took the lead against Vichy France resistance. Overall, Torch proved to be a great Allied success, with the Twelfth Airforce air cover and transportation. From March to May, 1943, Allied air units kept constant pressure on the overextended Luftwaffe, effective ending resupply of German Army units in Northern Africa.

In January 1943, even as operation Torch occupied much of the combined air power of the USAAF and RAF, Roosevelt and Churchill began to push forward with bombing attacks on Germany. With a combination of day attacks preferred by the Americans and night attack by the British, leaders expected the combined operations to "soften the Hun for land invasion and the kill." Luftwaffe marshalled resistance, which included attacking bomber squadrons head on, produced high casualties and less destruction than orig-

These men flew with the 322nd Fighter Group and become known as the Tuskegee Airmen. They represented a front-line fighter unit which flew and fought with distinction during the air war. From left to right are: Bertram Levy, Henry Moore, Dr. Eugene Richardson, John Harrison.

Their commander was Ben Davis who became the first African American General in the USAF.

inally expected. The air war was becoming a war of attrition. Ambitious attacks of high interest targets such as the Ploesti oil refineries in Rumania and the Schweinfurt bearing factories in Germany are cases on point. On August 1, 1943, B-24s, operating from Northern Africa, attacked Ploesti across the Ionian Sea. Of the 177 planes deployed, 54 were lost. Damage to surviving aircraft was such that only 30 planes were fit for service the next day. The attack reduced production at the Ploesti refineries by forty percent, short term,

but at a tremendous cost. Later that month, B-17s of the Eighth Air Force attacked the ball bearing factories at Schweinfurt and the Messerschmit plant at Regensburg. Delayed by heavy fog, the bombers encountered heavy opposition over Belgium and then all the way to their intended targets. Poor weather kept the force from identifying targets and accurately delivering its bombloads, so damage to the industrial plants was light. In September and October, the Allies struck these targets again, improving their effectiveness but again, at horrendous cost.

The NMUSAF features a combat veteran Consolidated B-24D Liberator, *painted as it served.* This bomber flew over fifty combat missions from North Africa during September of 1943 through June of 1944 with the 512th Bomb Squadron of the 376th BG.

The B-24 was employed in operations in every combat theater during World War II. Because of its great range, it was particularly suited for such missions as the famous raid from North Africa against the oil industry at Ploesti, Romania, on August 1, 1943. This feature also made the airplane suitable for long over-water missions in the Pacific Theater. More than 18,000 Liberators were produced.

One of the distinctive twin rudders of the B-24; centered between them, the powered tail gun turret.

The "front office" of the Liberator. The glazed nose compartment was where the aircraft bombardier was stationed, his Norden bombsight mounted just behind the Plexiglass. The .50 caliber nose guns were added in the combat theater to provide defense against oncoming enemy fighters.

The most famous of dangerous missions for the B-24 crews was the raid on the oil refineries at Ploesti, Romania. Launched from the USAAF air base in Tunisia at Benghazi, the bombers flew across the Mediterranean and attacked at low level. The mission was led by Major Ramsay Potts, who went on to become the youngest General in the Army Air Forces during the war. In this photo Ramsay Potts is once again in the cockpit of the B-24.

Right: *Tom Browning from Clinton County, Ohio, was also on a Ploesti mission and received the Distinguished Flying Cross, along with all of the survivors.*

Far Right: *A combat photo of a formation of B-24s from the 15th AF attacking the Ploesti oil complex from high altitude on May 31, 1944.*

In his painting artist Gil Cohen illustrated the scene at Benghazi when the last B-24 returned from Ploesti. *Utah Man*, piloted by Lt. Walt Stewart, was seriously damaged in the air battle and was over an hour later in returning than the rest of the bomb group. In the painting, Walt is describing the air battle to Col. Ramsay Potts, as only pilots can.

The first versions of the P-51 Mustang included the A-36 "Apache" dive-bomber.

An A-36 with the 86th (dive-bomber) BG stationed in Italy.

A B-26 Marauder over France.

144

The B-26 Marauder built by Martin is a very capable medium bomber, and by the end of the war had recorded the lowest loss rate of any USAAF bomber. The circular fuselage was streamlined and the high wing design left almost the entire midsection for a large bomb bay.

Gil Cohen's painting The Eyes of the Eighth *portrays a pilot from the 653 BS, 25th BG, USAAF, about to depart on his next mission.*

The de Havilland "Mosquito" provided the USAAF the fast and high-flying aircraft required for aerial reconnaissance. In a wartime acquisition from the British in a reverse Lend-Lease arrangement. The mostly plywood twin-engine fighter-bomber was powered by two Rolls-Royce Merlins of 1,690 hp each. It could achieve well over 400 mph and altitude above 40,000 feet. In the reconnaissance role it was unarmed and relied on performance alone for protection.

V-mail was a well-used method of writing home for American airmen and soldiers.

Gil Cohen's After the Mission *illustrates the post-mission debriefing of the bomber crews who had survived the harrowing mission of the day.*

Right: *Combat photos of the deadly missions undertaken by the Eighth Air Force.*

B-24 "Little Warrior" in flames over Europe.

SSGT George Little witnessed the B-17 as it was hit:

"I observed [the bomber] receive a direct flak hit approximately between the bomb-bay and the No. 2 [in-board motor on the left wing] engine. The aircraft immediately started into a vertical dive. The aircraft fuselage was on fire and when it had dropped approximately 5,000 feet the left wing fell off. It continued down and when the fuselage was about 3,000 feet from the ground it exploded, and then exploded again when it hit the ground. I saw no crew members leave the aircraft or parachutes."

B-24s from the 491st Bomb Group.

A P-47 "Thunderbolt" of the 361st Fighter Group forms up in close formation with a B-24.

B-17s from the 390th Bomb Group.

A P-51B "Kalamazoo Kid" flown by Charles Pearson of the 363rd Fighter Squadron closes up with a B-17: it is showing the invasion stripes added to all fighters the day before the D-Day assault on the French coast in June, 1944.

Catherine Wyler, who produced the film Memphis Belle, *which premiered in 1991. Her father William Wyler made the original film of the same name in 1943. She is holding the same type of 16mm movie camera her father would have used while making the wartime film.*

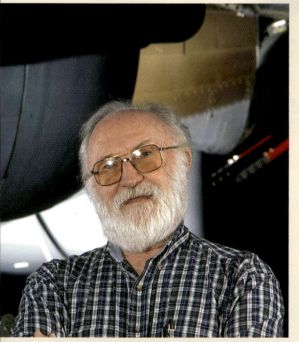

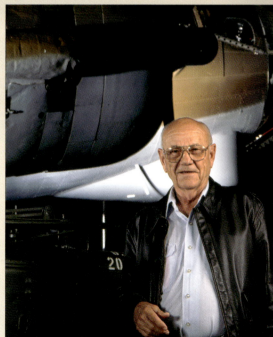

100th Bomb Group veterans Harry Crosby, "Cowboy" Roane, and Bomb Group Commander Tom Jeffries, whose stories were featured in the recent television series Masters of the Air.

Gil Cohen's Rosies Crew *depicts a scene at Thorpe Abbots, the air base of the 100th Bomb Group in the UK, as the crew of Capt. Robert Rosenthal gets their briefing before climbing into their B-17F.*

A B-17 departs the runway flying into the afternoon sun, casting the distinctive shadow of the Flying Fortress.

The NMUSAF's new iconic exhibit which features the B-17F Memphis Belle. After a lengthy restoration of more than 10 years, the Belle represents the thousands of B17s, which along with the B-24 were the USAAF's primary offensive weapons. The Eighth Force's mission was to strategically attack Hitler's occupied Europe. The invasion in June 1944 mounted the total war to defeat the Nazis.

Glenn Stroud flew C-47s and C-46s and accumulated over 12,000 flying hours.

The airborne troops were supplied with the more portable 75mm "Pack" howitzer. The 75mm could be broken down into several pieces for transport. These 75mm artillery pieces were also used by the 10th Mountain Division. Author Dan Patterson's late father-in-law, Jack Barnard, was an artillery man in the 10th and saw combat in Italy.

The Douglas C-47 "Skytrain" is the military version of the venerable DC-3. The rugged twin-engine transport served in every theater of the war. The Museum's C-47 is in the markings of the 88th TCS, 438th, TCG. for the D-Day invasion.

The 82nd Airborne and the 101st Airborne were the point of the spear for American forces on 5 June, 1944. More than 15,000 paratroopers were dropped behind the invasion beaches.

Left: Jack Reames of Company "C" 1st Bn. 508th Parachute Infantry Regiment, 82nd Airborne. Division. On D-Day he went out the door of the C-47 at "19 years old at 03:17" and jumped into the war near the town of Sainte-Mère-Église.

Right: Jim "Pee Wee" Martin of the G Company, 3rd Battalion, 506th Parachute Infantry Regiment, 101st Airborne Division. At 12:30 a.m. on D-Day he jumped into Normandy near the village of Saint-Côme-du-Mont, behind Utah Beach.

Both men also fought in Holland during the Market Garden Operation.

The tide turned early in 1944. The heavy losses sustained by both sides hurt the Germans more than the Allies. The inability of German industry to keep up with Allied production capacity took its toll. The new P-51 fighter, could accompany B-17s all the way to Berlin with drop tanks and outperform ME109s and FW-190s flying against them. Additional raids against the factories, the area bombing advanced by the RAF, attacks on oil production advocated by the Americans, all increased the Allied advantage. Air support for the D-Day invasion helped tip the narrow balance in favor of the invaders. More that a thousand B-17s and B-24s accompanied the landing forces at Omaha and the British beaches with

oil plants. As winter turned to spring, the Germans were effectively out of fuel. Russians and the Western Allies made their way to Berlin against limited resistance. The "area bombing" advocated by Marshal Arthur Harris of the RAF, produced significant civilian casualties and much controversy, particularly in the postwar years, for

its failure to destroy targets of military value and reduce the morale of the German homefront.

For the USAAF, the extent of its effort can be measured in a few of the statistics accumulated over the course of the war.

For the USAAF, 1942-45

Number of sorties flown

1,693,565

Bomb tonnage dropped

1,554,463

Enemy aircraft downed in combat (claimed)

29,916

USAAF aircraft lost (all causes)

27,694

Total USAAF casualties (killed, wounded missing, captured) 94,565

Total USAAF deaths (all causes) 30,099

limited effect due to weather and the reluctance of the bombardiers to drop bombs that might hit the landing troops. At Utah beach, with good visibility, a combination of B-26s, A-20s, and P-47s scored direct hits on coastal defenses. The Luftwaffe was conspicuous only by its absence.

Through the end of 1944 to the final capitulation of the Germans in early May 1945, the effectiveness of the bombing campaign increased, particularly due to the American focus on transportation infrastructure, including new raids on the Ploesti refineries and the synthetic

The war of attrition in Europe proved that, in the words of United States Strategic Bombing Survey (USSBS), Allied air poiser was decisive in the war in Western Europe. Hindsight inevitably suggest that it might have been employed differently or better in some respects. Nevertheless, it was decisive." The USSBS report offered an immediate evaluation of what worked and, just as important, what did not work. But the unassailable fact remained. The Allied air effort have removed the enemy's ability to defend itself from aerial attacks well before ground troops could finish the job.

American band leader Glenn Miller led his "big band" to the air bases across the UK to entertain the troops and the aircrews. The Museum exhibits his trombone and personal items, including his glasses and some of his arrangements.

The Eighth Air Force was flying hundreds of bombers over Hitler's Germany in 1944 and 1945. The introduction of the Rolls-Royce Merlin-powered P-51 Mustang turned the tide and created Allied air superiority.

The circular slide rule E6B was standard issue to all aircrews, used to compute all of the essential elements of aviation: fuel usage, time to navigational waypoints, wind factors, and much more.

The NMUSAF also has on exhibit some of the aircraft which the opposition flew against the USAAF.

Pages from a gunners information manual.

A restored wartime Messerschmitt Bf 109G banks away, displaying it's slender design.

ME 109G FIGHTER
SPAN—32' 7"
LENGTH—29' 4"
MAX. WEIGHT—7,230

SMALL TAILPLANE
BULLET SHAPED FUSELAGE
ROUNDED TIPS SQUARE TIPS ON ME 109E

HIGH SET ELEVATOR
SUPERCHARGER AIR INLET

TWIN RADIATORS AND OIL COOLER UNDER WINGS
LOW COCKPIT
SMALL FIN & RUDDER

RANGE IN MILES   500   1000   1500   2000   2500
ALTITUDE IN FEET
40,000
30,000
20,000
10,000
GROUND
SPEED IN MPH   100   200   300   400   500
MINS. OF CLIMB   5   10   15   20   25
RESTRICTED   Wing guns reduce : speed 25 mph, service ceiling 1000 ft., climb 8%
GIF 7-5

JU 88-C6 INTRUDER, NIGHT FIGHTER
SPAN—66'
LENGTH—47'
MAX. WEIGHT—28,500

TAIL PROJECTS BEYOND ELEVATOR
CIGAR SHAPED FUSELAGE
WING EDGES "BREAK" BOTH FRONT & REAR

ANGULAR NACELLES EVEN WITH NOSE

OFF CENTER GUN GONDOLA

"BULGED" GREENHOUSE FORWARD
SOLID NOSE
TAIL ROUNDED AFT

RANGE IN MILES   500   1000   1500   2000   2500
40,000
30,000
20,000
10,000
GROUND
SPEED IN MPH   100   200   300   400   500
MINS. OF CLIMB   5   10   15   20   25
RESTRICTED
GIF 7-9

Facing page top: The Junkers Ju 88 on show was flown by a defecting Romanian pilot in 1943 to Cyprus and turned over to British forces there. The British Royal Air Force turned over the Ju 88 to the US Army Air Forces. This fully intact example of one of the Luftwaffe's mainstay aircraft was flown by an American crew from the front across Africa, across the Atlantic Ocean to South America, and then north to Wright Field, where it was fully test-flown to determine the best methods to defeat the Ju 88 in combat.

Facing page bottom: The Focke-Wulf 190 D-9 was one of the Luftwaffe's deadliest opponents to the Allied air efforts. This Fw 190 was captured after the war and brought back to the USA for test flights and analysis. Those flights were managed by the Foreign Technology Office based at Wright Field. The Fw190 D-9 was powered by a Junkers Jumo 213 of 2,240 hp with methanol-water injection, it was armed with two deadly 20mm MG 151 cannons in the wings and

The very simple cockpit of the Fw 190 D-9 showing the flight instruments in front of the pilot. The other essential instruments for engine operations and fuel management were alongside the pilot's seat.

The Messerschmitt Me 163 Komet is a rocket-powered interceptor featuring a "tailless" design. The interceptor only had a range of 50 miles but was faster than any Allied fighter. Armed with two 30mm MK 108 cannons the rocket engine was the Walter HWK 509A-2, with 3,748 lbs. thrust, and had a maximum speed of 596 mph.

German test pilot Rudi Opitz also flew the Komet on some combat operations. Opitz, a lifelong glider pilot, was gathered up by the US Army's Operation Paperclip and was settled in Dayton, Ohio, and Wright Field after the war. He taught glider flying in the southwest Ohio region for decades.

Operation Paperclip was fully engaged late in the war to find and bring to the USA German aeronautical experts as well as rocket scientists for their acquired knowledge, but also to keep them out of the hands of the Russians, who were doing the same thing.

This German jet fighter, the Messerschmitt Me 262 was the world's first operational jet-powered fighter; of the more than 1,400 Me 262s produced, fewer than 300 saw combat. The two Junkers Jumo 004s of 1,980 pounds thrust each were very fragile and had about 20 hours of flight time before becoming unusable. The ME-262 had a maximum speed of 540 mph. It was armed with four 30mm MK 108 cannons and could carry 1,000 pounds of bombs.
On July 25, 1944, an Me 262 became the first jet airplane used in combat when it attacked a British photo-reconnaissance Mosquito flying over Munich. As a fighter, the German jet scored heavily against Allied bomber formations.

On display at the Museum since it was flown to Dayton in September, 1961, the B-29 on display, Bockscar, dropped the "Fat Man" atomic bomb on Nagasaki on Aug. 9, 1945, three days after the atomic attack against Hiroshima. Bockscar was one of fifteen specially modified "Silverplate" B-29s assigned to the 509th Composite Group.

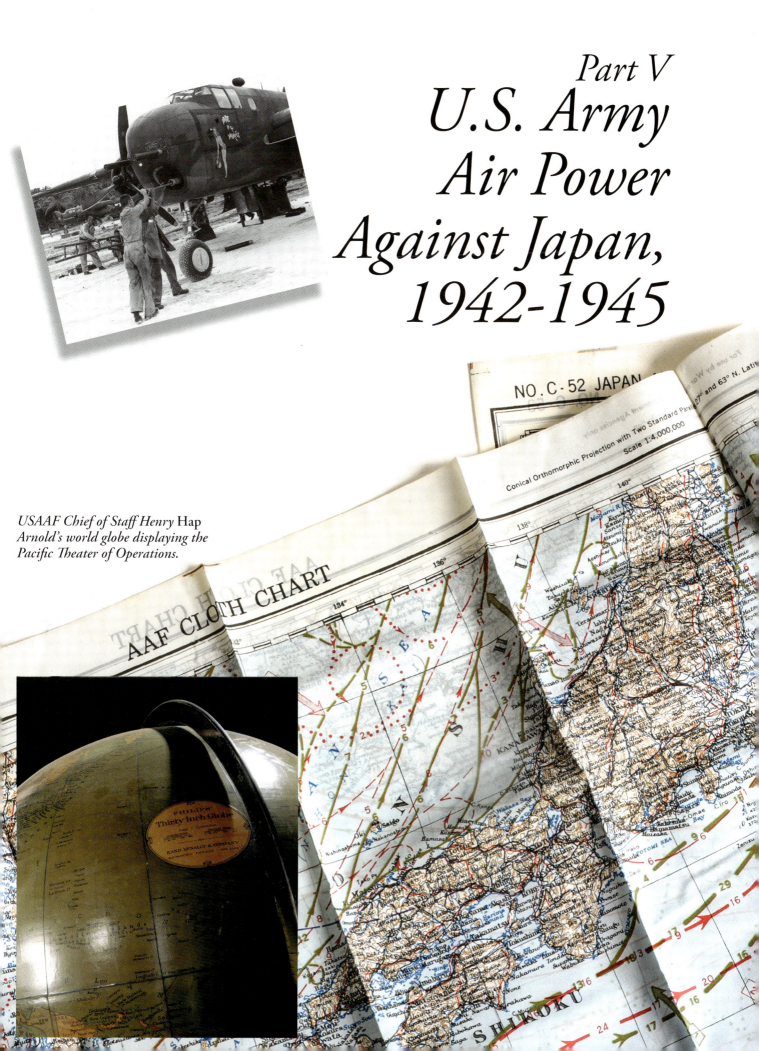

Part V
U.S. Army Air Power Against Japan, 1942-1945

USAAF Chief of Staff Henry Hap *Arnold's world globe displaying the Pacific Theater of Operations.*

The Doolittle raid on Tokyo of April 1942 had stung the Japanese high command. The raid had produced little damage, but it had reminded the military and civilian populations that the Americans were nothing if not resourceful. Military leaders knew they had not been seriously hurt, but they also knew that if the Americans could attack Tokyo only four months after Pearl Harbor, it was critically important to follow up on that success. They launched a four-pronged attack to make it difficult for the Americans to bring anything more than a nuance raid against the burgeon-

ing Japanese Empire. They intended to establish bases at Port Moresby in New Guinea, and Guadalcanal in the Solomon Islands, both intended to interrupt the America/Australia threat to the empire. Further north, capturing Midway Island in the Central Pacific and establishing a forward base in the Aleutian Islands would force the United States to keep its distance while the Japanese consolidated their positions throughout the Western Pacific.

In May, the Japanese sent an invasion force aimed at taking Port Moresby. To further the invasion, the Japanese needed to stop American aircraft carriers operating nearby. In the Battle of the Coral Sea, the first naval battle fought with aircraft carriers out of sight of each other, the two fleets struggled to a tactical draw, but since the Japanese were forced to abandon the invasion, the strategic victory belonged to the Americans.

At Midway Island, in early June, the Japanese suffered the defeat from which it could not recover. Initial success against island installations and aircraft attacks on the fleet by torpedo bombers were reversed, the Americans sinking four irreplaceable aircraft carriers, forcing Admiral Yamamoto to retreat to the west. The USAAF played only a small role in the battle and not a particularly distinguished role at that. B-17s of the 7th Air Force flew fifty-five sorties against the Japanese fleet, without effect. But the initiative in the air war passed to the Americans at Midway. The Japanese had certainly created an impressive empire on the Asian mainland and in the Western Pacific, but in six short months, the Americans had turned the tide, although it would take three more years for it fully to ebb.

The Japanese had no trouble securing a foothold in the Aleutians, but could gain no real advantage from their success. Too far away from any targets in the continental United States, and subject to intolerable weather most of the year, the small outposts on Attu and Kiska served mostly as defensive observation posts and little more. Attempts by the 11th Air Force to drive the Japanese away failed, sometimes worse than others. Perhaps the greatest success for the USAAF in the Aleutians came from an unexpected quarter. One of the bedeviling surprises of the Japanese war had been the great success of the Mitsubishi A6M fighter, known to the Allies as the Zero. It outperformed the American fighters, yet the USAAF knew almost nothing about it. After a raid one Zero pilot tried to land on soft ground, flipping the plane when he tried to do a standard wheels-down landing, killing himself in the process. The Americans were able to retrieve the plane and ship it to California for tests and evaluation, using what was learned to devise tactics to counter the Zero and adopt technology in later versions of American fighter aircraft.

General George Churchill Kenney, during his service in the Southwest Pacific in World War II, proved to skeptics the tremendous value of air force tactical support of ground and naval forces, demonstrating the new technique of skip bombing, to the pain of the enemy.

General Kenney directed the successful air war against the enemy in the Southwest Pacific during the long haul from Australia to the Philippines over a period of more than three years.

Fifth Air Force Lockheed P-38s attacking in the South Pacific.

Bell P-39 Airacobras lined up along a runway on Makin Island, one of many which were turned into air bases.

A North American B-25 on the attack against Japanese shipping.

The versatile P-38 Lightning performed many different missions during World War II, including dive-bombing, level bombing, bombing through clouds, strafing, photo reconnaissance, and long range escort. It first went into large-scale service during the North African campaign in November 1942, where the German pilots named it Der Gabelschwanz Teufel (The Forked-Tail Devil). When the Lightning began combat operations from England in September 1943, it was the only fighter with the range to escort bombers into Germany.

The Lightning truly shined in the Pacific theater; seven of the top eight scoring USAAF aces in the Pacific flew the P-38. On April 18, 1943, the long range of the P-38 enabled USAAF pilots to ambush and shoot down an aircraft carrying Admiral Isoroku Yamamoto, who was the planner of the Pearl Harbor raid and the commander of the Imperial Japanese Navy. The P-38 became the standard USAAF fighter in the Pacific theater until the closing months of World War II.

This single-pilot twin-engined fighter was powered by two Allison V-1710s of 1,475 hp each and had a maximum speed of 414 mph ands was heavily armed with four .50 caliber machine guns and a single 20mm cannon.

169

Weighing approximately 10,000 pounds, the stone roller on display aided in the construction and maintenance of the central Cheng Gong airfield in Kunming. One hundred workers normally pulled the stone rollers back and forth on mile-long runways to compress earth and rock, smoothing the runways for use by 14th Air Force fighters and bombers as well as transport aircraft flying the "Hump Route" over the Himalayas from India to China.

Using only hand tools, thousands of Chinese workers constructed hundreds of air bases and airfields. These handmade runways normally measured 5,000 to 7,000 feet long, 150 feet wide, and up to five feet thick.

The airfields constructed by the Chinese people proved to be a critical factor in the success of the US air campaign against Japanese forces. The simple stone rollers stand today as symbols of Chinese determination, toil, and sacrifice in resisting Japanese aggression and in defending freedom.

The C-46 gained its greatest fame during World War II, transporting war materials over the "Hump" from India to China after the Japanese had closed the Burma Road. C-46 flights on the treacherous air route over the Himalayas began in May 1943.

Air Transport Command was a unit that was created during World War II as the strategic airlift component of the US Army Air Forces.

George Kenney became the point man in countering the Japanese. Kenney, known for his visionary practical approach to the problems he faced, did whatever he could to keep his aircraft operational and adapt to circumstances he had never previously encountered. Finding that, in his words to General Arnold, "the artillery in this theater flies," Kenney allowed his crews to modify aircraft to make them more deadly. Major Paul "Pappy" Gunn fitted heavier armament, .50 caliber machine guns and 75mm cannon, to the B-25, to improve its ability to strafe enemy positions, turning a moderately effective plane into something fearsome. Having established air superiority in a matter of months, the Japanese withdrew from Buna. Shortly thereafter, an attack on a Japanese convoy reinforcing remaining installations on Western New Guinea sank eight troop transports and four destroyers, killing 3,000 soldiers, and destroying 100 of the 150 Japanese fighters engaged. The 5th Air Force, under General Kenney, ruled the air.

In the Solomons, the now-familiar pattern of the Japanese enjoying initial success only to fall victim to the ability of the Americans to overwhelm them with men, aircraft, and munitions prevailed once again. By February 1943, after six months of intense fighting and aerial combat, the Japanese left Guadalcanal. Unwilling to just abandon the Solomons, Admiral Isoroku Yamamoto tried to regain the initiative with a series of air raids beginning in April. By this time American air superiority countered the attacks, inflicting significantly more casualties than it suffered. In order to inspire the struggling units, Admiral Yamamoto made the fatal decision to visit in person. Code breakers had been reading Japanese communications and analyzing traffic with increasing success and knew Yamamoto would be visiting Ballale near the southern end of Bougainville and knew his complete itinerary. Sixteen P-38s with drop tanks, flying without radio for navigation nor communication, made the attempt to intercept the Admiral's squadron, two Betty bombers and six Zero. The P-38s took down both bombers, killing the architect and visionary of Japanese naval success.

Frank Lampe is a 308th BG pilot who flew combat missions in the B-24J in the China-Burma-India Theater of World War II. He recounted that at ninety-nine, he was here representing "all the other guys in the three-oh-eighth." He is holding a photo of the B-24 he flew back to the USA after the war ended. He remarked that "he had been given the chance to fly around the world twice and got paid for it."

Frank returned to regular life in Ohio, which included being married to Mary Louise for over seventy years.

Island hopping was difficult, intensive, and costly, and proceeded with a sense of inevitability. Japanese persistence and valor gave way to American superior resources and gritty determination. Ending the war, however, meant that the United States would have to take on Japan itself. Even if the home islands were invaded, the USAAF would be needed for aerial

support preceded by bombing operations. The strategic bombing weapon of choice was the new B-29, the "Superfortress." General Hap Arnold decided to form a new air force specifically for the B-29, the 12th, under Arnold's personal command, to keep the deployment focused on what was considered to be the most important targets.

American B-29s had been able to reach targets on Honshu for some time, but aerial attacks at high altitude had not been effective. General Curtis LeMay, fresh from the China-Burma-India theater, decided to switch to low-altitude night attacks using incendiary bombs to more accurately deliver payloads and increase the damage they caused. On March 9, 1945, 334 B-29s carrying E-46 cluster bombs delivered 1,665 tons on Tokyo from altitudes of 4,900 to 9,200 feet. Fanning out to drop bombs on areas not yet aflame, the raid produced one of the greatest conflagrations in human history.

Bell P-39 the Airacobra, *saw combat throughout the world, particularly in the Southwest Pacific, Mediterranean, and Russian theaters. Because its engine was not equipped with a supercharger, the P-39 performed best below 17,000 feet altitude. It often was used at lower altitudes for such missions as ground strafing. When P-39 production ended in August 1944, Bell had built 9,584 Airacobras, of which 4,773 were sent to the Soviet Union through lend-lease. Russian pilots appreciated the cannon-armed P-39 for its ground attack capability. Other P-39s served with Free French and British forces.*

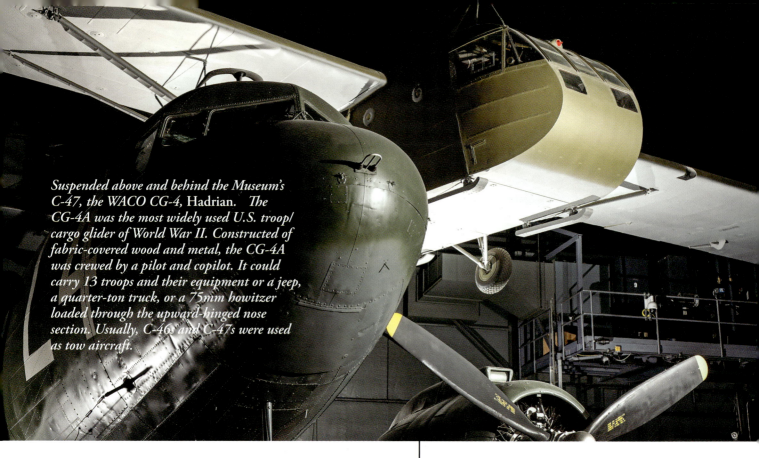

Suspended above and behind the Museum's C-47, the WACO CG-4, Hadrian. The CG-4A was the most widely used U.S. troop/cargo glider of World War II. Constructed of fabric-covered wood and metal, the CG-4A was crewed by a pilot and copilot. It could carry 13 troops and their equipment or a jeep, a quarter-ton truck, or a 75mm howitzer loaded through the upward-hinged nose section. Usually, C-46s and C-47s were used as tow aircraft.

The Air Commandos was a unique force with wide-ranging operations. Combat aircraft were mixed with Waco gliders and transport aircraft. Col. John Allison (right) seen here smiling broadly along with British General Orde Wingate and Col. Phil Cochran, CO of the Air Commandos.

Allison, a fighter pilot climbed into a Waco glider to fly the equipment necessary to construct an airstrip 10 miles behind the Japanese lines.

An Air Commando B-25.

died that night, more than 250,000 homes had been destroyed, and more than a million people were left homeless. LeMay confirmed the effectiveness of the new strategy and made plans to continue until redirected to support the invasion of Okinawa.

From May 1945 on, the B-29s worked their way through an extensive list of cities, from the largest down to smaller cities of 100,000 to 200,000 against light opposition. In July, LeMay began dropping leaflets over some cities, alerting residents that a raid would come soon, a tactic one Japanese official called "a very clever piece of psychological warfare." By August, most of the list of targets had been reduced to cities with populations of less than 40,000. Most of urban Japan lay in ruins, and some cities had been effectively obliterated. All expected an amphibious landing on the

Northrop P-61C Black Widow. *The heavily armed Black Widow was the first US aircraft specifically designed as a night-fighter. The P-61 carried radar equipment in its nose that enabled its crew of two or three to locate enemy aircraft in total darkness and fly into proper position to attack.*

World War II Pierced Steel Planking. The PSP landing mats represent the most commonly used form of World War II prefabricated runway material. They could be joined together with hand tools and provided a hard runway surface suitable even for bombers, where lack of time, materials, or equipment prevented the use of normal runway construction methods. Each 10-foot section weighed 64 pounds and the average laying speed was 125 square feet per man hour.

major islands to follow before Japan would eventually surrender.

The apocalypse came from a direction none of the USAAF had imagined. The United States had been developing atomic weapons through the top-secret Manhattan Project for several years. Successfully tested at Alamogordo, New Mexico, in July, the bomb was quickly approved by President Truman, who hoped to avoid the cost, human and financial, of an invasion of Japan itself. Even before the successful test, preparations were being made to deploy the new weapon. At Tinian, in the Northern Marianas Islands, specially modified B-29s of the 393rd Bombardment Squadron suddenly appeared and were isolated from the other units operating at Tinian's North Field. Only Colonel

An aerial camera like this was used to record the effectiveness of the B-29 missions over Japan.

A B-29 over Tokyo at high altitude.

176

The Boeing B-29 "Superfortress" was designed to be the replacement for the B-17 and the B-24. Pushed into production before the prototype had flown, the early B-29s were saddled with serious development issues which had to be worked out in operations.

B-29 operations were relocated to the Marianas Islands after the US forces captured that territory and airfields were constructed to base the 20th Air Force. The airfields on Saipan and Tinian were closer to the Japanese home islands than the bases in China.

B-29 GUNNER'S INFORMATION FILE

GENERAL ⊛ ELECTRIC

1400 YDS.

duration of att...

3½ second

170 YDS.

ON NOSE ATTACKS open fire at longer range because of the extremely high relative speed between your bomber and the fighter. Fire to kill at 1,400 yards. You will have to be plenty sharp on these attacks because in some cases the relative speed will be as high as 1,000 feet per second. This means that the duration of the attack will only be approximately 3½ seconds. Brother, think that over!

RESTRICTED

GIF 5-23

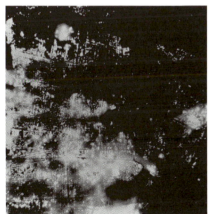

Tokyo in flames as the nature of the missions changed.

The culmination of the entire war effort: over five billion dollars invested in two projects. The Manhattan Project *delivered the atomic bombs and the Boeing B-29 provided the aircrews the ability to deliver the bombs on the targets.*

This B-29 Bockscar *delivered the bomb called* Fat Man *on August 9, 1945. Three days earlier the* Enola Gay *had delivered the bomb called* Little Boy.

When the B-29 strike aircraft took off the atomic weapons were not armed. There was a worry that if the B-29 crashed on take-off there could be a nuclear explosion. Each bomb was fitted with wooden plugs which were removed in flight to arm the bombs.

The result of the Manhattan Project, begun in June 1942, Little Boy was a gun-type weapon that detonated by firing one mass of uranium down a cylinder into another mass to create a self-sustaining nuclear reaction. Weighing about 9,000 pounds, it produced an explosive force equal to 20,000 tons of TNT.

Fat Man was an implosion-type weapon using plutonium. A subcritical sphere of plutonium was placed in the center of a hollow sphere of high explosive (HE). Numerous detonators located on the surface of the HE were fired simultaneously to produce a powerful inward pressure on the capsule, squeezing it and increasing its density. This resulted in a supercritical condition and a nuclear explosion.

When constructed in 1945, the Little Boy and Fat Man on display were operational weapons, but have been completely demilitarized for display purposes. In 2004 the Department of Energy repaired and repainted the artifacts at its Sandia National Laboratories in Albuquerque, New Mexico.

Paul Tibbets, a B-17 pilot with a distinguished record in Europe, knew what their purpose might be. A coded messaged delivered on July 18 alerted Tibbets that the test in New Mexico succeeded and that, pending approval, the secret mission would proceed.

A diplomatic warning issued on July 26 warned the Japanese that a "special bomb" would be deployed unless the Japanese surrendered immediately. As expected, Japan declined and final preparations were made to deliver the bomb. Hiroshima was selected as the primary target. The B-29 Enola Gay, with Tibbets at the helm, left Tinian at 02:45 on August 6, arriving over Hiroshima at 09:15 to drop the first uranium bomb, "Little Boy," from 31,600 feet. Detonation killed nearly 70,000 Japanese immediately, injuring at least 70,000 more, and destroying most buildings in a 5-square-mile area. Many more died of bomb-related injuries and radiation exposure over the years. On August 9, with no hint from the Japanese that they might surrender, a second B-29, Bockscar, piloted by Major Charles Sweeney

RESTRICTED

mbardier's
standing operating procedures
for the B-29 superfortress

RESTRICTED

27.

The forward bomb bay of Bockscar from which
the "Fat Man" bomb was released over Nagasaki
on August 9, 1945.

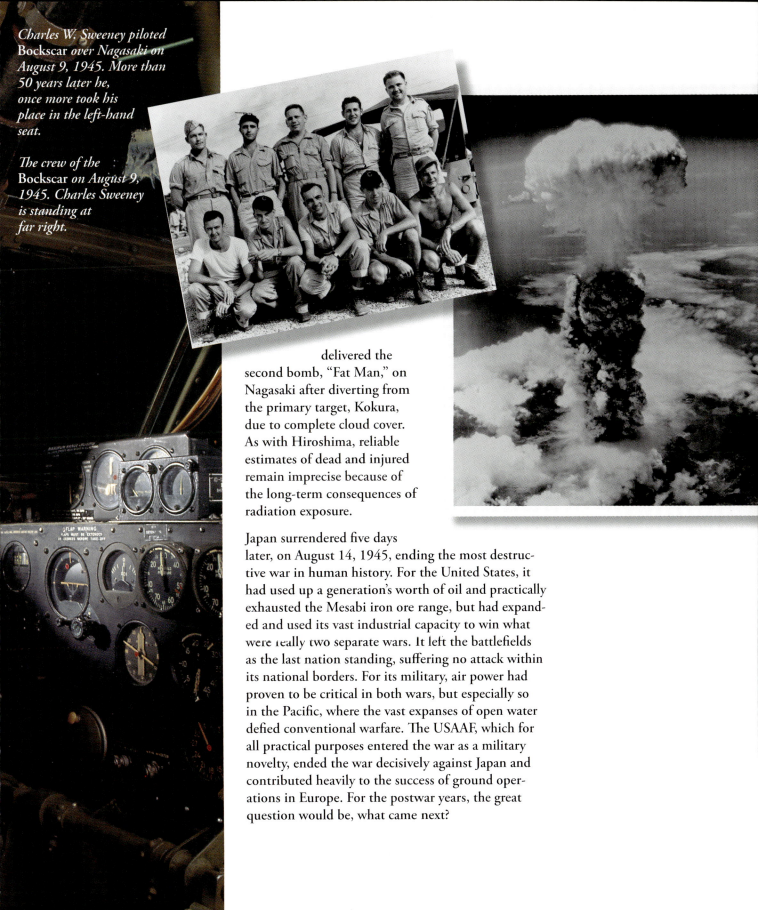

Charles W. Sweeney piloted Bockscar *over Nagasaki on August 9, 1945. More than 50 years later he, once more took his place in the left-hand seat.*

The crew of the Bockscar *on August 9, 1945. Charles Sweeney is standing at far right.*

delivered the second bomb, "Fat Man," on Nagasaki after diverting from the primary target, Kokura, due to complete cloud cover. As with Hiroshima, reliable estimates of dead and injured remain imprecise because of the long-term consequences of radiation exposure.

Japan surrendered five days later, on August 14, 1945, ending the most destructive war in human history. For the United States, it had used up a generation's worth of oil and practically exhausted the Mesabi iron ore range, but had expanded and used its vast industrial capacity to win what were really two separate wars. It left the battlefields as the last nation standing, suffering no attack within its national borders. For its military, air power had proven to be critical in both wars, but especially so in the Pacific, where the vast expanses of open water defied conventional warfare. The USAAF, which for all practical purposes entered the war as a military novelty, ended the war decisively against Japan and contributed heavily to the success of ground operations in Europe. For the postwar years, the great question would be, what came next?

On July 26, 1947, President Truman sat at this desk aboard the C-54 Sacred Cow and signed the legislation titled The National Security Act. which created a single Department of Defense and an independent United States Air Force. Sacred Cow is now a part of the new exhibits at the NMUSAF in the fourth Building, the Presidential Gallery.

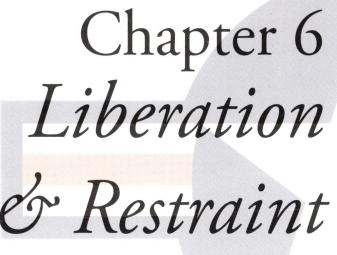

Chapter 6
Liberation
& Restraint

In one of the first milestones of the new USAF, on October 14, 1947, Captain Chuck Yeager flew the experimental Bell X-1 past the sound barrier.

"The real barrier wasn't in the sky, but in our knowledge and experience of supersonic flight."

(Chuck Yeager after flying faster than sound in the Bell X-1, October 14, 1947)

"It is hereby declared to be the policy of the President that there shall be equality of treatment and opportunity for all persons in the Armed Services without regard to race."

(President Harry Truman, Executive Order 9981 July 26, 1948)

The C-54 Presidential aircraft, Sacred Cow.

The end of hostilities against Japan increased the rate of change rather than diminished it. Of the 2 million-pl personnel, nearly all were volunteers, ea to return to civilian life. Aircraft, nearly 70,000 of all types, would be reduced t small fraction. Aircrews, numbering me than 400,000 at war's end would be cu 24,000. Returning to the days of 1939 not considered possible, but at the sam time, the USAAF was no longer in a po to engage in overseas combat only mon after concluding peace.

New problems arose almost immediate The Soviet Union, always a contentious insisted on maintaining political contro all lands it had come to occupy. The Ur States, the last nation standing in 1945 found itself in what would become kno as the "Cold War" against its beaten-do but not beaten former ally. The nuclear monopoly lasted only a couple of years. and the arrival of the jet engine as the r method of propulsion put the USAAF very different but just as difficult situati Increased speed produced aerodynamic instability, solved in part by swept-back wings. Further research on more power engines produced a rocket-powered eng incorporated into the X-1 by Bell Aircr which Captain Charles Yeager flew bey

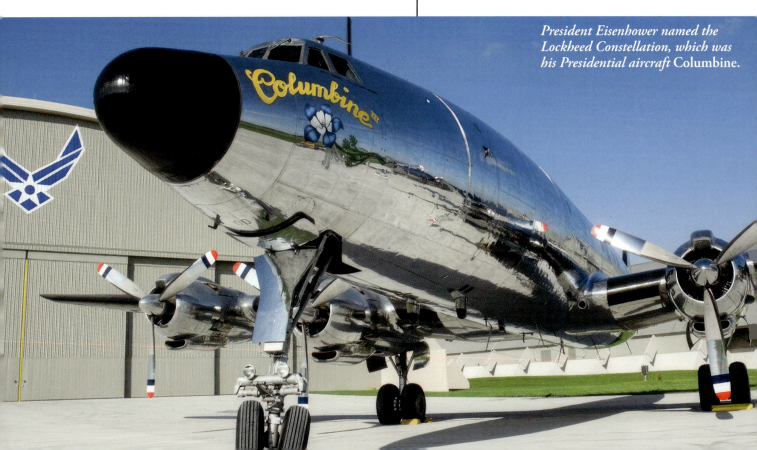

President Eisenhower named the Lockheed Constellation, which was his Presidential aircraft Columbine.

Designed and built in great secrecy during World War II, the P-59 was America's first jet aircraft. Although it never saw combat, the Airacomet *provided training for USAAF personnel and invaluable data for the development of higher-performance jet airplanes.*

The P-59 was powered by two General Electric turbojets developed from the British Whittle engine. Unfortunately, the relatively low thrust of the XP-59's engines and its heavy, conventional airframe design resulted in disappointing performance. The two GE J-31 engines powered the P-59 to a maximum speed of 450 mph.

the speed of sound for the very first time.

Carl Spaatz, who had replaced Hap Arnold as commanding general, Army Air Forces in February 1946, proposed that the long-range bomber be the backbone of American air power. In anticipation of an independent air force, Spaatz divided the USAAF into three new functional commands: Strategic Air Command, Tactical Air Command, and Air Defense Command. To support these three, Air Materiel, Air Proving Ground, Air Transport, Air Training Command, and Air University were set up to complete the reorganization. All the while hearings in Congress and meetings behind the scenes addressed the larger issue of the American military and most importantly, to the USAAF at least, whether or not the air sorces would become an independent entity.

Finally in February 1947 President Truman sent to Congress a draft of the National Security Act of 1947, which included a Cabinet-level secretary of national defense and a separate Department of the Air Force. More hearings and discussion produced a final bill signed into law by the president on July 26, 1947. On September 18, 1947, Stuart Symington took office as the first secretary of the United States Air Force and Carl Spaatz became chief of staff. An independent air force, long the vision of many flyers, especially Billy Mitchel,

The first postwar challenge to the Allies now facing the former ally, the Soviet Union, was the aerial lifeline known as the Berlin Airlift. For nearly a year the city was supplied the essentials of daily life with a continuous stream of cargo aircraft.

USAF General Curtiss LeMay

Developed by Igor Sikorsky from his famous VS-300 experimental helicopter, the R-4 became the world's first production helicopter, and the US Army Air Force's first service helicopter.

Gil Cohen's painting, Staying Power - Berlin 1948-1949 *illustrates the incoming USAF cargo aircraft as the women survivors of Berlin methodically cleanup the debris left after the actions of World War II.*

Facing page: Airlift relics from the NMUSAF collections division. The residents of the city of Berlin were supplied essential survival materials that included coal, sacks of flour, bags of beans and POM, (potato in dehydrated form).

Another Operation Paperclip *scientist was Hans von OHain the German inventor of the axial -flow turbo-jet engine. This portrait was made by author Dan Patterson's father, Bill Patterson.*

Originally developed by the General Electric Co. for the Lockheed P-80 Shooting Star, the J33 engine is a direct descendant of the British Whittle engine of the early 1940s. In November 1945 the Allison Division of General Motors assumed complete responsibility for the development and production of J33 series engines.

The rugged F-84 Thunderjet *gained its greatest renown during the Korean War. Initially sent to escort B-29s on long-range missions over North Korea, the* Thunderjet *excelled as a close air support and daytime interdiction strike aircraft. In Korea, F-84 pilots attacked enemy railroads, dams, bridges, supply depots, and troop concentrations with bombs, rockets, and napalm.*

During its service life, the Thunderjet *served in several roles, including day fighter, long-range escort fighter, fighter-bomber, and as the USAF's first tactical nuclear bomber. The USAF also supplied F-84s to fourteen other countries.*

The F-84E on display came to the Museum in 1963. It is marked to represent the F-84G flown by Col. Joseph Davis Jr., commander of the 58th Fighter-Bomber Wing in 1953.

Gil Cohen's painting Mission from Taegu *illustrates front line fighter base life during the Korean War. F-84s receiving maintenance parked on the ubiquitous PSP airfields laid around the world by USAF crews.*

The Shooting Star was the first American aircraft to exceed 500 mph in level flight, the first American jet airplane manufactured in large quantities, and the first US Air Force jet used in combat.

Although designed as a high-altitude interceptor, the F-80C was flown as a day fighter, fighter-bomber, and photo reconnaissance aircraft during the Korean War.

The F-80C on display is one of the few remaining Shooting Stars that flew combat missions during the Korean War. Restored and painted as it was in 1950 while assigned to the 8th Fighter-Bomber Group, it was placed on display in 1979.

191

The F-86H on display is exhibited with part of its stressed skin removed to show the internal structure and placement of equipment. Compare the complex interior of the 1950s USAF jet fighter with the spartan interior of the World War I SE-5A on page 58, to get an idea of the evolution of the airplane from 1918 to 1953.

had become a reality.

In a matter of months the new USAF faced its first challenge, not in combat, but in delivering food and fuel to Berlin. Citing "technical difficulties," the Soviets cut off all road and rail traffic into and from Berlin and Western Germany, expecting the Allied partners to withdraw. President Truman ordered an airlift of food and fuel to relieve the city. Curtis LeMay, commander of the USAFE, (US Air Force Europe), organized the effort. Starting with a fleet of mostly C-47s and replacing them with C-54s as quickly as possible, the airlift delivered some 2,325,000 tons of supplies on 277,804 sorties, more than 75 percent of which were delivered by the USAF. Any doubt that the United States had to maintain a peacetime readiness unlike anything it had

done previously was now gone. The Soviets also learned a lesson—that their expansion in Europe was a thing of the past. To counter any new threats, the United States helped organize the North Atlantic Treaty Organization (NATO) to jointly defend the twelve member nations against any future Soviet aggression.

In August 1949, the Soviet Union tested in own atomic weapon at a remote site in Kazakhstan. President Truman, dissatisfied with the way the United States had responded to the challenges of the Cold War so far, organized a study group in the National Security Council to examine what the United States should do going forward. The group presented its findings to the president in early April 1950 in a top-secret, sixty-six-page report that would become the framework for

American Cold War policy going forward.

The report, authored for the most part by director of policy planning for the State Department, Paul Nitze, emphasized military preparedness over diplomacy. While praising the concept of containment as argued by George Kennan, Nitze wanted a military ready to defend the United States and its allies and hold off any Soviet attack in the short term. The report called for aggressive increases in military spending, acknowledging that this would require increased taxation which it expected would be offset by stimulating the economy. A robust economy built around expenditures on national defense would necessarily force the Soviet Union to redirect resources away from rebuilding its economy toward countering American action. Truman originally opposed the conclusions offered by NSC-68, but soon came to realize it was the foundation of a coherent Cold War policy to counter the Soviet Union. Of course, such a policy would add considerable funds to the coffers of the USAF, the success of which in the previous world war made its readiness and performance central to the future of the American military.

Weeks later, on June 25, 1950, preparedness became the issue once again. Ten divisions from the People's Democratic Republic of Korea (North Korea) crossed the frontier intent on conquering the Republic of Korea (South Korea). The USAF quickly established air superiority over the North Koreans, who were limited to Soviet aircraft of World War II vintage, but air superiority did not translate into instant success in the ground war. The United States had seriously reduced its military capacity, and no matter how strongly Congress and the president embraced the conclusions of NSC-68,

The C-119 Flying Boxcar was developed shortly after World War II to carry heavy loads of cargo, paratroopers, or medical patients. Its wide rear doors and a fuselage parallel to the ground made it easy to load and unload. It first flew in 1947.

Flying Boxcars played an important role in the Korean War, carrying troops and supplies. The most important airlift mission in Korea came in the bitter winter of 1950 when USAF C-119Bs air-dropped bridge sections to US troops trapped by communist forces at the Chosin Reservoir. The sections replaced a destroyed bridge across a deep chasm, allowing thousands of soldiers and marines to escape.

The H-5, originally designated the R-5 (H for Helicopter; R for Rotorcraft), was designed to provide a helicopter with a greater useful load, endurance, speed, and service ceiling than the earlier R-4.

The YH-5A on display was obtained from Eglin Air Force Base, Florida., in March 1955.

The F-86, the US Air Force's first swept-wing jet fighter, made its initial flight in October 1947. The first production model flew in May 1948, and four months later, an F-86A set a new world speed record of 670.9 mph.

As a day fighter, the F-86A (and later F-86Es and F-86Fs) saw service in Korea as the primary opponent of the Russian-built MiG-15. By the end of hostilities, F-86 pilots had shot down 792 MiGs, with a kill ratio of about 8:1.

preparedness was some ways away, and resources were limited.

For the United States and, by extension, the United Nations, the Korean War was more about the Cold War political reality than defeating the enemy. The United States fought a limited war, more concerned with avoiding a nuclear reaction from the Soviet Union than winning outright on the battlefield. After the back-and-forth, nearly being driven off the peninsula by August 1, then reversing the momentum through the amphibious assault at Inchon, fighting toward the Yalu River, suffering the Chinese invasion to support the defeated North, and what amounted to a military stalemate, the parties settled for a negotiated settlement that changed

very little.

For the new USAF, Korea became the first test of the service and a jet-engine-powered fleet. Originally, the F-80C "Shooting Star," from Lockheed, the first American jet supplied in any quantity, proved to be not as suitable as it might have been. With no airfields in Korea to handle jets, many pilots chose to revert to the F-51, a propeller plane that could carry bombs which the F-80s could not do. The Mustang served the Far East Air Force (FEAF) well until newer jets could be pressed into service. Even with the Mustangs, the FEAF ruled the air war, but superior air power did not translate into instant success on the ground.

The Soviets supplied one plane, the MiG-15, that stood

The Soviet Union developed the MiG-15 following World War II and the fighter entered service in 1949. By 1952 the Soviets provided the MiG-15 (NATO code name "Fagot") to a number of communist satellite nations, including North Korea.

A defecting North Korean pilot flew the airplane on display to Kimpo Air Base in South Korea on September 21, 1953.

USAF F-80s lined up on the left and the F-82 Twin Mustang *on the right.*

Maintenance on an F-86 on this Korean airfield was performed in all kinds of weather.

some chance against the American fighter jets. Using a jet engine design taken from the British, the swept-wing fighter achieved higher speeds than the F-80, but well-trained American pilots were generally able to counter the MiG-15. Once the F-86 Sabre became available in number, the Americans went unchallenged.

But air superiority was never enough. Both the military and its political leaders faced a new problem: the idea of "limited war." With the ability to use nuclear weapons and having to defend against the Soviet Union, an opponent that now had nuclear capabilities, what was the lowest level of force that would produce victory yet not provoke a nuclear response? It became a constant consideration for both parties. That consideration had to be a part of every military decision made by the United

States or the Soviet Union when they allied themselves with another belligerent for the rest of the Cold War.

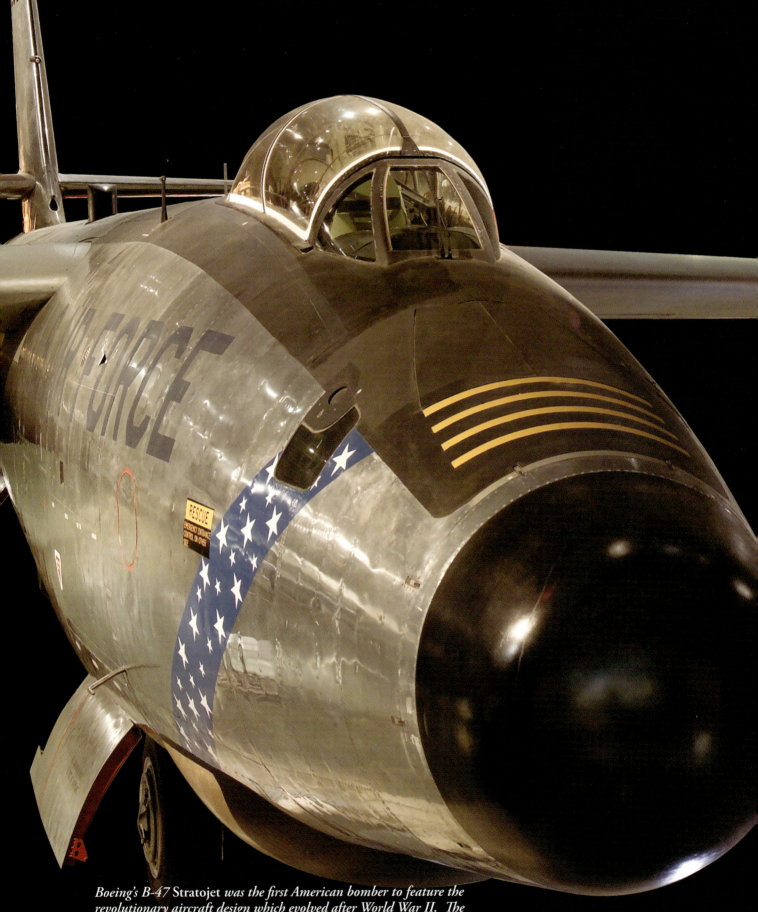

Boeing's B-47 Stratojet was the first American bomber to feature the revolutionary aircraft design which evolved after World War II. The features of thin swept wings and engines in pods were among many of the lessons gathered from German aeronautical scientists who were brought to the USA.

Chapter 7
Strategic Air Command & the Centuries

"We intend to have a wider choice than humiliation or all-out nuclear action."

(President John F. Kennedy, July 25, 1961)

"I am unable to distinguish between the unfortunate and the incompetent."

(General Curtis LeMay on his intolerance of failure to meet his standards)

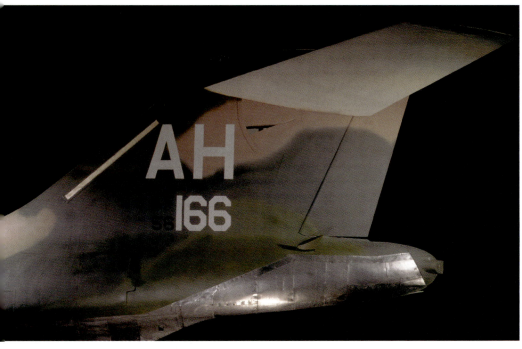

The USAF development of the Century Series *jet fighters is called the* Second Golden Era *of aircraft development by USAF retired Colonel William Harrell (see Bill's portrait on page 233). The distinctive tails of four of the series illustrate the wide range of aircraft design. Clockwise from the top left: North American F-100* Super Sabre; *Convair F-106* Delta Dart; *Lockheed F-104* Starfighter; *McDonnel F-101* Vodoo. *All the Century Series of fighter are*

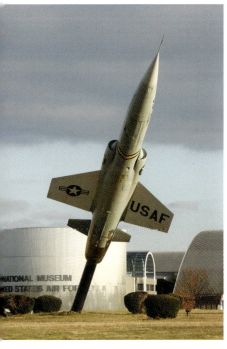

supersonic with a broad range of capabilities.

The F-100 Susan Constant *was on exhibit at the NMUSAF when the first edition of this book was published. It is now on loan to the Southern Air Museum in Birmingham, Alabama.*

The RF-101 *flew several impactful reconnaissance missions including the overflights of Cuba in 1962, which revealed the Soviet missiles which were the catalyst for the Cuban Missile Crisis.*

The F-104 *served with the USAF in California, West Germany, Spain, Taiwan, Vietnam, and Thailand. It also was flown by the winning pilot of the 1962 USAF* William Tell *Fighter Weapons Meet competition. It was flown to the Museum in August 1975.*

This F-106 *was involved in an unusual incident. During a training mission from Malmstrom Air Force Base on February 2, 1970, it suddenly entered an uncontrollable flat spin, forcing the pilot to eject.*

Unpiloted, the aircraft recovered on its own, apparently due to the balance and configuration changes caused by the ejection, and miraculously made a gentle belly landing in a snow-covered field near Big Sandy, Montana After minor repairs, the aircraft was returned to service. It last served with the 49th Fighter Interceptor Squadron before being brought to the Museum in August 1986.

The museum's Convair F-106 exhibits the dramatic design changes in its evolution from the F-102. More knowledge which came from the research done during and just after World War II. The "pinched" coke bottle shaped fuselage illustrates the area rule in fast jet technology.

Area Rule reduces drag at transonic speeds and is reflected in the "coke bottle" or "wasp waist" shaped fuselage of the F-106. Area ruling enabled the YF-102A to easily exceed the speed of sound and subsequently led to the go-ahead for the advanced version which became the F-106. The significance of area ruling was recognized by the National Aeronautic Association which awarded the originator, Richard T. Whitcomb, its prestigious Collier Trophy for the greatest achievement in aeronautics in 1955.

In the short period of time between the creation of the independent air force and the hard recommendations of NSC-68, followed immediately by the onset of the Korean war, which seemed to confirm everything in NSC-68, the USAF faced the unappealing dilemma of living on tight budgets with expensive new technologies to be developed and integrated into the plan to defend the United States and fight its wars. Prior to the North Korean invasion of the South in 1950, the USAF's front line consisted of 48 combat groups. Mid-war reorganization and expansion made the wing (one or more groups) the principal combat unit, increasing

The cockpit of the F-106 Delta Dart.

the number of combat units to 137 wings by 1957, approximately three times the size of the 1950 force, with substantial improvements in technology and capability.

The Strategic Air Command (SAC), responsible for strategic bombing and ballistic missiles from 1946 to 1992, consisted of 70,000 personnel and 868 aircraft in 1950, with 390 B-29s as the strongest component of its strike force. In 1955, personnel had increased to nearly 200,000 and aircraft to 3,068, with more

than a thousand B-47 axial-flow jets backed by 700 tanker aircraft. For much of this period of tremendous expansion and acquisition of new technology, General Curtis LeMay led SAC. LeMay had risen in the command structure for his service in the China-Burma-India Theater and as the architect of the low-altitude strategic bombing campaign against Japan. He would later command the Berlin Airlift. He was a demanding officer who expected much of his subordinates. If something did not work, he expected everyone to find a better way. Training was critical to mission readiness in his mind. He expected the SAC to be the most important element in the American military should World War III break out, delivering the knockout blow to the Soviet enemy in a matter of weeks, if not days.

The heavy bomber was the main weapon of the SAC, and the transition from radial piston engines to jets was the most important part of maintaining air superiority. The B-29, which was first flown in September 1942, was no longer state of the art in 1950. The interim replacement for the B-29 was another Boeing design, the B-47. A swept-wing, futuristic design with axial-flow jet engines and a fighter-like cockpit and a crew of three, the B-47 reflected the new focus on being able to deliver nuclear weapons to distant enemy targets. Much larger than the B-29, carrying half again as much weight as its predecessor, the B-47 performed well in flight, but its sleek airframe limited the amount of fuel it could carry on board, and necessarily, its range. Able to fly about 1,500 miles without refueling, B-47 units required their own complement of air tankers, the KC-97 to keep the bomber fueled on long flights. The original tanker was difficult to match with the B-47. The KC-97, based on the B-29, required a precise set of circumstances to refuel the B-47. To fly fast enough to allow the B-47 to maintain operational control, the KC-97 had to be in a gradual descent—not an ideal situation.

As good as the B-47 might be compared to the B-29, it soon became clear that the B-47 was an interim step. Even before the B-47 began its service, Boeing had already designed and was building the prototype B-52 as the replacement for the B-47. The B-52 gave the SAC the bomber it wanted. Originally designed as six-engine turboprop aircraft with straight wings, the final design incorporated eight podded turbojet engines hanging below swept wings, expected to carry a complement of nuclear weapons to distant targets. The prototype first

This panoramic photograph created by author Dan Patterson and brother Tom Patterson was made in 2010 and reflects the floor layout of the NMUSAF at that time. The entire Cold War Gallery is the subject. Seen here in one image is almost 50 years of USAF history. From left: Boeing KC-97, Convair B-58, Convair B-36, Boeing B-47, Northrop B-2, Northrop F-89, Lockheed SR-71, North American B-1, Lockheed U-2, Douglas C-133, and many more.

Responding to the US Army Air Forces' requirement for a strategic bomber with intercontinental range, Consolidated Vultee (later Convair) designed the B-36 during World War II. The airplane made its maiden flight in August 1946, and in June 1948 the Strategic Air Command received its first operational B-36.

Powered by six Pratt & Whitney R-4360 engines, the B-36J cruised at 230 mph, but for additional bursts of speed its four General Electric J47s increased the maximum speed to 435 mph. It carried 86,000 pounds of nuclear or conventional bombs. When production ended in August 1954, more than 380 B-36s had been built for the US Air Force. In 1958-1959, the USAF replaced the B-36 with the all-jet B-52. Although never used in combat, the B-36 was a major deterrent to enemy aggression. Making the last B-36 flight ever, the aircraft on display flew to the Museum from Davis-Monthan Air Force Base, Arizona, on April 30, 1959.

The Convair B-36, showing the bombardiers position from the inside and out.

Midair refueling provides the USAF the extension of air power across the globe. Flying experiments were begun at McCook Field shortly after World War I to prove the theory and develop the procedures (see chapter 3). Here a Boeing KC-97 refuels a Boeing B-47.

Gil Cohen's painting, Operation Creek Party *illustrates the all-weather mission of the USAF, a New York Air National Guard KC-97 receiving engine and propeller maintenance.*

Northrop SM-62 Snark
The Snark, *a pilotless nuclear missile, represented an important step in weapons technology during the Cold War. The SM-62 (Strategic Missile) program lasted from 1945 to 1961, and it gave the US Air Force valuable experience in developing long-range strategic nuclear missile systems. The SM-62 was a significant forerunner of cruise missiles developed many years later.*

flew in April 1952, and the first production aircraft began service in 1955. On a full load of fuel, the B-52 had a range of some 8,800 miles and a weapons payload of 70,000 pounds, later increased to accommodate new weapons, navigation, and defense systems. The B-52 remains in service to this day.

Strategic warfare required tactical capabilities as well. In the 1950 reorganization the new USAF formed both the Tactical Air Command (TAC) and the Air Defense Command (ADC) as separate commands to address the other areas of readiness expected in an ongoing Cold War that might become hot at any moment. The more important of the two, the TAC, was to prepare fighter-bombers for combat readiness and deploy them overseas. Even while preparing to send F-84 "Thunderjets" for Korea, the TAC sent two waves of the fighter-bombers to Germany to be ready to counter anything the Soviets might be up to. A variety of other fighter-bombers were introduced and each filled some but not all the requirements. The "Century Series" fighters, beginning with the F-100, were fast, but not particularly agile. Other new designs were brought in regularly so that by 1957, the TAC had a full complement of fighter-bombers to handle all the expected situations. But the TAC was not limited to fighter aircraft. By the end of the Korean War the TAC had more than a

thousand aircraft, 60 percent of which were transport planes, which were going through their own technical development and expansions. The venerable C-46 gave way to the Fairchild C-119 and Lockheed C-130 Hercules. The Military Air Transport Service (MATS) fleet included some 1,400 aircraft, including 610 four-engine transport planes, most of them C-54s, but also the heavy and slow C-124, which were ultimately replaced by Boeing's C-135 and Lockheed's C141.

Airborne surveillance of the Soviet Union was critical to the Cold War mission of the USAF, particularly after the Soviets acquired their own nuclear capability. Beginning with modified B-29s and a variety of other aircraft, the USAF conducted high-altitude surveillance overflights for photographic documentation and electronic surveillance of radar and radio transmissions. So-called "ferret" missions were flown to provoke a reaction from Soviet defenses. At high altitude, the ferret aircraft would fly close to Soviet airspace, fully expecting Soviet search and height-finding radar to lock in, followed by missile guidance and ground-controlled interception radar to acquire the ferret. All the while, the ferret monitored the electronic signals. This activity was quite dangerous. In the 1950s, the Soviets brought down some two dozen aircraft of the Western powers, at least eight from the USAF.

1962 Bendix Trophy

Convair B-58A Hustler

The US Air Force's first operational supersonic bomber, the B-58, made its initial flight on November 11, 1956. In addition to the Hustler's delta wing shape, distinctive features included a sophisticated inertial guidance navigation and bombing system, a slender "wasp-waist" fuselage, and an extensive use of heat-resistant honeycomb sandwich skin panels in the wings and fuselage. Since the thin fuselage prevented the carrying of bombs internally, a droppable, two-component pod beneath the fuselage contained a nuclear weapon, along with extra fuel, reconnaissance equipment or other specialized gear. The B-58 crew consisted of a pilot, navigator/ bombardier, and defense systems operator.

The B-58A on display set three speed records while flying from Los Angeles to New York and back on March 5, 1962. For this effort, the crew received the Bendix and Mackay trophies for 1962. It was flown to the Museum in December 1969.

Postwar development of large jet aircraft by Boeing provided the USAF with intercontinental capability. The B-47 Stratojet was followed by the B-52 Stratofortress. A parallel aircraft development created the Boeing KC-135, which led to the commercial version, the Boeing 707. The B-47s were retired in the 1980s while the B-52 and the KC-135 soldier on now over seventy years since being introduced.

The restored cockpit of the B-47H on display at the NMUSAF. The RB-47H first entered service in August 1955. Over the next decade, RB-47H crews of the 55th Strategic Reconnaissance Wing (SRW) flew thousands of dangerous "ferret" missions. Flying in radio silence at night along-and sometimes over-the border of the Soviet Union and other communist nations, RB-47Hs collected essential intelligence about the size and capability of Soviet air defense radar networks.

In an attempt to limit the risk of strategic reconnaissance, the USAF sought to build aircraft that could operate beyond the range of enemy countermeasures. Lockheed's Advanced Development Program, colloquially known as the "Skunk Works," built two aircraft that filled the bill for a time. The first, the U-2, appeared much like a "jet-powered sailplane," able to operate at altitudes as high as 70,000 feet, later increased to as high as 90,000 feet. For a time this put the U-2 beyond Soviet air defenses. In conjunction with the Central Intelligence Agency, U-2 pilots acquired otherwise unknowable information on Soviet air defense systems, bomber deployment, and submarine development. The ability to fly with impunity ended on May 1, 1960, when Francis Gary Powers was shot down by SA-2 Soviet missiles. Chairman Nikita Khrushchev used the incident to embarrass the United States and cancel a long-planned summit meeting with President Dwight Eisenhower. The "Skunk Works," undeterred,

built a replacement, the SR-71 Blackbird, which could operate at 85,000 feet and fly at three times the speed of sound.

By the end of the Eisenhower administration, the new USAF was well prepared to engage any enemy it might encounter. With flush budgets, the newest technologies, and strong partnerships with manufacturers—so strong that President Eisenhower, in his farewell address, cautioned the nation about the growing Military Industrial Complex, the USAF faced the new challenges of the 1960s.

The NMUSAF South-East Asia (SEA) gallery features a wide range of the USAF capacity during the Vietnam War. Two of the most iconic are the McDonnell Douglas F-4 Phantom II *and the* Republic F-105 Thunderchief.

Chapter 8
Cold War Hot Combat

"I won't let those air force generals bomb the smallest outhouse without checking with me."

(President Lydon Johnson on his command of Operation ROLLING THUNDER, 1965)

"Thank God for the U.S. Air Force"

(U.S. Army survivor rescued under fire by an HH-53 helicopter at Quang Tri, 1972)

The most recent addition to the SEA Gallery is the newly restored Douglas A-1H Skyraider.

The expansion of the USAF throughout the 1950s would be tested throughout the 1960s, most dramatically through the conflict in Vietnam. The negotiated ceasefire in Korea kept the USAF occupied in Northern Asia while events in the former French colony of Vietnam slowly rose to be the greatest challenge it faced during the Cold War. The German occupation of France allowed Japan to occupy its Southeast Asia without opposition. Vietnamese nationalists sought to expel the Japanese and create an independent Vietnam free of French colonial rule. The United States supported the return of the French to Vietnam, in part to avoid the possibility of a communist takeover. Cold War ideology subscribed to the idea of the "domino theory," that the fall of one country in a region would lead to the fall of others. The United States came to render what little support it could to the French in Vietnam as early as 1950, an innocuous first step toward unlimited support.

The Vietnamese nationalist and communist, Ho Chi Minh, who had once appealed to the United States for aid in creating an independent Vietnam, waged guerrilla war against the French colonial regime, ultimately surrounding a French force at Dien Bien Phu in May 1954. France accepted the new reality and recognized

Vietnam, Cambodia, and Laos as independent countries. Ho's communists controlled the northern portion of Vietnam and a new regime led by Ngo Dinh Diem, a former French colonial official, was formed in the south. Elections scheduled for 1956 were postponed, and soon thereafter, communist guerrillas began a constant and conscious effort to reunite Vietnam under the control of the Communist Party, with support from Ho's government in the North. The United States sent military advisors and military equipment to strengthen and train the Army of the Republic of Vietnam (ARVN) as it resisted Communist advances. By 1961, the Communist insurgency in the South was on the verge of succeeding, thanks to support from the Soviet Union funneled into the South by Ho's Northern army.

But before Vietnam could break out into the morass it became, trouble much closer to home directed attention away from Southeast Asia. Less than a hundred miles away from Florida, the Cuban Revolution had ended a long-standing American relationship with the Cuban government. Revolutionary forces led by Fidel Castro overthrew the American-backed government of Fulgencio Battista. Battista's government was notoriously corrupt, but had very close ties to American business interests

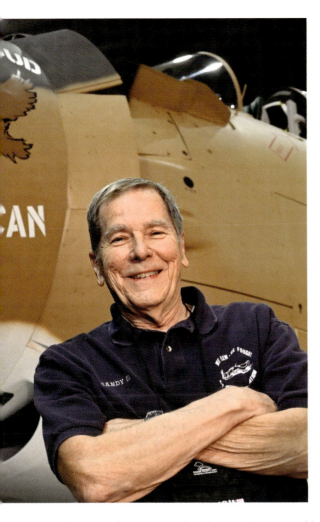

that owned much of the land and industry. Castro quickly aligned himself with the Soviet Union, nationalizing foreign-owned assets. President Eisenhower authorized the Central Intelligence Agency (CIA) to conduct a covert operation against Cuba, using exiled Cuban recruits.

Before the invasion could be launched John F. Kennedy replaced Eisenhower as president. Preparations continued until the invasion was ready to go in April 1961. On the night of April 14, eight B-26 bombers, disguised as Cuban air force planes, with Cuban pilots, attacked Cuban airfields from Nicaragua, intending to destroy Cuban air support on the ground. The attacks were partially successful, but not enough to offset the disastrous land attack at the Bay of Pigs. The failure to liberate Communist Cuba embarrassed the United States and its president, enhanced the position of Castro as the leader of a Communist Cuba, and convinced the Soviets to look toward Cuba as an advanced outpost in the ongoing competition with the United States in the still escalating Cold War.

Eighteen months later, the seriousness of the failed Bay of Pigs invasion became clear as the US and Soviet Union faced off in the Cuban Missile Crisis, the closest the two superpowers came to a direct nuclear war. Premier Nikita Khrushchev had been increasing Soviet military support to

Douglas A-1H Skyraider, The Proud American

US Air Force Skyraiders in Southeast Asia are often remembered for their support of search and rescue (SAR) missions. Operating under the call sign Sandy*, the A-1's extended loiter time and massive firepower offered pilots the ability to protect downed airmen for extended periods. Whereas jet aircraft often had to leave the battle area for refueling, the A-1s provided nearly continuous suppressing fire until helicopters extracted downed airmen.*

The aircraft on display represents Captain Ronald Smith's A-1H The Proud American *(Serial Number 52-139738) as it appeared during his SAR mission in June 1972 as part of the 1st Special Operations Squadron, Nakhon Phanom (NKP) Royal Thai Air Force Base, Thailand. Captain Smith was awarded the Air Force Cross for the rescue of a downed F-4 Phantom crewman near a North Vietnamese airfield.*

USAF Col. (Ret.) Ron Smith, Air Force Cross recipient, flew The Proud American *(Douglas A-1H Skyraider) on the deepest-ever SAR into North Vietnam on June 2, 1972. Smith is viewed here as part of the aircraft opening ceremony.*

Cuba to equalize perceived advantages the United States had by stationing nuclear missiles in Turkey. Nuclear bases in Cuba would allow the Soviets to reach many targets in the United States, offsetting at least part of the American advantage. Shortly after construction of the missile bases commenced the CIA acquired intelligence of their existence. On October 14 and 15, 1962, the SAC sent two U-2 reconnaissance aircraft from the 4080th Strategic Wing to overfly Cuba and confirm that missile sites were being built. Confirmation prompted the SAC to put all missiles and a fleet of nuclear-armed bombers on full alert and began a flurry of lower-altitude intelligence fights which validated U-2 gathered intelligence. On full alert, the USAF prepared for nuclear war at any moment.

President Kennedy confronted the Soviets, placing an embargo against military shipments to the island. With nuclear war hanging in the balance for the next two weeks, and a Soviet supply convoy turning back at the last moment in the face of American blockading ships, diplomats negotiated an end to the crisis. The Soviets removed the missiles from Cuba in exchange for the United States removing its PGM-19 missiles from Turkey. The two sides had stared each other down. Only the Soviets blinked, but neither side liked what they saw, and avoided similar incidents in the future. The rest of the hot Cold War would be fought by proxy. The USAF

Douglas A-1E Skyraider

Rarely does an aircraft which was flown on a Medal of Honor mission survive the flight.

The A-1E on display (Serial number 52-132649) is the aircraft flown by Major Bernard Fisher on March 10, 1966, a mission for which he was awarded the Medal of Honor. He rescued a fellow pilot shot down over South Vietnam by landing in enemy territory under heavy fire and flying him to safety. This is believed to be the only surviving fixed-wing Medal of Honor aircraft. The airplane on exhibit, severely damaged in further combat in South Vietnam and later repaired, came to the Museum in 1968 for display.

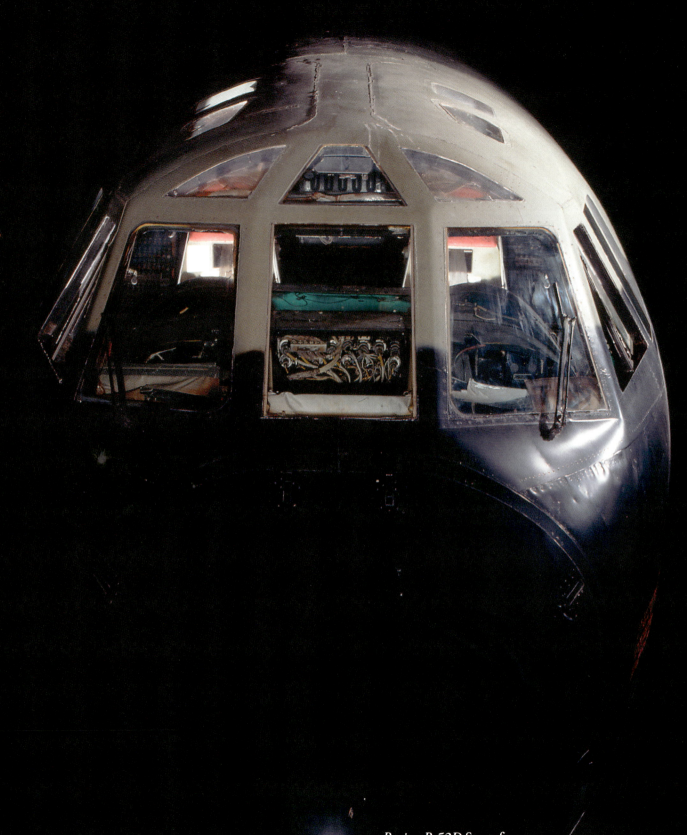

Boeing B-52D Stratofortress

The looming presence of the NMUSAF B-52D.

Right: *Underwing pylons added to the B-52s already enormous bomb-carrying capacity.*

acquitted itself well by all accounts in the Missile Crisis. A full defense of the southern coast was implemented in a matter of days, with only a few lessons to learn.

For the USAF, the greatest proxy fight of the Cold War was about to get serious. By 1961, the Communist insurgency in Vietnam had grown to the point that it threatened the stability of the South Vietnamese government. Soviet premier Khrushchev declared that the USSR supported "wars of national liberation," a statement the included Vietnam, Cuba, and a number of conflicts in Africa. In response, President Kennedy assured the nation and its allies that he intended to meet the Communist challenge head-on. Vietnam, of course, had now advanced to the top of the list. The air war in Vietnam can be divided into five distinct phases. Phase one was more covert than anything else. From 1961 to mid-1964 USAF planes flew reconnaissance

over Vietnam and Laos, while deploying support personnel to help train pilots and crews of the VNAF. Newer planes, A-1s and T-28s, replaced F-8s, but USAF participation remained low-key. In phase two, from the Gulf of Tonkin Resolution to 1969, the USAF presence expanded dramatically as the United States entered the war directly. The USAF provided air support for all ground operations in South Vietnam and bombing forays into North Vietnam and Laos. The third phase, from mid-1969 to 1972, saw the USAF pull back from the high level of engagement of the previous five years, withdrawing many units and transferring airfields and equipment to the VNAF. Phase four, a short phase from the North's spring offensive of 1972 until the peace accords of March 1973, saw the USAF conducting concentrated attacks in the South and on the Northern port areas surrounding Hanoi and Haiphong. The last phase saw the USAF complete the process of completely withdrawing operations within Vietnam.

The cockpit of the Museum's B-52D. The handful of eight throttles seen on the pedestal centered in between the pilot and copilot's controls. Behind those the instruments for all eight engines.

In June 1965, B-52s entered combat in Southeast Asia. By August 1973, they had flown 126,615 combat sorties with seventeen B-52s lost to enemy action. The aircraft on display saw extensive service in Southeast Asia and was severely damaged by an enemy surface-to-air missile on April 9, 1972. In December 1972,

In the covert phase, after expanding participation in reconnaissance over Vietnam and Laos, the USAF deliberately kept enough distance to plausibly deny direct participation in the war, if so accused. In response to President Kennedy's concern about the ability to fight counterinsurgency campaigns, General LeMay established the 4400th Combat Crew Training Squadron to develop tactics and select aircraft for action in Vietnam. By November, USAF T-28s, SC-47s, and B-26s were deployed to Bien Hoa, outside Saigon, to train the VNAF. These planes flew VNAF markings and USAF pilots always flew with VNAF pilots on board so that it could be said that the Americans acted only as "instructors." Additional units joined the 4400th to provide tactical airlift support and to deploy "Agent Orange" and other defoliants on the rain forest to make ground operations easier. T-28s, which had been in service since the 1950s, were soon replaced by A-1Es, another propeller-driven aircraft. Replacing one prop-driven plane with another in an air force of jets might

after being repaired, it flew four additional missions over North Vietnam. Transferred from the 97th Bomb Wing at Blytheville Air Force Base, Arkansas, this aircraft was flown to the Museum in November 1978.

SA-2 Surface-to-Air Missile.

Developed in the mid-1950s, the V-750 Dvina was the first effective Soviet surface-to-air missile. The missile was better known by the NATO designation SA-2 Guideline. The Soviets began exporting it to

many countries worldwide in 1960, with many remaining in use into the 21st century.

North Vietnam began receiving SA-2s shortly after the start of Operation Rolling Thunder in the spring of 1965. With Soviet help, they built several well-camouflaged sites, regularly moving SA-2s and their equipment among them. The North Vietnamese also ringed SA-2 sites with anti-aircraft artillery (AAA), making them even more dangerous to attack.

221

First flown in May 1958, the Phantom II originally was developed for US Navy fleet defense. The US Air Force's first version, the F-4C, made its first flight in May 1963, and production deliveries began six months later. Phantom II production ended in 1979 after over 5,000 had been built-more than 2,600 for the USAF, about 1,200 for the U.S. Navy and Marine Corps, and the rest for friendly foreign nations.

In 1965 the USAF sent its first F-4Cs to Southeast Asia, where they flew air-to-air missions against North Vietnamese fighters as well as attacking ground targets. The first USAF pilot to score four combat victories with F-4s in Southeast Asia was Col. Robin Olds, a World War II ace. The aircraft on display is the one in which Col. Olds, the pilot, and Lt. Stephen Croker, the weapons system officer, destroyed two MiG-17s in a single day, May 20, 1967.

In the fall of 1966, Olds took command of the 8th Tactical Fighter Wing (TFW) at Ubon Royal Thai Air Force Base. Old's charisma and courage endeared him to his people, and under his leadership, the Wolfpack became the USAF's top MiG-killing wing in Southeast Asia. Olds also played a key role in the creation of the Red River Valley Fighter Pilots Association, which improved coordination between USAF wings in Southeast Asia and became a lasting fraternal organization.

U.S. AIR FORCE F-4C-24-MC
A.F. SERIAL NO. 64-829A

Olds led from the front-he shared the same risks as his aircrews by flying on the most dangerous missions. He received many decorations for his audacity in combat, including the Air Force Cross for a mission in August 1967, when he led a strike force against the heavily defended Paul Doumer Bridge in North Vietnam.

seem odd, but pilots found the A-1E ideal for the conditions in Vietnam. Pilots found it easy to fly, able to absorb battle damage, accurately deliver payload, and operate in weather which grounded other planes. Operations expanded gradually, but by June 1964 USAF aircraft had attacked AAA targets in Laos with the expectation of additional operations to follow.

The role of the USAF changed dramatically in mere weeks. Congress gave President Lyndon Johnson blanket authorization to use whatever force necessary to assist South Vietnam against both the Viet Cong and North Vietnamese regular units in response to attacks on American destroyers on August 2, 1964, which did in fact happen, and August 4, which did not. Blank check in hand, the TAC deployed a Composite Strike Force of B-57s, F-110Ds, and F-105Ds while the SAC sent additional tanker aircraft. The "show of force" had no discernible effect, if any, and emboldened the Viet Cong to initiate mortar attacks on American airfields and officers' quarters, prompting a debate between the Joint Chiefs of Staff (JCS) and the State Department about its effectiveness.

The huge jet pipes of the F-4's J-79s contrast with the small Sidewinder tails strapped alongside. Between the exhausts is an arrester hook, a reminder of the F-4's naval heritage.

The JSC wanted a quick and decisive response. General LeMay, the USAF chief of staff went even further, advocating a bombing campaign of North Vietnam with more to follow if the North refused to deescalate and negotiate. The State Department argued that the United States should respond with incremental increases, so as not to take negotiations off the table. President Johnson sided with the State Department, setting off an ongoing disagreement between the military and the president over conduct of the war. The initial response, Operation Barrel Roll, was by any measure indirect, bombing missions over Laos in support of Laotian forces against Communist insurgents. Increased activity by the Viet Cong attacks at various points in the South made it clear that the North was not intimidated by the American expansion.

President Johnson kept close control over air operations, which frustrated USAF commanders. No target in Vietnam could be attacked without Johnson's personal approval. The next step, "a measured and limited air action against selected military targets," as described by Ambassador Maxwell Taylor, was intended to be another incremental expansion of the American role in air combat. Operation Rolling Thunder required a long series of orders passed along from the president, to the secretary of defense, to the JCS, the Commander in Chief, Pacific (CINPAC), who finally determined targets and routes before sending the orders to the USAF, USN, and VNAF. Such a rigid protocol kept ground commanders from reacting quickly to changing

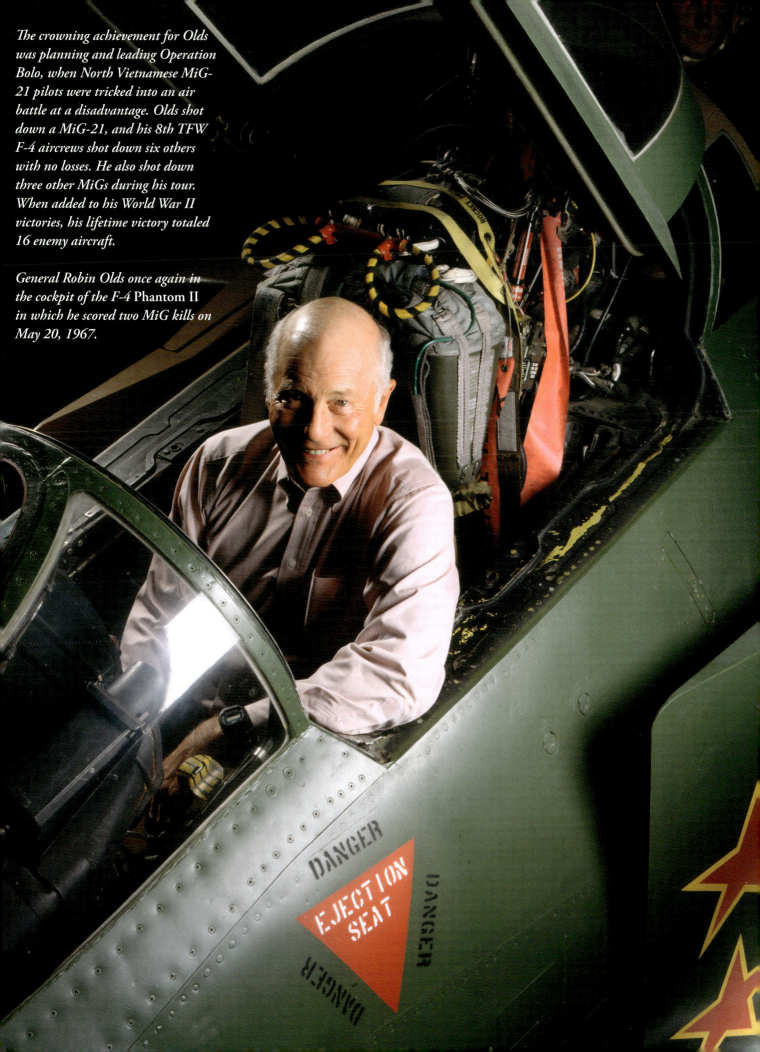

The crowning achievement for Olds was planning and leading Operation Bolo, when North Vietnamese MiG-21 pilots were tricked into an air battle at a disadvantage. Olds shot down a MiG-21, and his 8th TFW F-4 aircrews shot down six others with no losses. He also shot down three other MiGs during his tour. When added to his World War II victories, his lifetime victory totaled 16 enemy aircraft.

General Robin Olds once again in the cockpit of the F-4 Phantom II in which he scored two MiG kills on May 20, 1967.

DANGER

EJECTION SEAT

DANGER

DANGER

Capt. Charles Chuck *DeBellevue*

With six victories (four MiG-21s, two MiG-19s), weapon system officer Capt. Charles "Chuck" DeBellevue, 555th Tactical Fighter Squadron, was the highest-scoring USAF ace in Southeast Asia. He achieved his victories between May and September 1972, and had two double-victory missions.

situations and allowed the North to figure out what targets were off limits. Permissible targets were selected from a list, principally infrastructure such as bridges, railways, and roads. Great care was taken to avoid targets that would harm the civilian population or Chinese and Soviet citizens.

The North Vietnamese managed to counter Rolling Thunder with a combination of dispersing its resources into small storage locations while using Soviet anti-aircraft guns and missiles. The USAF squadrons had been particularly effective in taking out the most obvious targets, rail lines, bridges, oil storage capacity, and military installations, using a variety of aircraft, including F-4Cs, F-105s, F-100s, F-104s, F-5As, B-57s, and others. The heat-seeking, air-to-air Sidewinder missile proved to be effective against Soviet MiG fighters. But airborne success was offset by significant losses. Of the 273 fixed-wing aircraft lost in 1965, 158 belonged to the USAF, the majority of which were hit by AAA and small-arms fire.

Into 1966, President Johnson kept his tight rein on the USAF and the targets it was allowed to engage. In hopes of bringing the North to the negotiating table, Hanoi and Haiphong remained off-limits as did the airfields around Hanoi which housed the newly deployed MiG-21. The North, understanding the limits of heavy

bombing, dispersed their resources so that any single strike, no matter how accurate, could only inflict a small amount of damage. The pace of the air offensive expanded dramatically over 1966, peaking with more that 12,000 sorties flown over North Vietnam in September. Pilots became increasingly good at hitting targets, but the North Vietnamese countered with increasingly accurate air defenses. Over the course of 1966, the US fixed-wing losses in combat amounted to 465 planes, 296 from the USAF.

After the 1967 Lunar New Year truce, the president opened up a number of previously off-limits targets in North Vietnam. Industrial targets in and around Hanoi and Haiphong were now subjected to concentrated bombing. The North's only steel mill at Tai Nguyen, the MiG airfields around Hanoi, new bridges, and surface-to-air missile sites all took direct hits from USAF squadrons that increasingly controlled the skies over North Vietnam. The effect on the ground war in the South proved to be relatively light. Losses for the year increased to 515 fixed-wing aircraft, 325 belonging to the USAF, AAA and small arms accounting for about half the total number of planes lost in combat.

As dissatisfaction with the slow rate of the overall success of the war grew at home, Rolling Thunder became the subject of a number of studies looking to evaluate how effective the concentrated attacks had been in reducing the North's ability to fight. The damage to Hanoi's military-industrial infrastructure had been significant, but there was little evidence that the damage had diminished the North's ability to support the Viet Cong in the South. Nor did it appear that the intensity of the air war had any detrimental effect on morale, military or civilian. Defense Secretary Robert McNamara calculated that the US was spending about ten dollars for every dollar of damage the bombing causes. But despite the successes, even weighed against the costs, one glaring exemption remained: The port of Haiphong and the Soviet supply line were still off-limits.

The "In-Country" War against the Viet Cong and North Vietnamese regular forces required its own air support. Originally, all USAF sorties were accompanied by a VNAF aviator to reinforce the idea that the United States was in Vietnam in an advisory capacity. Beginning in February 1965, at the request of the South Vietnamese government, USAF pilots flew missions in American planes. By the end of 1965 more than 500 aircraft and 21,000 personnel were stationed at eight air bases in South Vietnam. The air war fell under the command of General William Westmoreland, commander of the Military Assistance Command, Vietnam (MACV), with control of the air units under Maj. Gen. Joseph Moore.

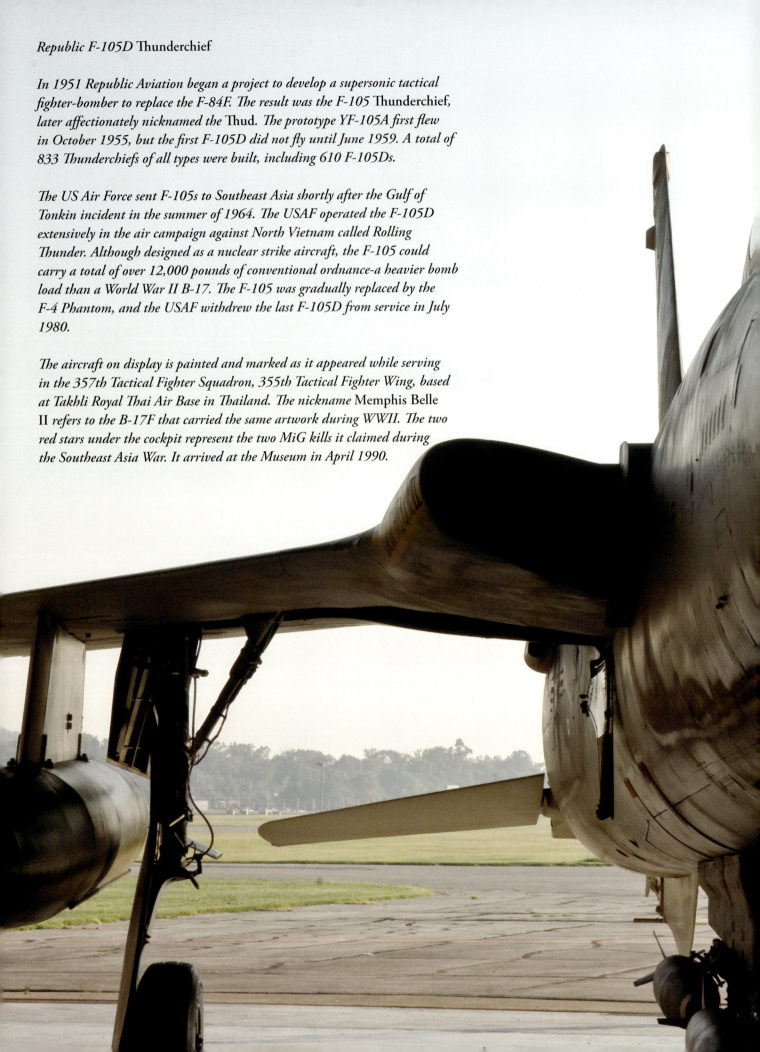

Republic F-105D Thunderchief

In 1951 Republic Aviation began a project to develop a supersonic tactical fighter-bomber to replace the F-84F. The result was the F-105 Thunderchief, later affectionately nicknamed the Thud. The prototype YF-105A first flew in October 1955, but the first F-105D did not fly until June 1959. A total of 833 Thunderchiefs of all types were built, including 610 F-105Ds.

The US Air Force sent F-105s to Southeast Asia shortly after the Gulf of Tonkin incident in the summer of 1964. The USAF operated the F-105D extensively in the air campaign against North Vietnam called Rolling Thunder. Although designed as a nuclear strike aircraft, the F-105 could carry a total of over 12,000 pounds of conventional ordnance-a heavier bomb load than a World War II B-17. The F-105 was gradually replaced by the F-4 Phantom, and the USAF withdrew the last F-105D from service in July 1980.

The aircraft on display is painted and marked as it appeared while serving in the 357th Tactical Fighter Squadron, 355th Tactical Fighter Wing, based at Takhli Royal Thai Air Base in Thailand. The nickname Memphis Belle II *refers to the B-17F that carried the same artwork during WWII. The two red stars under the cockpit represent the two MiG kills it claimed during the Southeast Asia War. It arrived at the Museum in April 1990.

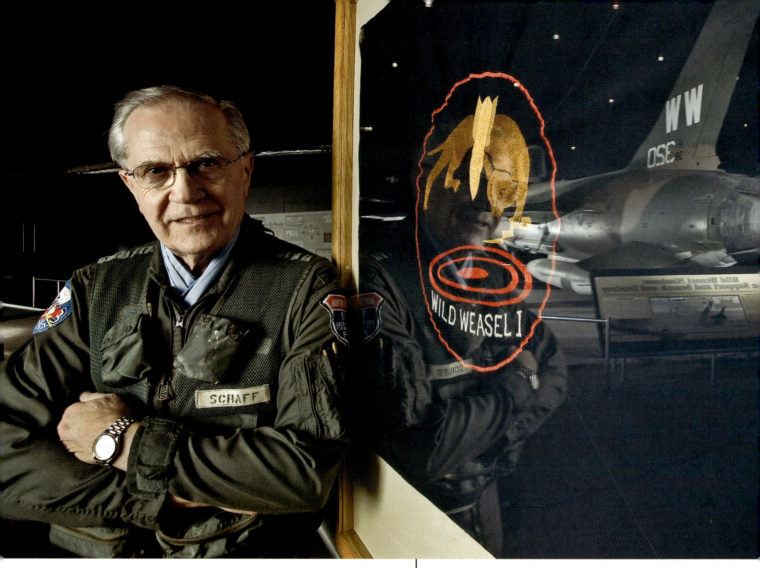

Bill Schaff , F-105 Wild Weasel *Pilot*

Bill Schaff wearing his flight suit from his missions over North Vietnam and his flight jacket with the 100

Missions North patch; 4 Silver Stars; 4 Distinguished Flying Crosses; 14 Air Medals; 67 very intense missions into the heart of the air defenses; 31 years of USAF service, 1955–1986.

Part of Moore's responsibility was to the MACV but he reported to CINPAC on out of country missions. The conflicting responsibilities made it difficult to coordinate activity throughout the Southeast Asian theater. Further complicating matters, Moore had no control over army or marine aircraft.

Once in the air, the forward air controller (FAC), flying single-engine Cessna O-1Es, often took responsibility for directing aircraft to their targets. With a top speed of 115 mph and unarmed, the O-1s had one of the most difficult and dangerous tasks, because they had to see the enemy to mark targets, which meant they could also be seen and attacked. FACs directed a formidable array of aircraft to close-in targets. F-100s, F-4s, and B-57s delivered any combination of bombs, cluster bombs, fragmentation bombs, gunfire, napalm, rockets, and missiles. Ground soldiers preferred napalm to other close-support weapons, as it penetrated rain

forest foliage better than anything else and created no shrapnel. They were also quite partial to the prop-driven A-1 Skyraider, which could carry an incredible amount of ordnance, more than four tons on fifteen attachment points, and stay in contact with the enemy far longer than their jet-powered counterparts. While most close-support missions were planned attacks on known targets, guerrilla strongholds, supply routes, staging areas, and the like, on many occasions aircraft responded to desperate calls for help from besieged ground units, and a prompt, accurate response made the difference between survival and destruction.

The arrival of SAC's B-52s in June 1965 increased the firepower for tactical operations under MACV. This was a surprising shift in strategy that shows the flexibility multiple platforms added to a growing and learning air force. Strategic bombing of North Vietnam was being done with fighter-bombers while the high-flying bomber of nuclear deterrence supported tactical operations. Modifications allowed the B-52D to carry eighty-four 500-pound bombs in the bay and an additional twenty-four 750-pound bombs externally. With the bombers operating at 30,000 feet, enemy on the ground had no advance notice of incoming ordnance, and captured Viet Cong reported that the uncertainty of knowing such an attack might be coming caused them the greatest fear. At Khe Sanh during the Tet Offensive, B-52s dropped nearly 100,000 tons of bombs on North Vietnamese regulars and Viet Cong who had hoped to make their siege of Khe Sanh a second Dien Bien Phu. Intelligence estimates suggested that, at minimum, two full divisions of North Vietnamese regulars had been effectively destroyed by the B-52 campaign at Khe Sanh.

One of the major problems to address in the air war was how to stop the flow of men and materiel from the North into the South via the Ho Chi Minh Trail. Moving supplies directly across the Demilitarized Zone between North and South was not an option, so the North developed clandestine routes that passed through neutral Laos and Cambodia. Without stopping, or at least diminishing the traffic along these routes, the South had little chance of victory over the North. Protected by the thick forest canopy, Northern convoys could move at will until the Americans began air raids, which forced the convoys to operate at night or take other evasive action. Beginning in 1965, F-100s, F-105s, and B-57s helped

reduce the flow of supplies, but not nearly enough to affect the ability of the Viet Cong and North Vietnamese regular forces operating in the South. Once again, innovation created some new and interesting solutions to the ongoing problem. B-52s joined the attack, complete with the Combat Skyspot radar, which directed the bombers to their targets. B-57s fitted with low-light television, infrared sensors, forward-looking radar, and laser-target marking made identifying targets along the trails easier, forcing the enemy, once again, to adapt to new circumstances.

The combination of platforms and weapons systems proved formidable, but one of the most effective, surprisingly, came from the venerable AC-47 cargo plane. The AC-47, the military version of the Douglas DC-3, was modified into a true gunship, armed with three 7.62mm machine guns which fired from the cargo door and windows. The plane circled the target with the guns held centered in a sight located next to the pilot in the cockpit. "Puff the Magic Dragon," as it became know in the media, proved to be highly effective against stationary and mobile targets along the trail. Later, more sophisticated aircraft like the AC-119K, the C-130, and the AC-130E refined the tactic, combining machine guns, cannon, and howitzer, all fired with the aid of a computer.

A Douglas EB-66 Destroyer *acts as ECM escort for an F-105 formation as bombs are released over North Vietnam. EB-66s provided threat warnings and jamming protection against gun-laying radars and SAMs.*

Above: Medal of Honor recipient Col. Joe Jackson served as a career officer in the US Air Force and received the Medal of Honor for heroism above and beyond the call of duty during the Vietnam War. On May 12, 1968, he volunteered for a dangerous impromptu rescue of three remaining USAF members trapped at an overrun Army Special Forces camp. While the camp was still under heavy enemy fire from North Vietnamese and Viet Cong troops, he skillfully piloted his C-123 cargo plane and rescued the three men.

Below: FAC pilot and author of the book, Naked in Danang, *USAF Col. Mike Jackson.*

Right: USAF Col. Bill Harrell flew the Cessna A-37 Dragonfly over Vietnam and Southeast Asia on 366 missions.

Bill Harrell in the center along with his unit the 8SOS, which flew from Bien Hoa air base.

The North American Rockwell OV-10 Bronco. The large cockpit gave exceptional all-around visibility.

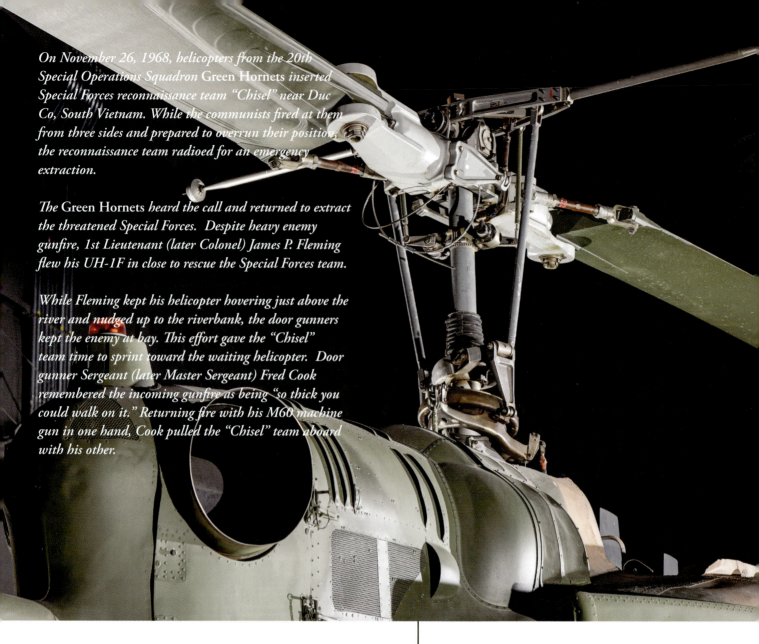

On November 26, 1968, helicopters from the 20th Special Operations Squadron Green Hornets inserted Special Forces reconnaissance team "Chisel" near Duc Co, South Vietnam. While the communists fired at them from three sides and prepared to overrun their position, the reconnaissance team radioed for an emergency extraction.

The Green Hornets heard the call and returned to extract the threatened Special Forces. Despite heavy enemy gunfire, 1st Lieutenant (later Colonel) James P. Fleming flew his UH-1F in close to rescue the Special Forces team.

While Fleming kept his helicopter hovering just above the river and nudged up to the riverbank, the door gunners kept the enemy at bay. This effort gave the "Chisel" team time to sprint toward the waiting helicopter. Door gunner Sergeant (later Master Sergeant) Fred Cook remembered the incoming gunfire as being "so thick you could walk on it." Returning fire with his M60 machine gun in one hand, Cook pulled the "Chisel" team aboard with his other.

With Richard Nixon as president after January 1969, the United States pursued a policy known as "Vietnamization," by which the United States would reduce its participation in the war as the South Vietnam military forces took over responsibility for its own defense. When United States ground forces invaded Cambodia in April 1970, American troop strength had been reduced significantly from its highest levels and USAF numbers had been brought down as well. The bombing campaign against the North had been suspended when Nixon took office, and by the time the North attacked the South directly through the DMZ in March 1972, fewer than 100 combat aircraft remained in Vietnam. Nixon ordered new strikes against the North and then expanded into operation Linebacker on May 8, 1972. Linebacker was not subject to the target restrictions that held Rolling Thunder back. USAF commanders, for the first time, were allowed to select targets that would hurt the North the most. New "smart" bombs, guided to the target, increased the effectiveness

of the attacks. By the end of June, more than 400 bridges had been destroyed, the harbor at Haiphong had been mined, and the supply chain to the South had been reduced to a trickle. The North Vietnamese had significantly increased their air defenses and air force so that while it suffered crushing losses from Linebacker it also inflicted severe damage on the attacking Americans. But in all, the unleashed aerial war stopped the Northern invasion, almost in its tracks and brought the North back to the negotiating table with a new set of peace proposals.

The bombing campaign continued through the end of the year. After a brief Christmas truce, concentrated air strikes began again on December 26. B-52s and F-111s took dead aim at Northern airfields and radar, SAM, and anti-aircraft sites. The North condemned the "extermination bombing" but returned to the negotiating table, this time to conclude a cease-fire document on January 23, 1973. Linebacker, despite the

For his efforts, Fleming received the Medal of Honor. The two door gunners, Cook and Sergeant Paul Jensen, received the Distinguished Flying Cross. Fleming's copilot, Major (later Lieutenant Colonel) Paul McClellan, received the Silver Star. Gonzales received the Air Force Cross. The other participating Green Hornets received eleven Distinguished Flying Crosses, one Silver Star, and two Air Medals.

From left to right: SSgt. Paul Jensen, Capt. Randy Harrison, MSgt Fred Cook. These veterans took part in the November 26, 1968 mission that is depicted in the 20th SOS Green Hornets exhibit

Sikorsky CH-3E

The CH-3E is the US Air Force's version of the Sikorsky S-61 amphibious transport helicopter developed for the US Navy. The USAF initially operated six Navy HSS-2 (SH-3A) versions of the S-61 in 1962, eventually designating them CH-3A/Bs. They were so successful the USAF ordered seventy-five modified versions, designated CH-3C.

Later, fifty CH-3Es were modified for combat rescue missions with armor, defensive armament, self-sealing fuel tanks, a rescue hoist and in-flight refueling capability. They were redesignated HH-3Es and used extensively in Southeast Asia under the nickname Jolly Green Giant.

The museum's CH-3E–known as Black Mariah*–is a veteran of the Southeast Asia War. In 1965 it was attached to the 20th Helicopter Squadron. Painted flat black (hence the nickname), it was used for highly classified special missions.*

cost, had done what it needed to do, bringing the North to the table to get an agreement.

The final cost for the United States in Vietnam was enormous. For the USAF, from 1962 to 1973, 1,679 fixed-wing aircraft and 58 helicopters were lost. Another 495 aircraft and 18 helicopters were lost in accidents. Five million sorties had been flown. Six million tons of ammunition were expended on the enemy, three times the amount delivered in all theaters of World War II. The USAF suffered 2,118 deaths and 3,460 wounded by official count. Overall, the USAF had served well by most accounts, and many of the senior leadership believed, that left to their own devices and judgment, the final outcome might have been quite different.

The Republic A-10 on show at the NMUSAF is a combat aircraft that flew and fought in Operation Desert Storm. The A-10A on display was flown on January 21, 1991, by Capt. Paul Johnson on an eight-hour rescue support mission during Operation Desert Storm, for which he was awarded the Air Force Cross, the USAF's second-highest award for valor. The aircraft was delivered to the Museum in January 1992.

Chapter 9
The
Professionals

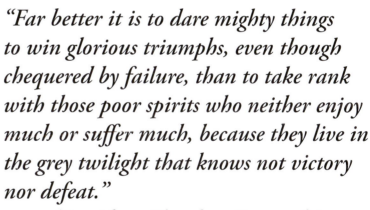

"Far better it is to dare mighty things to win glorious triumphs, even though chequered by failure, than to take rank with those poor spirits who neither enjoy much or suffer much, because they live in the grey twilight that knows not victory nor defeat."
(President Theodore Roosevelt)

"Thank God for the U.S. Air Force

(U.S. Army survivor rescued under fire by an HH-53 helicopter at Quang Tri, 1972)

After Desert Storm the Museum received a letter from a soldier who had seen action in Iraq. He asked that when he came to visit the Museum, if he could just touch the A-10, one of which was flying support and saved his unit.

Lockheed F-117A

The first F-117A flew on June 18, 1981, and the first F-117A unit, the 4450th Tactical Group (renamed the 37th Tactical Fighter Wing in October 1989), achieved initial operating capability in October 1983.

The F-117A went into action during Operation Desert Shield/Storm in 1990-1991, when the 415th and the 416th squadrons of the 37th TFW moved to a base in Saudi Arabia. During Operation Desert Storm, the F-117As flew 1,271 sorties, achieving an 80 percent mission success rate, and suffered no losses or battle damage. A total of fifty-nine F-117As were built between 1981 and 1990. In 1989 the F-117A was awarded the Collier Trophy, one of the most prized aeronautical awards in the world.

Top right: *The cockpit of the Museum's F-117A.*

The long debriefing after the Vietnam War produced a number of studies, reflections, and critical examinations with the hope that when called upon again, the USAF would be more than ready, having learned whatever lessons had been there to learn. Overall, the USAF felt it had performed well doing the job it was asked to do. When left to their own devices and allowed to attack the enemy when and where the USAF decided it could do the most good, the USAF believed it had kept the North Vietnamese and Viet Cong poorly supplied and on the defensive. Obviously there were problems, but overall, the air war always belonged to the Americans. At the same time, the United States left the combat arena with the enemy still in place and that rankled. Many Americans, particularly young Americans had come to strongly oppose the war and that opposition extended to poor treatment of those who had given life and effort to the cause.

For the latter years of the Cold War the USAF modified and developed aircraft to suit the needs of particular situations. Fighters became more sophisticated with computer-controlled cockpits and weaponry. The A-10

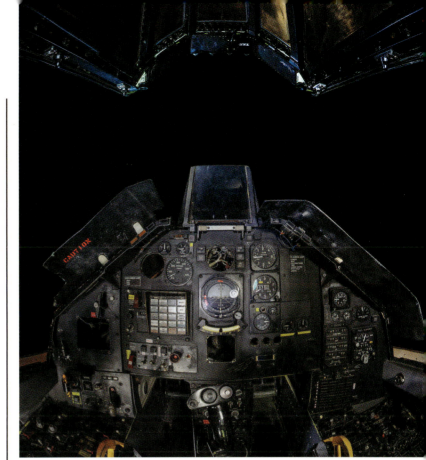

An important ally during Desert Storm was the Royal Air Force. The aircraft on display flew with the RAF's 17 Squadron from Dhahran, Saudi Arabia, where it sported desert camouflage and the name Miss Behavin'. The aircraft is currently painted as an aircraft assigned to 617 Squadron. It came to the Museum in October 2002 as a donation from the RAF.

USAF F-15s and F-16s carried the bulk of the missions in Desert Storm.

Lockheed AC-130A Spectre

The AC-130A Spectre *is a C-130 converted to a gunship, primarily for night attacks against ground targets. To enhance its armament's effectiveness, it used various sensors, a target acquisition system, and infrared and low-light television systems.*

The crew of this AC-130A Spectre *gunship, named* Azrael *(Azrael, in the Koran, is the angel of death who severs the soul from the body), displayed courage and heroism during the closing hours of Operation Desert Storm. On February 26, 1991, Coalition ground forces were driving the*

EF-111A Ravens, known affectionately as Fat Tails *and* Spark Varks *(the F-111 is known as the* Aardvark*), served as tactical electronic jamming aircraft in the 1980s and 1990s. The US Air Force received forty-two EF-111As between 1981 and 1985, and the aircraft supported several USAF operations in the 1980s and 1990s.*

...rmy out of Kuwait. Azrael was sent to the Al Jahra highway between Kuwait City ...asrah, Iraq, to intercept the convoys of tanks, trucks, buses, and cars fleeing the battle. ...numerous enemy batteries of SA-6 and SA-8 surface-to-air missiles, and 37mm and ...radar-guided anti-aircraft artillery, the crew attacked the enemy skillfully, inflicting ...cant damage on the convoys. The crew's heroic efforts left much of the enemy's ...nent destroyed or unserviceable, contributing to the defeat of the Iraqi forces. On ...ry 28, 1991, Iraq agreed to a cease-fire.

...rcraft on display was assigned to the 919th Special Operations Wing and was retired ...Museum in October 1995.

AZRAEL
"Angel of Death"

Operation Nickel Grass, *by Gil Cohen*

The SR-71, unofficially known as the Blackbird, *is a long-range, advanced, strategic reconnaissance aircraft developed from the Lockheed A-12 and YF-12A aircraft.*

Throughout its nearly twenty-four year career, the SR-71 remained the world's fastest and highest-flying operational aircraft. From 80,000 feet, it could survey 100,000 square miles of Earth's surface per hour. On July 28, 1976, an SR-71 set two world records for its class - an absolute speed record of 2,193.167 mph, and an absolute altitude record of 85,068.997 feet. On March 21, 1968, in the aircraft on display, Maj. (later Gen.) Jerome F. O'Malley and Maj. Edward D. Payne made the first operational SR-71 sortie. During

Coronet Oak, *by Gil Cohen*

its career, this aircraft accumulated 2,981 flying hours and flew 942 total sorties (more than any other SR-71), including 257 operational missions, from Beale Air Force Base, California, Palmdale, California, Kadena Air Base, Okinawa, and RAF (Base), Mildenhall, England. The aircraft was flown to the Museum in March 1990.

Above: *One of the SR-71's powerful engines, a Pratt & Whitney J58s of 32,500 pounds thrust each, with afterburner.*

Thunderbolt, more often known as the "Warthog," became the plane of choice for close support. Maneuverable and able to absorb heavy battle damage, the A-10 could also carry a variety of weapons on its eleven pylons. Despite all that, its most impressive piece of armament was "the gun," a seven-barrel, 30mm, GAU-8A cannon that could fire as many as 4,200 rounds a minute. When armed with depleted uranium rounds it was capable of destroying armored tanks.

The B-52 continued to be the strategic bomber. Any number of upgrades to the basic airframe, first used in

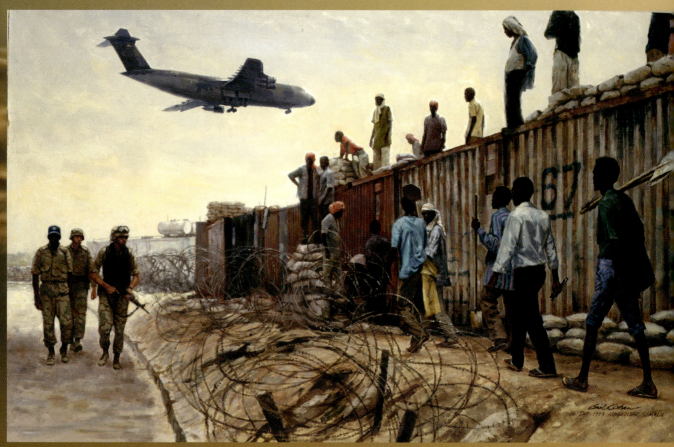

Mission Somalia, by Gil Cohen

The USAF operates across the globe and depends on the "professional" air force personnel who keep the machinery operational. The non-commissioned officers, the sergeants, who manage the legions of enlisted men and women who turn the wrenches, connect the cables, fuel the aircraft, and keep the complex systems working.

The Chief Master Sergeants are the top of that chain and no one represents those professionals better than CMSGT Harrison "Bud" Golem. His life was dedicated to the air force and "his" aircraft, and those who served with him. Bud entered the service during World War Two, served combat duty in Korea and Vietnam, and retired at the top of his profession in 1968. He became a civilian contractor and worked at the aircraft modification center at Wright-Patterson Air Force Base. Bud was involved with the original AC-130A gunships (see page 243) and Advanced Cruise Missile programs.

1952, kept the venerable aircraft at the center of Cold War preparedness. Its replacement, the Rockwell B-1, began as a proposal in the 1960 and suffered cancellation by the Carter administration as being too expensive. Revived under the military expansion of the Reagan administration, the B-1B was slower than the original design but could carry more weaponry with a full fuel load. Improved avionics and a much reduced radar cross-section made the B-1B a formidable all-weather bomber capable of service to the SAC command or in support of tactical operations.

By the mid-1980s, the Reagan administration's strengthening of the military brought the USAF back to 8,200 aircraft and 630,000 personnel. The sudden end of the Cold War found the USAF well prepared for whatever came next. It retained its traditional division into SAC and TAC commands with a variety of other support units. The Soviet Union had failed as a government, but the new Russian Federation retained its nuclear capability. Other nations had acquired nuclear capabilities, leaving the US alone at the top militarily in a way it had not been since the years immediately after WWII. In effect, the USAF was given a breather from the active threat of a Soviet nuclear attack, but it also had to remain prepared for whatever new threat which might appear on the horizon.

The Cold War had barely reached room temperature before the US found itself involved in international combat once again. In August 1990, the Iraqi military under Saddam Hussein invaded its oil-rich neighbor, Kuwait. The US demanded that Iraq withdraw while assembling a coalition to counter liberate Kuwait. When Iraq failed to leave Kuwait, the US and it allies initiated an air campaign in January 1991 that produced almost instantaneous results. Critical infrastructure was destroyed immediately and the Iraqi leadership sought shelter from the air attack. The USAF was able to test its ability to use new equipment and tactics on an enemy, which had little ability to offer significant resistance. When the ground campaign began in late February, the Iraqi military had been weakened to the point President Bush could declare a ceasefire in a matter of four days. The USAF had brought any number of new technologies to the campaign, including precision-guided bombs and missiles, stealth technology, and global positioning electronics, and learned much to be digested over the relative peace of the 1990s. With a new century just a few years away, the USAF had reason to both reflect and prepare.

The North American XB-70 looms above the Northrop YF-23, when both were in the Museum annex.

Chapter 10
At the Leading Edge

"To strive, to seek, to find, and not to yield."
(Alfred Lord Tennyson, 1809-1892)

"In research, the horizon recedes as we advance."
(Mark Pattison, 1813-1884)

McCook Field Wind Tunnel

This wind tunnel was designed and built at McCook Field, Ohio, in 1918. Using a 24-blade fan of 60 inches diameter, the tunnel developed a maximum airspeed of 453 mph at its 14-inch diameter choke-throat test area.

It was used for calibrating airspeed instruments and testing airfoils.

Legendary USAF **Big** *aircraft test pilot, Lt. Col. Fitzhugh "Fitz" L. Fulton was flying the XB-70 when it was flight delivered to the Museum in February, 1969.*

Author/photographer Dan Patterson was at the end of the runway in 1969 when the XB-70 landed at the Museum. He was a sophomore in high school.

The Bell X-1B furthered the supersonic test flights for the USAF.
Reaction Motors XLR-11-RM-6 four-chamber rocket engine of 6,000 pounds thrust.

North American XB-70 Valkyrie

The futuristic XB-70A was originally conceived in the 1950s as a high-altitude, nuclear strike bomber that could fly at Mach 3 (three times the speed of sound). Any potential enemy would have been unable to defend against such a bomber.

Engines: Six General Electric YJ93s of 30,000 pounds thrust each, with afterburner
Maximum speed: 2,056 mph (Mach 3.1) at 73,000 feet.

Brigadier General Jay Jabour, USAF (Ret.) General Jabour served as systems program director for both the F-22 and B-2 programs, as well as a test pilot and director of the F-22 / Advanced Tactical Fighter (ATF) Combined Test Force, seen here with the Northrop X-4 Bantam.

Don Lopez filled many roles as an American aviator in a career which spanned decades. He was a US Army Air Forces and US Air Force fighter and test pilot, and, until his death the deputy director of the Smithsonian National Air and Space Museum. He wrote two great books about his life in the cockpit: Into the Teeth of the Tiger Fighter *and* Pilot's Heaven: Flight Testing the Early Jets.

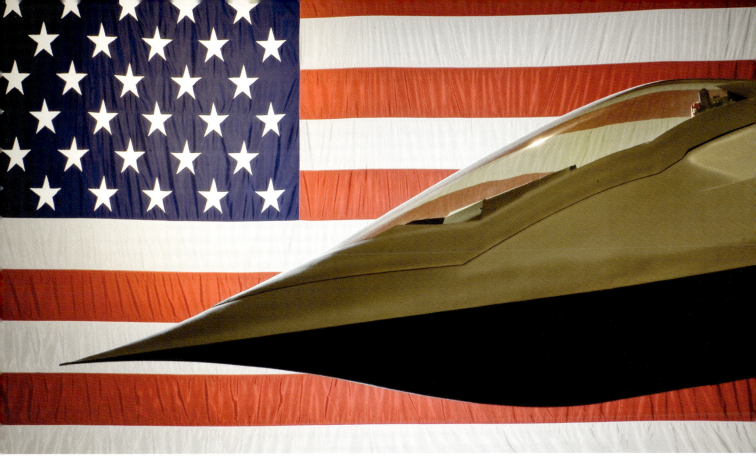

Boeing Bird of Prey

The Bird of Prey *is a single-seat stealth technology demonstrator used to test "low-observable" stealth techniques and new methods of aircraft design and construction. The secret* Bird of Prey *project ran from 1992 to 1999, and the aircraft first flew in the fall of 1996. The* Bird of Prey *was named for its resemblance to the Klingon spacecraft from the science-fiction series Star Trek.*

Boeing X-45A J-UCAS

The pioneering X-45A demonstrated that highly autonomous uninhabited aircraft could be used to attack opposing surface-to-air defenses (called Suppression of Enemy Air Defense, or SEAD).

In 2005 the X-45As autonomously flew a preplanned SEAD mission against simulated Surface-to-Air Missile (SAM) systems. The X-45As then used their on-board, decision-making software to avoid a new, unplanned SAM threat. They independently determined which aircraft would attack the new target based upon their position, weapons and, fuel. After the pilot-operator at Edwards AFB, California, checked the plan created by the UCAS's software, the X-45As successfully attacked and returned to base..

NASA

66671

North American X-15

The X-15 is a famous and significant part of aviation history. Its purpose was to fly high and fast, testing the machine and subjecting pilots to conditions that future astronauts would face. It made the first manned flights to the edges of space and was the world's first piloted aircraft to reach hypersonic speeds, or more than five times the speed of sound. The X-15 was an important tool for developing spaceflight in the 1960s, and pilots flying above 50 miles altitude in the X-15 earned astronaut wings.

This aircraft is the second of the three X-15s. North American modified it for even greater speed, adding the large orange-and-white propellant tanks and lengthening the fuselage about 18 inches. This was the fastest X-15, reaching Mach 6.7 in October 1967. It was delivered to the Museum in 1969.

In the two years beginning in October 1963, Joe Engle flew the X-15 sixteen times, reaching Mach 5.71 on his tenth flight and an altitude of 271, 000 feet on his fifteenth. He later joined the Space Shuttle program commanding Columbia in 1981 and Discovery in 1985.

In 2011, Joe Engle an enshrinee in the National Aviation Hall of Fame, talks with young student pilot Danny Bush about flying, as only pilots can. Now Lt. Danny Bush flies FA-18s for the US Navy.

Col. Albert Boyd with his P-80R.

Shaking hamds with Lockheed Chief Designer Kelly Johnson

Lockheed P-80R

On June 19, 1947, at Muroc Army Airfield (now Edwards Air Force Base), California, Col. Albert Boyd flew this P-80R to a new world's speed record of 623.753 mph, returning the record to the United States after nearly twenty-four years.

A high-speed variant of the standard P-80A Shooting Star, it had a smaller canopy, redesigned air intakes, and a shorter wing with an extended leading edge. In addition, the engine was modified, armament removed and replaced by a fuel tank, and all drag-producing openings sealed.

The P-80R on display is the only one built. It was shipped to the Museum from Griffiss Air Force Base, New York, in October 1954.

In the Museum's Missile Gallery education specialist Cindy Henry describes to a group of school kids the operations of the NASA space shuttle.

Chapter 11
Wild Black Yonder

The Museum's collections hold this rare piece of American space history. USAF test pilot Ed White became an astronaut and was the first American to "walk in space." Before his Gemini 4 flight he purchased this 35mm Contarex camera, which NASA engineers modified so that he could operate it while wearing the heavy gloves which were a part of his EVA (extravehicular activity) space suit.

Between Museum Buildings 3 and 4 is the Missile Gallery, where there is a dramatic display of the ICBMs which the USAF has kept on nuclear. Two of these rocket types were also modified for NASA to use for launch vehicles in the manned space program. The Atlas was used in the Mercury program, and the Titan II, to launch the Gemini spacecraft.

Opened to the public in 2004, the Missile Gallery is contained in a silo-like structure that stands 140 feet high. Visitors can view missiles such as the Martin Marietta Titan I and II and Chrysler Jupiter from ground level, or can take in an aerial view from an elevated platform that hugs the inside circumference of the gallery.
Additional missiles include:
Boeing LGM-30A Minuteman IA
Boeing LGM-30G Minuteman III
Douglas SM-75/PGM-17A Thor
Martin Marietta LGM-118A Peacekeeper
Thor Agena A

The next and logical step from powered flight through the atmosphere was to fly beyond the atmosphere, into space, a great unknown where pilots could not fly. Aviators saw the possibilities, as they did with atmospheric flight, of exploration and then, by extension, of using what was learned as a weapon of war. The Greeks had imagined space travel some two thousand years ago, Icarus had flown too close to the sun, and the Chinese had learned the rudiments of rocket propulsion by the 12th century AD, if not before. The use of rocket propulsion as a weapon was little more than an extension of the firearm and cannon, although translating idea into practical application took more time and ingenuity.

The first American effort at the idea of the guided missile came in the form of a pilotless aircraft known as the Bug. Made by the Dayton-Wright Company, the Bug carried a 180-pound warhead as part of a biplane that dropped its wings after traveling a distance determined by the number of propeller revolutions turned. Inaccurate by design, the Bug was no more than a curiosity. The German V-1 and V-2 demonstrated that guided missiles were possible. The V-1 was little more than a jet-powered bomb, flying subsonic. The V-2 used a solid fuel and traveled at supersonic speeds, but was only marginally more accurate than the V-1. Both served as much as terror weapons than anything else, raining from the sky without warning.

The USAF saw no real need to develop a missile program with any speed. With the military downsizing and lack of enthusiasm from many of the commanders, the missile programs languished until the Soviet Union delivered several wake-up calls. The detonation of the first Soviet atomic bomb in 1949 and a hydrogen bomb in 1953 meant that, technologically, the Soviets had closed the gap on the United States so far as weapons capability was concerned. Intelligence reports that the Soviet rocket program was making great progress with the size and power of their experimental designs. By 1955, the USAF had begun a program to produce both intercontinental (ICBM) and intermediate-range (IRBM) missiles, but tight budgets limited its progress. The Soviet launch of the Sputnik satellite in October 1957 shocked the United States into action. All of a sudden, the most important issue facing the nation was the "missile gap," a problem that ran all the way through American society, right down to elementary school science textbooks.

It did not take long for the United States to reverse the trend despite the short-term panic over the Soviet success. By the time of the Cuban Missile Crisis in the fall of 1962, the United States had deployed 126 Atlas and 54 Titan ICBMs and Thor and Jupiter IRBMs in Europe. Ten Minuteman Is were already in service,

the first solid-propellant rockets which would become the backbone of the American land-based arsenal. Development of the Minuteman II and Minuteman III missiles followed quickly, in 1965 and 1970. The older Atlas and Titan I liquid-fueled rockets were retired in the mid-1960s, leaving just the Titan II and Minuteman as the basis for the land-based fleet. The Minuteman was another of the technical marvels of the day. Only 60 feet long and weighing 80,000 pounds, it was both inexpensive and easy to deploy, with a range of 8,000 miles.

Robert McCall's paintng of Gordon Cooper's launch of Mercury-Atlas 9, on May 15, 1963.

The USAF viewed missiles as an extension of air power and a natural extension of its mission, and took that position against arguments of the other services to the contrary. But unmanned aircraft required a rethinking of any number of factors, including, but not limited to, new bases, training, career paths, logistics problems, and integration of doctrine and tactics. The end product of an effective missile system meant that the greatest fears of the earliest theorists had come to fruition. Air war could end the world as it had come to be known.

From the early 1950s on, even before the Soviet satellite Sputnik threw down the gauntlet, it was apparent that manned space flight would be the next extension of flight. For the United States, the USAF assumed, reasonably, that exploring space fell under its purview, as the service devoted to advancing the nation's ability to explore the limits of flight. The Kennedy administration assigned the USAF the task of providing early-warning and space-based defense, detecting incoming ICBM attacks and developing a system to counter such aggression. Later that would expand to include the Defense Satellite Communications System (DSCS), to provide an extensive military communication network of voice, data, and imagery. The USAF designed its own

Joe Kittinger Jr.

After starting his USAF career as a fighter pilot, Joe Kittinger became a test pilot for **Project Man High,** *where a high altitude balloon was used with a pressurized gondola and partial pressure suit. In 1957, Joe piloted the balloon,* **Man High One,** *to an altitude of 96,000 feet.*

He moved to **Project Excelsior** *in 1958. The goal of the project was to put a man into space and test a person's ability to survive extremely high-altitude bailouts. In 1959, Joe made a parachute jump from* **Excelsior I** *from an altitude of 76,000 feet.*

Kittinger set a world record for the highest balloon ascent and the longest parachute freefall in **Excelsior III,** *where he piloted the gondola to an altitude of 102,800 feet in 1960. This jump established that it was possible to put a man into space.*

Joe was awarded the Harmon Trophy by President Eisenhower in 1960 for outstanding accomplishments in aeronautics.

weather satellite system separate from NASA's to provide real-time accurate weather reporting for all military operations. The development of the Global Positioning System (GPS) by the Department of Defense took longer. Begun in the 1970s without any sense of urgency, the initial stage was not complete until 1994, with twenty-four satellites providing data.

These new systems paid off handsomely for the Allies in the Gulf War, the first war in which satellite communication was a part of all levels of planning and operations, essentially giving the Allied operation the virtual "high ground" against Iraq. On the ground, coalition forces could operate independently of each other with full confidence that coordinated attacks could attack precisely as planned, night or day, in any weather. Artillery fire predictable made direct hits on its targets. In the air, aircraft trained on targets with or without line-of-sight aiming. Lt. General Donald Cromer, Commander of the Space Division, comment in the debriefing that "…space is as much a part of the Air Force and the military infrastructure as airplanes, tanks, and ships. All future wars will be planned and executed with that in mind."

The USAF expected it would play the most important role in manned space exploration, but that was ultimately given to the National Aeronautics and Space Administration (NASA), to keep space exploration

services and civilian crew.

The shuttle program expanded the scope of the scientific research performed in space and extended more opportunities for military pilots and a small number of civilians to contribute to space exploration. Sally K. Ride became the first woman to fly as a 1983 member of a shuttle crew in June 1983. Guion Bluford became the first African American to travel in space two months later. Eileen Collins would be the first woman to pilot a shuttle mission in 1995 before commanding two additional missions, in July 1999 and July 2005.

Apollo 15 was the All Air Force *crew on the mission to the moon. Their spacecraft is on display at the NMUSAF. One of the items they carried to the moon was the music and lyrics to the Air Force song, signed by the crew.*

separate from the military. The army had directed its research into rocket technology based on the German V-2. The USAF expected that space exploration would be accomplished with pilots flying into space in aircraft specially designed for the task. With that in mind, North American developed the X-15, a hypersonic, rocket-powered aircraft that could reach the arbitrary frontier of space some 50 miles up and at speed as fast as 4,500 mph. When it became time to begin training for the first space mission, President Eisenhower approved the rocket and capsule plan over the winged aircraft, but chose military test pilots as the first astronauts. Three USAF captains (Deke Slayton, Gus Grissom, and Gordon Cooper), three US Navy lieutenant commanders (Walter Schirra, Alan Shepard, and Scott Carpenter), and one USMC lieutenant colonel (John Glenn) were appointed as the astronauts for the Mercury program. Throughout the Mercury-Gemini-Apollo missions that took the United States to the moon, USAF astronauts participated in every aspect of the lunar missions. Likewise, when NASA switched its focus to the laboratory environment of the space shuttle, USAF pilots joined the other

Tom Stafford had a long career in the space program flying in nearly every spacecraft after Mercury. He was chief of the astronaut office, and later became deputy director of flight crew operations for NASA. He commanded the American half of the Apollo-Soyuz joint space mission with the Soviet Union and assumed command of the Air Force Flight Test Center in 1975.

McDonnell Douglas F-15A Eagle

The F-15 is a twin-engine, high-performance, all-weather air superiority fighter. First flown in 1972, the Eagle entered US Air Force service in 1974. The Eagle's most notable characteristics are its great acceleration and maneuverability. It was the first US fighter with engine thrust greater than the basic weight of the aircraft, allowing it to accelerate while in a vertical climb. Its great power, light weight, and large wing area combine to make the Eagle very agile.

Chapter 12
Air Power

"Air technology has finally caught up to air theory"

(Lt. General Charles Horner, USAF, Joint Force Air Component Commander, DESERT STORM)

"You cannot lose a war with air supremacy, and you cannot win one without it."

(Carl Vinson, Chairman of the House Committee on ther Armed Services)

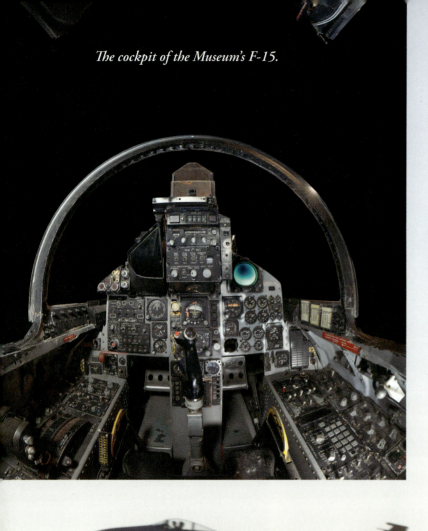

The cockpit of the Museum's F-15.

The relative quiet of the post—Cold War years of the 1990s did not extend far beyond the turn of the century. The USAF supported NATO forces in establishing no-fly zones over parts of the former Yugoslavia, particularly Bosnia and Serbia. Several minor operations in Iraq enforced no-fly zones, but for the most part, the USAF quietly continued to be the watchful sentinel it was expected to be. No longer required to defend the United States at a moment's notice, the USAF focused on a strategy that had it ready to respond to any threat requiring an airborne response, at any distance, with overwhelming power. A reduction in force accompanied the new focus, but more than that, the USAF took a hard look at how it could address the new mission. Budgets dropped about 20 percent between 1990 and 1993, not all of it reductions, but also due to a conscious streamlining of operations. The distinctions between tactical and strategic blurred. Bombers could support ground troops and fighters could drop precision-aimed bombs. The Air Combat Command replaced the SAC, MAC, and TAC.

The world of the USAF changed on the morning of September 11, 2001, much in the same way it changed by the attack on Pearl Harbor, December 7, 1941. Four hijacked commercial airliners crashing into the World

Trade Center towers in New York City, the Pentagon outside Washington, DC, and in rural Pennsylvania turned ongoing anti-terrorism action into open warfare. Planes scrambled by the Northeast Air Defense Sector (NEADS) of the North American Aerospace Defense Command (NORAD) were in the air within minutes when they knew of the nature of the attack and were prepared to shoot down commercial planes if necessary.

In the wake of the attacks of September 11, the United States decided to respond against Afghanistan, which had sheltered the terrorist organization Al Qaeda. Al Qaeda had formed out of the remnants of the Afghan army that had driven the Soviet Union out of Afghanistan in the 1980s. A loose coalition partially affiliated with and protected by the Taliban, which controlled about two-thirds of Afghanistan in 2001, Al Qaeda had vowed to wage war against the United States and its allies after American support disappeared once the Soviets had withdrawn.

Airstrikes against Al Qaeda targets in Afghanistan began almost immediately. The USAF and USN combined to deliver the blows. B-52s and B-1s flying out of bases in

An F-15 launches from Nellis AFB; the Superstition Mountains, familiar to USAF pilots, make a stunning background, with F-16s in the foreground.

Above: The NMUSAF has several examples of the opposition and many are in this book. The Museum's MiG 29 aircraft on display was an early-model Soviet Air Force MiG-29A (S/N 2960516761) assigned to the 234th Gvardeiskii Istrebitelnii Aviatsionnii Polk (234th Guards Fighter Aviation Regiment) stationed at Kubinka Air Base near Moscow. It was one of the six MiG-29s that made a goodwill visit to Kuopio-Rissala, Finland, in July 1986.

The cockpit of the Soviet fighter.

Boeing B-1B Lancer

The Boeing (formerly Rockwell International) B-1B Lancer is the improved
variant of the B-1A, which was canceled in 1977. Initiated in 1981, the
first production model of this long-range, multi-role, heavy bomber flew in
October 1984. The first operational B-1B was delivered to Dyess Air Force
Base, Texas, in June 1985, and the final B-1B was delivered in 1988.

First used in combat against Iraq during Operation Desert Fox in 1998,
the B-1B has also been employed in Kosovo and Afghanistan. Starting in
2002, the US Air Force began reducing the number of B-1Bs as a cost-saving
measure.

The aircraft on display arrived at the Museum from the 7th Bomb Wing at
Dyess Air Force Base, Texas, on Sept. 10, 2002.

The B-1B's blended wing/body configuration, variable-geometry design, and turbofan engines combined to provide greater range and high speed -- more than 900 mph (Mach 1.2) at sea level. Forward wing settings were used for takeoff, landing, and high-altitude maximum cruise. Aft wing settings were used in high subsonic and supersonic flight, which also enhanced the aircraft's maneuverability.

Saudi Arabia and carried-based F-14s and Tomahawk missiles rained down on Al Qaeda training camps and Taliban sites that sheltered Al Qaeda forces. The Afghani Northern Alliance, a combination of tribes that united against the Taliban, joined the US and its allies, and much of the USAF action in the early months supported Northern Alliance ground action. By December 18, the Taliban had been forced out of power and the allied air campaign ended successfully.

Operations began again immediately after the new year as coalition forces joined in Operation Anaconda, an attempt to eliminate remaining Taliban / Al Qaeda strongholds in Eastern Afghanistan. Close-in air support succeeded in helping the Northern Alliance make advances, but by the time the United States had decided to go to war in Iraq, the situation in Afghanistan was not yet stable.

In Operation Iraqi Freedom, the war to remove Saddam Hussein as leader of Iraq, the USAF and USN were combined under a single command, the Combined Force Air Component Command (CFACC). Throughout the short campaign to drive Saddam out of Baghdad, the CFACC was not challenged, flying more that 41,000 sorties, 24,000 by the USAF alone. When combat operations ended on May 1, 2003, the United States had not developed a plan to replace the Iraqi government with a coalition of factions and the situation remained unstable going forward. The USAF would maintain an active presence in Iraq for years, providing a combination of combat support roles as well as security, logistics, and engineering assistance.

Northrop B-2 Spirit

The global spread of sophisticated air defense systems in the 1980s threatened the USAF's ability to destroy an enemy's most valued targets. To overcome this threat, the USAF incorporated the revolutionary low-observable, or "stealth," technology into a long-range bomber capable of delivering large payloads of conventional or nuclear weapons. The Northrop Grumman B-2 Spirit merged the high aerodynamic efficiency of the "flying wing" design with composite materials, special coatings, and classified stealth technologies. As a result, the B-2 became virtually invisible to even the most sophisticated air defense radar systems.

With a crew of only two -- the pilot in the left seat and the mission commander in the right -- a typical combat mission consisted of a nonstop flight from Whiteman Air Force Base to the target and back. During these missions, normally lasting more than thirty hours and requiring numerous aerial refuelings, each B-2 delivered up to 40,000 pounds of precision weapons.

Northrop

US Air Force materiel and suppliers.

The industry of providing the Air Force the weapon systems necessary to fulfill the missions builds not only aircraft but the entire spectrum of supporting information. These images are just a slice of what the Museum's collections has filed away for research and publications such as this.

Lockheed Martin

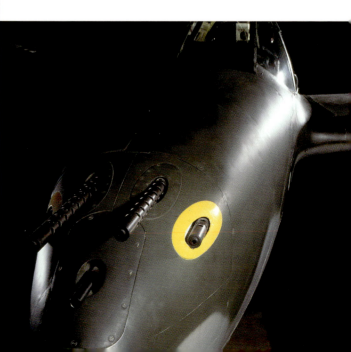

Boeing

The NMUSAF maintains a large and comprehensive archives of the technical drawings, flight manuals, technical field orders, and updates generated by the manufacturers of the aircraft flown by the US Army Air Forces and after 1947 the US Air Force.

The Museum's archives also includes thousands of photographs—not only manufacturers' photos, but also images from operations over the years.

General Electric

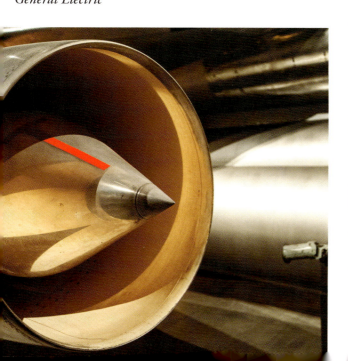

Since the end of combat operation in Iraq, the USAF has increasingly relied on Unmanned Aerial Vehicle (UAVs), sometimes known, incorrectly, as drones, to provide aerial support, especially in situations where manned

General Atomics Aeronautical Systems RQ-1 Predator

Technically, the RQ-1 Predator *is not just an aircraft but an entire system. Developed as an Advanced Concept Technology Demonstration (ACTD), this system consisted of four unmanned aerial vehicles (UAVs), a ground control station, a satellite communications terminal and, fifty-five personnel. The* Predator *UAV in the Museum -- the most recognizable part of the system -- provided military commanders with an intelligence, surveillance and reconnaissance (ISR) platform capable of flying over dangerous areas for extended periods without risk to a human pilot.*

Designed and built to be easily deployed worldwide, the Predator *systems operated from Creech Air Force Base, Nevada. In February 2001 the* Predator *demonstrated a new potential. In a test program, it successfully fired a laser-guided Lockheed Martin AGM-114* Hellfire *anti-tank missile at a stationary target.*

aircraft might be difficult to use. The US uses the UAVs particularly to attack targets in the larger war on terrorism. UAVs have become one of the most precise weapons that can be directed at small scale targets. So important has this new, adaptable technology been in engaging the enemy, the USAF now trains more UAV pilots than manned aircraft pilots.

IM-9 Sidewinder *Air-to-Air Missile*

The AIM-9 is a 200-pound supersonic air-to-air missile carried by A-10, F-4, F-15, F-16, and F-111 aircraft. It is a "heat-seeking" missile with a range of 1 to 2 miles and is generally used during the day in clear weather conditions. The Sidewinder *has been continually improved since entering service in the 1950s.*

The missile shown here is an AIM-9E; Desert Storm aircraft used improved AIM-9L and AIM-9M versions.

On the ramp at Nellis AFB, participating in USAF exercises to maintain razor-sharp readiness.

Left: *F-16s prepped for an early-morning mission.*

Right: *An F-22* Raptor *receiving line service, getting the front tires changed.*

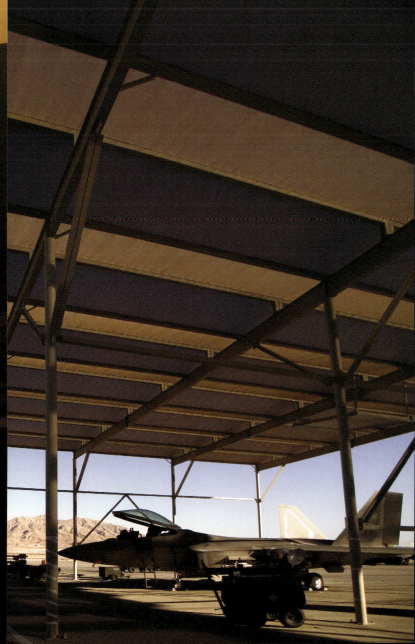

The US Air Force Memorial was dedicated on October 14, 2006, celebrating the service's 60th anniversary. In a rare clearance of very restricted airspace, USAF Thunderbirds overfly the new memorial.

Chapter 13
United States Air Force Since 1997

"Of the four wars in my lifetime none came about because the United States was too strong".

(Ronald Reagan)

"However absorbed a commander may be in the elaboration of his own thoughts, it is necessary sometimes to take the enemy into consideration".

(Winston Churchill)

One of the mainstays of the USAF, the F-15. The original manufacturer was McDonnell Douglas, who have since been acquired by the Boeing Company. The Eagle entered USAF service in 1974 and has evolved through the years, adapting to the changing roles necessary to maintain air superiority.

Until World War II, American military aviation had been exclusively reserved for white males, with the exception of those few women who held clerical positions, and the fewer still who served as mechanics. This corresponded, of course, with the cultural expectation that women, as keepers of the household, should be protected from the ravages of war, as should their children. For the United States, separated from the combat theaters by the Atlantic and Pacific oceans, civilian casualties were rare, with the exception of civilian sailors on merchant ships, of whom 9,500 died on the 700 plus ships sunk by the enemy during World War I. While women eagerly took the place of men in any number of the traditionally male occupations, there had been no pressing need to recruit women for combat or even for support roles going into World War II, despite the willingness of many women to volunteer.

Women's path to serving as USAAF pilots came through two separate organizations that merged to form the Women Airforce Service Pilots (WASP), which was formally recognized on August 5, 1943. The Women's Flying Training Detachment (WFTD) and the Women's Auxiliary Ferrying Squadron (WFS) had both been founded in September 1942, to move aircraft from place to place, particularly from the factory to the airfield. The WFTD, the idea for which had been presented to Eleanor Roosevelt by Jacqueline Cochran in 1939, trained women pilots to assist in the ferrying operations. Once the two organizations were operational, Cochran moved to get them united into a single group, the WASP. More than 25,000 women applied for consideration, but only 1,800 were accepted. Of that group, more than 1,000 completed the training. The vast majority of these pilots were white. Only a dozen or so of the pilots came from ethnic minorities.

Once trained, WASP pilots joined ferrying squadrons across the United States. Ferrying planes from the factory to their assigned bases was the primary duty for the women pilots, who delivered more than 12,500 aircraft. Other duties included test flying repaired aircraft and towing targets for airborne artillery practice. WASP pilots qualified in every plane flown by the USAAF. WASP pilots never earned military status during the war. They served as federal civil service employees, earning a regular salary, about two-thirds that of a military pilot, with deductions for room, board, and incidental expenses. They did not earn veteran's status unit 1977 and received Honorable Discharge certificates in 1979.

The Tuskegee Airmen, the USAAF's Black aviator program, was an extension of the Civilian Pilot Training Program (CPTF). The CPTF was created in 1938, to increase the number of civilian pilots who might be trained as military pilots in the future. From its founding and continuing during the war as the War Training Service (WTS), the CPTF/WTS taught more than 400,000 American civilians how to fly, including women and Black pilots. The original authorization for the CPTF included funds to train Black pilots in segregated units. In March 1941, the 99th Pursuit Squadron was established in Illinois and soon transferred to Tuskegee, Alabama, where training continued. In all, the Tuskegee program graduated 673 fighter pilots, 253 medium bomber pilots, and 132 navigators. The Airmen were led by Benjamin O. Davis, Jr., the first Black West Point graduate since 1889, who went on to a distinguished career, rising to the rank of lieutenant general.

The 99th deployed to North Africa in April 1943 and soon began flying combat missions in North Africa and Sicily. Despite initial complaints about their readiness from white officers, forcing Davis to defend the 99th before a committee on Negro troop policies, despite the fact that the units had been awarded a distinguished unit citation. By February 1944, three other fighter squadrons, the 110th, 301st, and the 302nd had joined the 99th to create the 332nd Fighter Group, now flying P-51 Mustangs instead of the older P-40s. Tuskegee trained bomber aviators served in the 477th Bombardment Group. Overall, the Tuskegee Airmen achieved a record commensurate with other flying units, sometimes better and rarely worse. The 332nd Fighter group served until April 26, 1945, flying some 15,000 sorties in two years, downing or damaging thirty-six German aircraft in the air and another 237 on the ground. Sixty-six Tuskegee airmen died in combat and another thirty-two spent time in prisoner of war camps after being shot down. The Tuskegee Experiment had vindicated the pilots, crews, and officers of the 332nd and the 477th, but it would not be until President Truman desegregated the armed services in 1948, before Blacks began to receive equal treatment.   ho

The creation and growth of the United States Air Force in many respects runs parallel to the American civil rights movement. At the heart of equal opportunity for women and minorities lay the problem of training and education. For under-represented groups, learning what it meant to be an air force aviator directly affected how well and how quickly members of these groups could become contributing members of the service.

The USAF, like the US Army and US Navy, has its own military academy to train officers and future leaders for the service. Prior to the founding of the USAF as a separate service in 1947, many of its senior officers had begun their careers at the United States Military Academy at West Point. No sooner had the

The Air Force Memorial located near the Pentagon was the last design project of American architect James Ingo Freed. Three spires soar into the Virgina sky, designed to reflect the flight pattern of the Thunderbirds as they perform the famous "bomb burst" maneuver. The plaza which makes the base is surrounded by simple and elegant structures and appropriate quotes.

The NMUSAF exhibits two of the most iconic air force fighters which were employed to carry the message of the precision performance team. These fighters and the pilots who fly them assemble a thrilling air show which is made up of standard operational maneuvers, albeit flown very close together.

North American F-100
The aircraft on display was used by the Thunderbirds, the official USAF Flight Demonstration Team, from 1964 until 1968. During that period, the team toured the Caribbean, Europe, Latin America, and nearly every state in the USA.

This F-100D was retired from service with the 114th Tactical Fighter Group, South Dakota Air National Guard, in 1977. It was restored by Thunderbird maintenance personnel at Nellis Air Force Base, Nevada, to its original appearance as a team aircraft. It was flown to the museum by the Air National Guard, and the Thunderbirds presented the aircraft to the Museum on July 22, 1977.

280

General Dynamics F-16. The F-16 on display (S/N 81-0663) was one of the first F-16s to be received by the Thunderbirds in 1982 when they transitioned from T-38s to F-16s. The Thunderbirds continued to fly this aircraft until 1992 when they converted to F-16Cs. It was then modified to operational condition and assigned to the Air Education and Training Command to train pilots at Luke Air Force Base, Arizona. In 1996 the Thunderbirds repainted it in Thunderbird colors at Nellis Air Force Base, Nevada. The Museum placed it on display in October 1996.

The Lockheed Martin F-22A Raptor is the world's first stealthy air dominance fighter. Its radar, weapons control, and electronic warfare systems work together as one integrated unit. The Raptor combines stealth, maneuverability, and the ability to fly long distances at supersonic speeds -- or "supercruise" -- in performance of air superiority and air-to-ground missions. Furthermore, it requires less maintenance than older fighters.

USAF become independent than discussions about the need for an air force academy began. It was not until 1954 that Secretary of the Air Force, Harold Talbott commissioned a team to select a site for the establishment of a permanent academy. From a short list of three finalists, the team chose a site outside Colorado Springs, Colorado. The first class of 306 cadets arrived in 1955, to be sworn in at temporary facilities at Lowry AFB, in Denver, Colorado. Admission was, and remains, highly competitive. Cadets are invited from each of the congressional districts and receive a bachelor of science degree on graduation. Post graduation, they have a five-year active service commitment with three additional years in the reserve. Many, of course, serve for a career.

The need for officers and pilots in Southeast Asia brought a significant expansion of the Academy in the 1960s. In 1961, the Academy commissioned 217 graduating second lieutenants. In March 1964, President Johnson expanded the United States Military Academy and the Air Force Academy to match the size of the Naval Academy's size of 4,417 midshipmen. From then

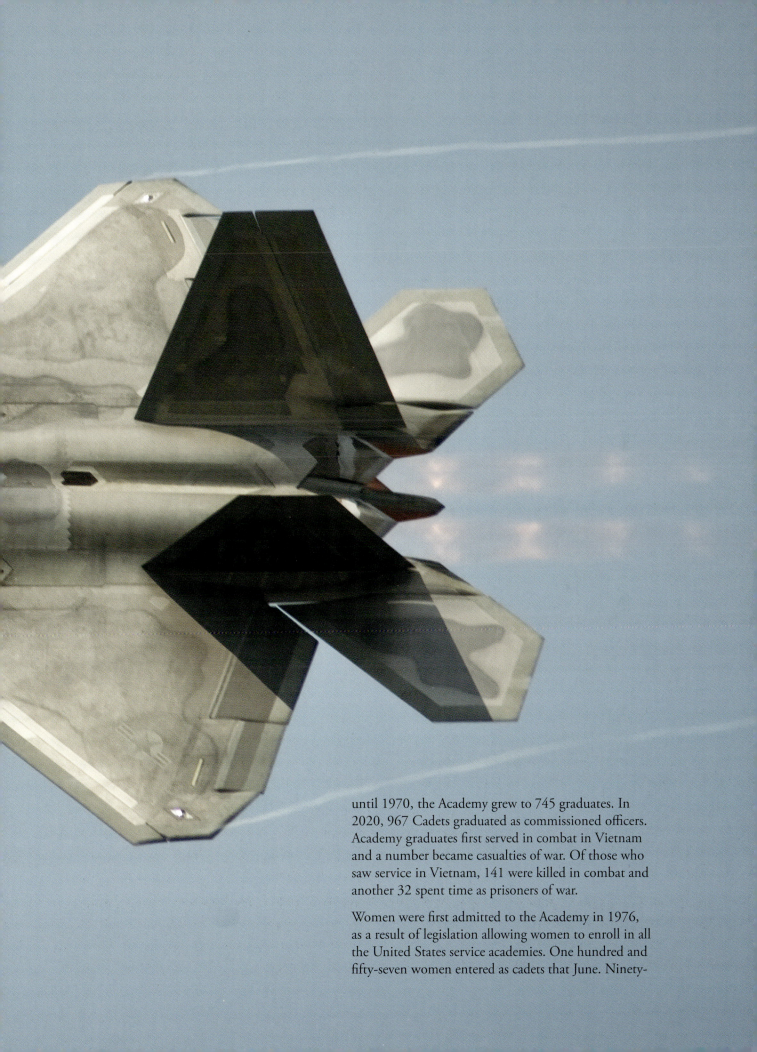

until 1970, the Academy grew to 745 graduates. In 2020, 967 Cadets graduated as commissioned officers. Academy graduates first served in combat in Vietnam and a number became casualties of war. Of those who saw service in Vietnam, 141 were killed in combat and another 32 spent time as prisoners of war.

Women were first admitted to the Academy in 1976, as a result of legislation allowing women to enroll in all the United States service academies. One hundred and fifty-seven women entered as cadets that June. Ninety-

Clay Pittman seen here with the C-141 66-0177 on exhibit at the NMUSAF, known as the Hanoi Taxi.

Clay Pittman has been a professor at Sinclair Community College since 2014 as the chair of the Aviation Technology Department. He has led the department through a rapid expansion its programs, facilities, and staff. This included the creation of the first two community college bachelor's degrees in the state of Ohio.

Clay has over 9300 hours of flight time in multiple types of Air Force heavy transport aircraft which includes 4200 hours in C-141B/C aircraft and 275 hours in the Hanoi Taxi *(66-0177).*

seven of the women in this first class graduated with the class of 1980. Despite inclusion as cadets, women were still excluded from combat roles. Combat exclusions had been in place since 1948, claiming to protect women from work situations deemed unsuitable. Although new rules and regulations were modified over time, it was not until April 1993 that the first three women were approved for fighter pilot training, although the combat exclusion policy would not be completely overturned until 2013. All military occupations would finally be open to women as of January 2016.

The issue of integration had been with the USAF since its inception. The USAAF had operated under the army's segregated policies so that technical training at Chanute Field, Illinois, and pilot training at Tuskegee, Alabama, were segregated although policy directed that facilities, equipment, training, and living conditions would be identical to other training. The service of the segregated squadrons indicates that, so far as training is concerned, Black pilots were fully prepared for the job at hand.

The formation of the USAF came at the same time the president, Congress, and senior military officers considered the issue of race in the postwar military. As might be expected, opinions differed, but in the USAAF, it became problematic to keep two air forces separate but equal. The first air force chief of staff, Gen. Carl Spaatz argued that the air force must "eliminate segregation" and use all personnel "for any duty…for which they may

USAF tanker boom operators flying in Boeing KC-135 aerial tankers.

TSgt Krista Guillotte (left) and SSgt Emily Ehrhart.
121st air refueling wing at Rickenbacker Air National Guard Base, near Columbus, Ohio. With the 166th air refueling squadron, they reprise the famous photo of WASP aviators made during World War II on the same airbase ramp.

qualify." Secretary of the air force, Stuart Symington, along with a strong group of advisors, concurred. President Truman's Executive Order 9981 required equal treatment for all military personnel regardless of "...race, color, religion, or national origin."

In a perfect world, that would have been the end of the desegregation of the Air Force. And to be sure, as early as 1949, African American pilots, officers, and enlisted personnel could be assigned to units based entirely on the needs of the service. But the blacks only units were not immediately disbanded. It took another three years to disband all the segregated units. The desegregation of the Air Force took place at a time attitudes were being challenged and the Truman administration promoted

equitable policies, but a significant number of officers opposed desegregation. Framing it as a simple matter of practicality, there was simply no way to have segregated units and a common purpose at the same time, helped ease the transition yet slowed it. Still, by 1952, the USAF had been fully integrated.

Integration did not mean immediately lead to color-blindness or equality in treatment. The USAF, as an extension of a diverse cultural America, has continued to deal with issues of race, perceived and real. A recent Racial Disparity Review conducted by the office of the Inspector General, identified sixteen separated areas in which African American airmen of all ranks might experience some type of discrimination which required

Leading a USAF Heritage Flight is the Lockheed F-35, followed by a Douglas A-1 Skyraider *and a North American P-51* Mustang.

Banking away from the setting sun, a USAF F-35 displays a dramatic afterburner air-show pass.

remediation. A second review went further to look into the possibility of discrimination among other ethnic groups such as, but not limited to, Hispanics, Asians, and Native Americans. The second study also examined gender equality, noting that a full third of all women airmen reported they had experienced some sort of sexual harassment at some time in their career. A high number, when asked anonymously, responded that they had not reported incidents because they feared negative consequences for having done so.

The conclusions reached by both studies noted that addressing issues of Diversity, Equality, and Inclusion would be an ongoing issue for the USAF. Recommendations asked for both continued and increased awareness including civilian participation in oversight activities.

The CV-22 Osprey is a tiltrotor aircraft that combines the vertical takeoff, hover, and vertical landing qualities of a helicopter with the long range, fuel efficiency, and speed characteristics of a turboprop aircraft. Its mission is to conduct long-range infiltration, exfiltration, and resupply missions for special operations forces.

The Osprey at the Museum was originally built as a preproduction aircraft for the US Navy (serial number 165839). In 2005 this aircraft was modified into a CV-22B and was designated an additional test asset (ATA). At Edwards AFB, California., it flew more than 200 developmental test missions. Transferred to the US Air Force in 2007, it received the serial number 99-0021 and was assigned to the 413th Flight Test Squadron, at Hurlburt Field. Completing over 400 additional test missions, it was flown to the Museum in December 2013.

The aircraft on display (S/N 91-4003) was one of nine F-22s built for engineering, manufacture and development (EMD) testing, and it rolled off the Lockheed Martin assembly line in Georgia on May 22, 1999. Assigned to the 412th Test Wing at Edwards Air Force Base, California, the aircraft made its first flight on March 6, 2000. After completing its phase in the test program, this aircraft came to the Museum in January 2007. It is painted to represent an F-22A flown by the 1st Fighter Wing at Langley Air Force Base, Virginia.

A few words from the Museum Director

Mr. David Tillotson, III

On behalf of the entire staff of the National Museum of the US Air Force, I want to thank you for your interest in this historical milestone in museum history. Much has changed over the last 100 years, but we continue to hold true to our mission to collect, research, conserve, interpret and present the Air and Space Forces' history, heritage and traditions.

One of the most frequent questions we are asked is "how can the National Museum of the USAF be older than the Air Force itself?" On the heels of World War I, American engineers were eager to improve on the technology of aircraft engines. In 1923 the museum started as a small engineering study collection and quickly grew to the world's largest military aviation museum. It is now a world-renowned center for air and space power technology and culture preservation.

Throughout this book you'll get a look at the tremendous

growth of our collection and campus over the last 100 years. With each new artifact or aircraft that has been added to the collection comes a tremendous sense of responsibility to honor our nation's Airmen and Guardians, and to share the rich heritage of the U.S. Air Force as it executes its mission to Fly, Fight and Win... Airpower Anytime, Anywhere.

As you look at the pictures, it's not hard to see why our aircraft often garner the greatest attention from visitors when they walk through the doors. Coming nose-to-nose with the storied Memphis Belle™ or walking aboard the historic SAM 26000 which carried President Kennedy's body from Dallas, Texas are experiences that can easily take your breath away.

The stories of the more than the 350 aerospace vehicles and thousands of artifacts in the museum immerses our visitors in our proud history and preserves it for

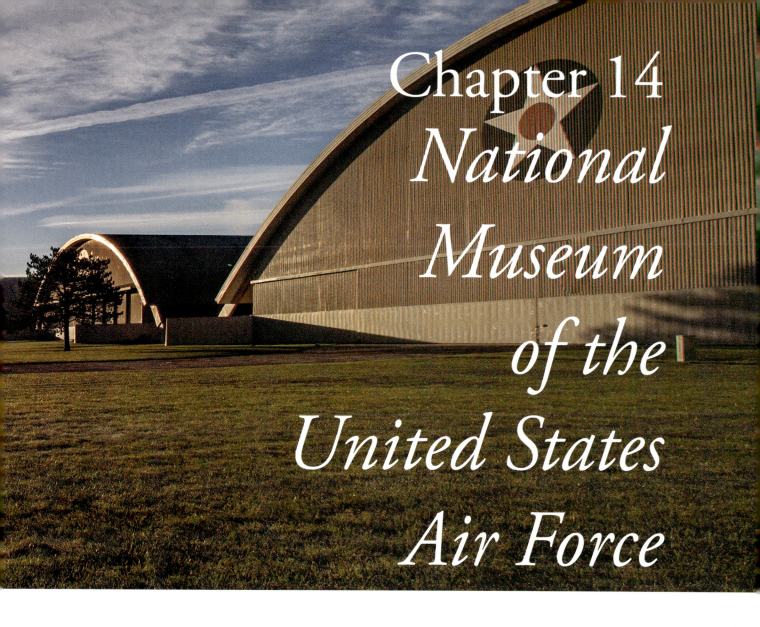

Chapter 14
National Museum of the United States Air Force

generations to come. But to us, these stories are about more than hardware. When we tell these stories we are also telling the stories of our nation's Airmen and Guardians, for they are the backbone of our past and the bedrock of our future. The stories of the brave men and women who proudly wear the uniform of our nation's Air and Space Forces are what are truly remarkable. Whether they are stories of wartime accomplishments and heroic actions, or day-to-day achievements that build to broader successes, they are the stories make our Air and Space Forces what they are today: ready, resilient, and capable. They are the stories of the men and women who raised their right hand and pledged an oath to a cause greater than themselves. Our museum staff and volunteers are dedicated to telling their stories in a way that resonate with all museum visitors.

Whether your last visit to the museum was last month, last year or longer, I encourage each of you to visit us again soon. The changes here are happening fast, and thanks to the hard work of our staff there is always something new to see when visiting the museum.

What began as a small display in a corner of a hangar of the Aeronautical Engineering Center in 1923, at McCook Field in Dayton, Ohio, is now the largest military aviation museum in the world, as well as the oldest. Known originally as the Engineering Division Museum, that small display preserved and collected artifacts of aviation technology from the United States and other nations, particularly from the World War. The original collections were largely hit or miss depending on what might have been available. In 1927, the museum, now known as the Army Aeronautical Museum, moved

The hangars at McCook Field were the first home of the Engineering Division Museum, which began collecting and preserving flying history.

A lineup of very early and very rare aircraft.

Wright Field opened in 1927 and everything from McCook Field found a new home. This elegant building was the first purpose-built home of the Museum. This building still exists, although repurposed around the time of World War II. It can be seen along Springfield Street. in the famous original downtown *section of Area B.*

to Wright Field east of Dayton, occupying some 1,500 square feet of a laboratory building. The small space did not allow for full display of the aircraft in the collection, so much so that most of the aircraft had to be displayed without wings. By 1935, the inadequacy of the small space led to the creation of a new museum, specifically designed to house the expanded collection. The new museum opened the next year with a collection of 2,000 items on display. As the base expanded and the threat of war loomed, the museum closed, the collections relegated to long-term storage until after the war.

In the 1950s the Museum reopened after the pause created by the war, housed in this building until the present Museum was built and opened in 1971. Much of the collection was displayed outside the building.

Aircraft displays were limited by ceiling height and building support columns.

The new US Air Force Museum opened in 1971 and was dedicated by President Richard Nixon. The XB-70 stood guard near the entrance for decades until it was moved to the Museum annex across the field. Museum visitors can now see the unique aircraft in Building 4 along with many other research and development aircraft.

It was 1946 before the idea of a new version of a museum took shape. An engine overhaul building at Patterson Field was designed as the home for the new facility. Mark Sloan was appointed curator and began for both the National Air Museum of the Smithsonian Institution and the Air Force Technical Museum. Opening the Museum was an arduous undertaking. It reopened to the public in April 1954, but still without complete aircraft on display. The building itself was inadequate to store aircraft indoors, leaving most of the collection outside to suffer the effects of the ever-changing Ohio weather.

Aircraft open events: In the fall of 2022 the Museum offered the opportunity to take a look inside the massive Convair B-36.

Building the Museum into what it is now came from a new source, the Air Force Museum Foundation, a group of private citizens led by Eugene Kettering, son of Charles Kettering, the famed automotive engineer and inventor. In 1964, the Foundation launched a $6 million fund-raising drive to build a new museum complex, beginning construction in 1970 and opening to the public in 1971. The new building, 800 by 240 feet, housed more than eighty aircraft on display, ranging from the Wright Type B Flyer to the Century Series jet fighters, including the Convair B-36, the largest piston-engine aircraft ever built and the

The Museum's education division offers a variety of hands-on workshops for visiting school groups. In the classroom/workshop students are building model rockets underneath a large- scale model of aviation pioneer Otto Lilienthal's glider.

295

In the early 1980s the Museum began installation of the Memorial Park in the open space at the southwestern end of Hangar 1. In 1984, Public Affairs Director Dick Baughman asked author/photographer of this book Dan Patterson to create some photographs for a promotional brochure. Interested groups and organizations were already requesting information about spaces and details.

The direction was to make some photos of a World War II veteran and a grandchild. "My dad, Bill Patterson, was a veteran who had served with the US Army Air Forces and I also had a 4-year-old-son, Nate, who loved a visit

to the Museum." The trip to the Musuem and the Park are shown here, along with some very recent photos of the now mature trees which have transformed the open field into a very pleasant place of reflection.

largest then housed inside a museum. Additional buildings, including an expanded administration and visitors' center and a much larger hangar facility, were complete by 1988. Total floor space to display and house aircraft had now risen to 10.5 acres, making the Museum the largest of its kind. Additional storage and renovation facilities occupied other areas of the base.

In the 1990s, as the Museum approached the 50th anniversary of the US Air Force, a number of new developments made the facilities more accommodating for visitors and enhanced the experience. A new IMAX theater, an expanded bookstore, and additional and updated space to house collections added to the attractiveness of the Museum to the general public. At the turn of the 21st century, the Museum supported any number of USAF and Department of Defense museums nationwide through loans of artifacts and aircraft. A collection of more than 50,000

artifacts, of which no more than 10 percent can be displayed at any given time, allows the staff of more than 100 and 300 volunteers to keep the Museum's displays fresh, constantly renewing interest.

The importance of Wright-Patterson AFB as a part of the United States' presence in world affairs became fully evident when the base was chosen to host the peace conference to negotiate an end to the Bosnian War. On November 21, 1995, the parties agreed that there would be a single sovereign state, Bosnia and Herzegovina, divided into two parts according to ethnic majority, with a joint capital at Sarajevo. WPAFB was chosen for its accessibility and separation from any of the warring parties. The formal peace agreement was ultimately signed in Paris, France, but holding the discussions away from the homes of any of the participants and away from access to the press contributed to a relatively early agreement.

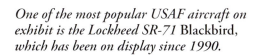

One of the most popular USAF aircraft on exhibit is the Lockheed SR-71 Blackbird, *which has been on display since 1990.*

Rocket workshop students ready to fly their creations in front of the Museum.

Part I
Collections

The Museum's collections hold a vast amount of artifacts, posters, publications, and photographs. This photo was created for the USAF 50th anniversary. Included here is a World War II flight jacket, and General Billy Mitchell's red pennant which he flew while bombing World War I battleships off the Virginia coastline. The medals in the center belonged to Don Gentile. To the left of those are photographs from the Wright demonstration of their military Flyer at Fort Myer, Virginia.

Right: An early version of a USAF spacesuit for the DynaSoar program.

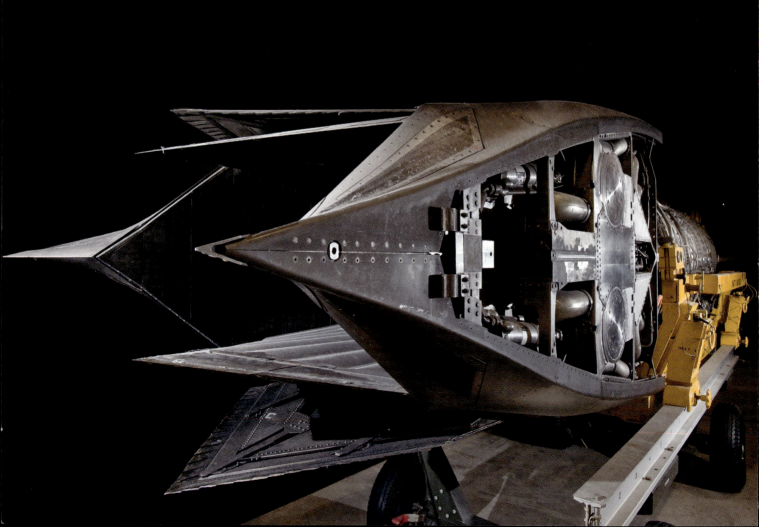

Collections include the hundreds of aircraft owned and maintained by the Museum, including all the aircraft and associated equipment which is on loan to museums across the USA and around the world.

The Martin B-10 is the only remaining example of the US Army Air Corps first all-metal bomber with retractable undercarriage, fully enclosed fuselage, and powered gun turrets.

The F-22's Pratt & Whitney F119-PW-100 turbofan engine of approximately. 35,000 pounds of thrust, each with afterburners and two-dimensional thrust vectoring nozzles.

The Northrop Grumman B-2 Spirit merged the high aerodynamic efficiency of the "flying wing" design with composite materials, special coatings, and classified stealth technologies. As a result, the B-2 became virtually invisible to even the most sophisticated air defense radar systems.

Piston-powered aircraft engines evolved into extremely complex multi-row in the endless quest to produce the power required to fly increasingly larger aircraft. The Wasp Major engine was developed near the end of World War II to power the Boeing B-50, an improved version of the successful B-29 Superfortress.

The R-4360 is a 28-cylinder, air-cooled radial engine that produces a maximum of 3,500 hp and weighs approximately 3,500 pounds.

303

The staff of any museum are who brings the institution to life. The staff and volunteers of the National Museum of the United States Air Force are the beating heart of this musuem.

Speaking now as not only the author and photographer of this book, but as a lifelong resident of Dayton, Ohio I grew up at this museum. I started taking the bus from the Greyhound bus station in Dayton, all the way to Fairborn (about 15 miles) when I was 11 or 12 years old. I learned years later that my Dad had taken the same bus to Fairborn to enlist in the Army Air Force after high school in 1944.

I returned often and after I started my career as a photographer and graphic designer I began to produce projects for the Museum. I got to know the staff and the leadership who built the national treasure it is today. I worked closely with Public Affairs Director Dick Baughman and the Musuem Director, Col. Dick Uppstrom. Their vision for the Museum has come to life.

The collections staff in a photo made for the Museum's 100th anniversary.
Front row: Melissa Shaw, Yvonne Gehring (Volunteer), Larry Skapin (Volunteer),
2nd row: Jennifer Myers, Amelia Fuller (Student), Alix Holmes (Student), Brett Stolle, Roberta Carothers,
3rd row: Trey Clifton (Volunteer), Sarah Sessions, Jeremy Gallogly, Jim Liddle (Volunteer), Tom Rohmiller (Volunteer), Krista Overman, Jackie Heiss, Jess Brinkman, Alyssa Edgington (Volunteer), John Luchin,
4th row: Sarah Sessions, Jeremy Gallogly, Jim Liddle (Volunteer), Tom Rohmiller (Volunteer, Krista Overman, Jackie Heiss, Jess Brinkman, Alyssa Edgington (Volunteer), John Luchin, Sherry Howard, Mike Rowland

Staff members come and go, and the folks seen here represent the staff as of May 2023. You'll notice that they all have a smile on their faces, which I know from getting to meet many of them is because they know the place they work is a world class museum.

MUO personnel Left to right: Tim Kolodziejczak, Jeff Becker (back), Ben Guptil, James Leach , Dennis Kleiner (back), Sam DeLong, Don Terpstra, Rob Hitchcock, Sean Landau (back, Mike Espedal, Dylan Spires, Caitlyn Riggs, Mark Murphy, Adam McFarland, Joe Shively

Special Events L-R: Danielle Almeter, Steve Jones Megan Helton, Lauryn Bayliff, JC Snediker, Taylor Gentry

MUA (Research Division) L-R: Ms. Christina Douglass, Manuscript Curator, Mr. Bryan Carnes, Research Curator, Ms. Meghan Anderson, Research Curator, Dr. Doug Lantry, Museum Historian and Research Curator, Mr. William McLaughlin, Reference Curator, Mr. Jim Liddle, Research Division Volunteer, Ms. Lonna McKinley, Acting Research Division Chief & Reference Curator, Mr. Wesley Henry, Retired Research Division Chief.

Museum Exhibits L-R: Caleb Still, Jerry Miracle, Bob Metering, Tony Cerra, Will Haas, Mitchell Dorsten, Quinton Johnson, Eric Infante, Bob Pinizzotto, Luis Machuca, Luke Maynard, Mike Foster, Steve Markman, Matt Card, Dave London

Museum Public Affairs L-R: Robert Bardua, Lisa Riley, Ken Larock, Ty Greenlees

Museum Management Support
L-R: John Marang, Deputy, Planning and Operations, Luke Liming, David Lockhart, IT (seated), Rick Bedwell, IT (standing), Francis Mathais, Human Resources (standing), Andrea Hall, IT (seated), Marzena Kluska-Maier, Finance(seated), Scott Rogers, Exec. (standing), Rob Aguiar, Management Support (standing), Mark Wertheimer, Plans & Programs (standing)

Education
L-R : Patrick Hannon, John Duren Jacob Monroe, Mike Brimmer

Part II
Restoration

The Museum's single-seat F-15A, nicknamed Streak Eagle, *broke eight time-to-climb world records between January 16 and February 1, 1975. In setting the last of the eight records, it reached an altitude of 98,425 feet just 3 minutes, 27.8 seconds from brake release at takeoff and "coasted" to nearly 103,000 feet before descending. It was flown in its natural metal finish to reduce weight for the record-setting flights. It is currently being returned to its natural metal configuration.*

Restoration Staff L-R: Francis Lymburner (Volunteer), Garry Guthrie (Volunteer), Willie Crawford (Volunteer), Tom Gardner (Volunteer), Ron Hunt (Volunteer), Larry Furrow (Volunteer), Zach Hunt (Restoration Specialist), Jason Davis (Restoration Supervisor), Joe Schoenling (Restoration Specialist), Brian Lindamood (Restoration Specialist), Chase Meredith (Restoration Specialist), Duane Jones (Restoration Specialist), Roger Brigner (Restoration Specialist), Casey Simmons (Restoration Project Lead), Brian Neill (Restoration Specialist), Matt Gideon (Restoration Specialist), Adam Naber (Restoration S, Elwood Dornbusch (Volunteer), Nick Almeter (Restoration Specialist/Bio-Environmental Manager), Bob Rehmert (Volunteer Coordinator), Tim Ward (Volunteer), Dale Burnside (Volunteer), Roger Deere (Division Chief)

Streak Eagle *from above displays the broad structure of the F-15.*

307

Special Air Mission 26000

The military version of the Boeing 707 and the first jet aircraft used by American presidents. Flown to the Museum in the colors of the USAF Executive flight wing. It was taken off exhibit in 2009 and totally restored to its configuration in the fall of 1963.

Restoration specialist Geno Toms applies the presidential seal to the repainted aircraft.

The aircraft elements which are unpainted required a complete polish, here being applied by Gerald Ewing.

Restoration specialists masking the underside of the starboard wing to apply the USAF national markings.

The painting crew (restoration staff) dressed for the job.

As parts of the aircraft were getting the final paint, previously finished elements must be masked and covered.

308

First Lady Jacqueline Kennedy worked with legendary designer Raymond Lowey to create the now-iconic look of the Presidential aircraft. The restoration staff accessed the original design studies to ensure the accuracy of the restoration.

The completed SAM 26000 rolled out and being towed back to exhibit in the Museum's annex. The newest structure, building Number, 4 now holds the Presidential Collection.

Boeing VC-137C SAM 26000

The Boeing VC-137C on display was the first jet aircraft built specifically for use by the President of the United States. During its 36 year flying career, it carried eight sitting presidents and countless heads of state, diplomats, dignitaries and officials on many historic journeys known as Special Air Missions (SAM).

On Oct. 10, 1962, the Boeing Co. delivered to the Air Force a highly modified civilian 707-320B airliner, serial number 62-6000. Bearing the unique call sign SAM Two-Six-Thousand, this aircraft illustrated the Air Force's commitment to providing safe, reliable and comfortable air transportation for the president and other key personnel to locations anywhere around the globe. Whenever the president was onboard the aircraft, the call sign changed to "Air Force One," a special designation established in 1953 to avoid confusion with other aircraft in flight.

At the request of President Kennedy, a new paint scheme was developed by First Lady Jacqueline Kennedy and famous industrial designer, Raymond Loewy. In addition to the vibrant blue and white colors, the words "United States of America" were emblazoned in tall letters along the fuselage and an American flag was placed on the tail. These distinctive markings reflect the stature of the Office of the President and serve as a highly visible symbol of American prestige.

The Boeing B-17F Memphis Belle was brought to the Museum in 2005 for preservation and restoration. The famous bomber had been exhibited outdoors in Memphis for decades and was in very poor shape. The airframe required a complete disassembly and corrosion mitigation before it could be returned to its combat appearance, which was an over-10-year undertaking.

Eventually the bomber began to take familiar shape. The Museum's dedication to accuracy is to ensure that an exact record example of the thousands of B-17s flown in World War II exists for display, but also for future research.

Restoration specialist Casey Simmons repaints the crew details and the iconic nose art.

When the Memphis Belle was towed across the grounds of historic Wright Field there was a moment when the Museum's previously exhibited B-17G Shoo Shoo Shoo Bay stood nose to nose. The B-17G was also restored to record copy status by a volunteer crew at Dover AFB before being flown to the Museum in 1988. Shoo Shoo Shoo Baby will be on exhibit soon at The National Air & Space Museum satellite facility Udvar-Hazy at Dulles Airport. Both of these 8th Air Force veteran bombers have extensive combat records.

The Museum's very early Curtiss JN-4 Jenny is being totally restored by restoration specialists. The aircraft's wooden structure has been refinished or re-created if necessary. Irish linen was imported to assure that this over-100-year old US Army Air Service aircraft is also a record copy.

Curtiss JN-4D Jenny

The Curtiss Jenny became America's most famous World War I training airplane. Generally used for primary flight training, some Jennies were equipped with machine guns and bomb racks for advanced training.

The JN series began by combining the best features of the Curtiss "J" and "N" models. A 1915 version, the JN-3, supported Pershing's Punitive Expedition into Mexico in 1916, but the aircraft proved unsuitable for field operations. Curtiss improved the JN-3 and redesignated in the JN-4.

With America's entry into WWI on April 6, 1917, the Signal Corps ordered large quantities of JN-4s, and by the time production was terminated after the Armistice, more than 6,000 had been delivered, the majority of them JN-4Ds.

After WWI, the Army sold hundreds of surplus JN-4s to civilians. The airplane soon became the mainstay of the "barnstormers" of the 1920s, and many Jennies continued flying into the 1930s.

The JN-4D on display was obtained from Robert Pfeil of Taylor, Texas, in 1956.

Part III
Air Force Museum Foundation

The Air Force Museum Foundation, Inc., is a private non-profit organization dedicated to the development and expansion of the Museum's facilities, and to assisting the Museum in its efforts to inform and educate the public about the history and role of the Air Force.

The Foundation raises funds through donations, planned giving, and major gifts handled by the Development department, and operations such as the Museum Store, Air Force Museum Theatre, Attractions including flight simulators, the Launchpad Café, and an Events department that helps individuals and organizations host events at the Museum. Since its incorporation in 1960, the Foundation has gifted $87.3 million to the Air Force for construction of the Museum's buildings – 94% of the total cost. In addition, the Foundation provides financial support for the Museum's programs – contributing $1.5 million in 2022. To date, total funding provided totals nearly $100 million.

The Foundation was incorporated in 1960. The first Board meeting was held in March 1962, and it decided to raise approximately $6 million for the construction of a new Museum building on space set

Foundation Staff

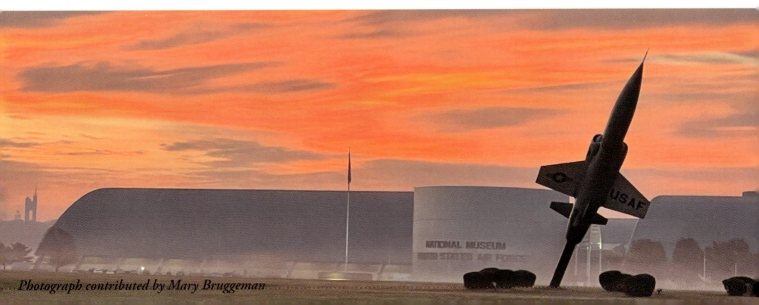

Photograph contributed by Mary Bruggeman

Wright Modified "B" Flyer

The airplane on display was used for flight instruction by Howard Rinehart at Mineola, New York, in 1916. It appears here almost exactly as it did when it was last flown by Lt. John A. Macready during the International Air Races at Dayton, Ohio, in October 1924. It was acquired by the Air Force Museum Foundation and donated to the Museum.

In 2011 the Radio City Rockettes *visited the Museum and made some appearances to support the Foundation.*

aside by the Air Force. On June 3, 1970, ground was broken at the site, and on September 3, 1971, President Richard Nixon formally dedicated the new Museum facility. In 1975, the Foundation funded construction of an addition to house a new Museum entrance, improved café, and larger gift shop. The facility was completed in 1976 and opened to the public in April.

In the early 1980s the Museum approached the Foundation about funding a second building. Groundbreaking took place in October 1985, and ribbon cutting for the second building, housing the Korea and Southeast Asia War galleries, took place in April 1988.

The 1990s saw the Foundation enhancing the visitor experience by undertaking the construction of an IMAX theater that was presented to the USAF and opened to the public in May 1991. And the Museum Café, built in 1976 and showing its age, underwent a nearly one-million-dollar renovation in 1996.

In 2003 the museum opened its third building – the Eugene W. Kettering Cold War Gallery, named for the first chairman of the Foundation Board. In 2004 the Missile and Space Gallery (now simply the Missile Gallery) opened. The Foundation funded roughly $24 million for these two projects.

During 2013 the IMAX theatre underwent an $800,000 upgrade and conversion to a 400-seat digital theatre. On June 8, 2016, the Museum opened the 224,000-square-foot fourth building. The $40.8 million cost was funded by the Foundation. The building houses the Space (separated and expanded from

318

The Museum features the vast aircraft model collection of Eugene Kettering, an early supporter of the Air Force Museum Foundation. The over 500 models are all handmade and in scale with each other, providing a very visible history of flight from the earliest days until Mr. Kettering passed away, in 1969.

In 2013 the Foundation's digital theatre received a new high-resolution screen and enhanced sound system.

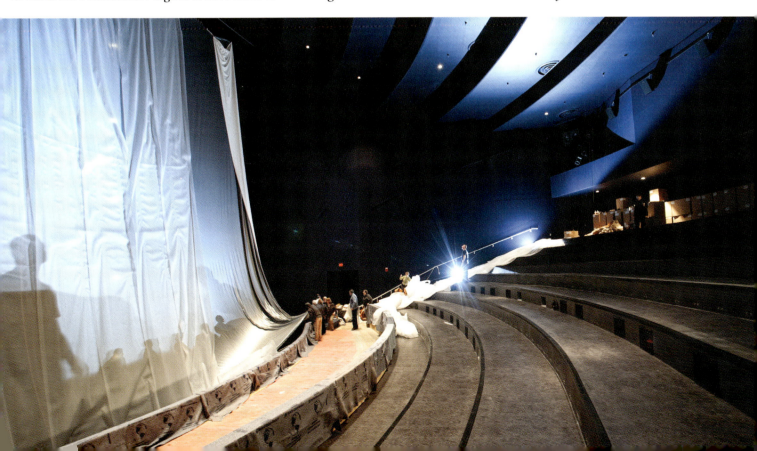

The Foundation encourages families from across the USA and from across the globe to visit the Museum and experience the American History that flies, represented by the collection of aircraft and exhibits. Here a family stops in front of the F-22 Raptor, the Wright Modified "B" Flyer overhead.

Full-motion flight simulators have added to the experience for kids of all ages.

the Missile Gallery) and Global Reach galleries, as well as the Presidential, and Research and Development galleries, and three science, technology, engineering, and mathematics (STEM) Learning Nodes. Also, to mark the 75th anniversary of D-Day in 2019 the Foundation presented D-Day: Freedom from Above, an exhibit enhanced by interactive augmented reality.

In 2021 the Foundation began funding special exhibits to attract visitors who might not otherwise come to the Museum. And beginning in 2022 the Events division organized adult-only After Dark events, offering visitors the opportunity to enjoy the Museum's galleries and exhibits in a more relaxed, kid-free atmosphere during the evening.

The uniform and hat that belonged to Lafayette Escadrille pilot Ted Parsons, along with a flying helmet from the squadron. On top of Parson's logbook are fellow pilot William Thaw's pocket altimeter and a French air force pilot's wings.

Facing page: Under the memorial near Paris there is a crypt where many of the Escadrille pilots are entombed. There are XX sarcophagi which fill the crescent shaped crypt, although many of the pilots are interred in other locations. Norman Prince is entombed in the National Cathedral in Washington D.C.

Epilogue

The archival photo you see here, is the same image on Page 35, and allows us to complete our circle of history. The USA entered the war in April of 1917, but Americans had been part of the air war well before then, fighting with and for France since the war began in 1914.

The five pilots in the photo were the beginning of a a squadron of American volunteer pilots who would fight for France in what would be known as the Great War or World War. This squadron would be known to history as the Lafayette Escadrille, named for the French aristocrat who lent his military talents to the new United States during the American Revolution. Of the five in this photo, only the commander, Captain Georges Thenault (center) survived to the end of 1916.

The Escadrille pilots, the first Americans to fly in combat, were motivated by the novelty and thrill of flight, the danger of combat, and the duty to help the French preserve the future of their democracy against German aggression. It turned out to be a heady combination, one they embraced even though the chance of death loomed increasingly possible as they added to their list of sorties.

On April 20, 2016, France celebrated the centennial of the formation of the Escadrille. The men who volunteered to die for France are once again revered by a grateful

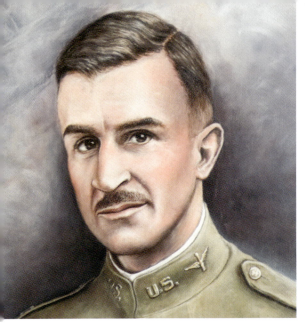

James Norman Hall joined the squadron after being dispatched to France to write an article about the unit for the Atlantic magazine. He survived the war after being shot down twice and was also a prisoner of the Germans.

His daughter Dorothy is seen here with her husband Nick Rutgers at the dedication of an exact replica of James Norman Hall's SPAD XIII.

Lt. Col. Nick Rutgers III flew F-15 Eagles with the Oregon Air National Guard until 2021. Seen here in front of one of the F-15s he flew and holding a die-cast model of an American Air Service SPAD XIII similar to the ones his great-grandfather flew over the battlefields of the Great War.

nation. In a leafy green park outside of Paris and close to Versailles the memorial created to honor these pilots had been fully restored to its original glory. The stone arch, a half-sized replica of the Arc de Triomphe, now gleams in the Paris springtime, celebrating the role of American names etched into the surface. The locations of the battles in which they flew, fought and died are memorialized as well.

The meadow in front of the memorial was arranged with seating for dignitaries and most importantly the descendants of the original 38 American pilots. The families came from the USA and across Europe.

Many of the family members are also aviators who carry on the legacy established 100 years before. Many had never met their contemporaries with who they shared a common bond and here they gathered. Some of the names were the same on the monument. Thenault, Lufbery, Rockwell. Other names different due to 100 years of family history. De Ramel descended from Norman Prince, Rutgers from James Norman Hall.

Regis and Guillaume De Ramel are the great grand-nephews of Norman Prince, who is pictured in the 1916 photograph and died in combat in October of that year. Both of them are aviators. Nick Rutgers III is the great grandson of James Norman Hall. Hall came to France to write an article about the Escadrille for The Atlantic magazine, and joined the squadron. He survived the war and wrote extensively about the grim realities of the newest form of men killing men . . . in the air.

After the war Hall had had enough

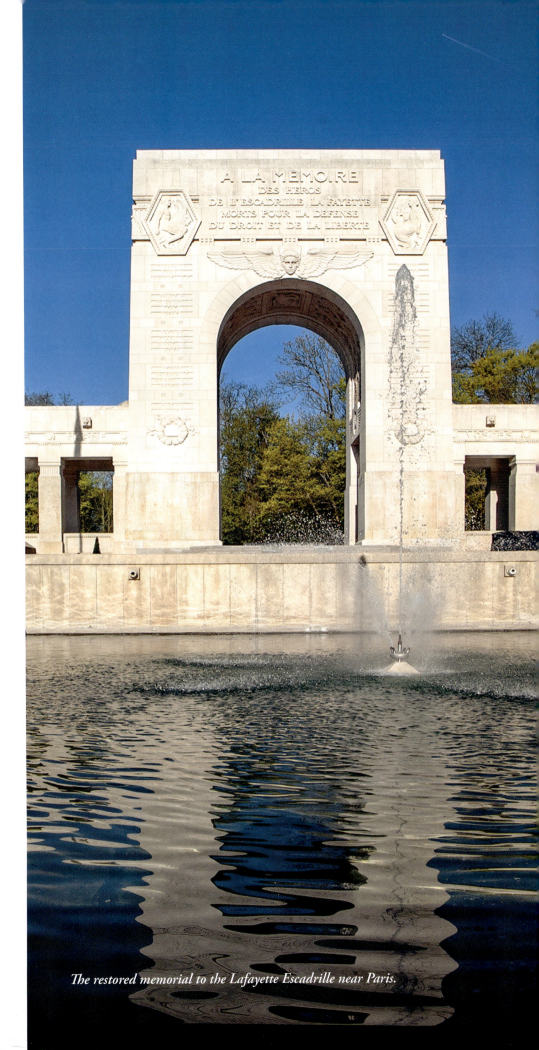

The restored memorial to the Lafayette Escadrille near Paris.

of western civilization and moved to the South Pacific to pursue his writing career. Along with Charles Nordoff he wrote the complete history of the unit, a two volume set. They also wrote the popular "Bounty" trilogy of the South Pacific which included "Mutiny on the Bounty," "Men Against the Sea," and "Pitcairn's Island." Hall lived out his life in the South Pacific and never flew again. His daughter, Dorothy was born there and married when she was 16 to Nick Rutgers.

During World War II Rutgers flew with the US Navy as a crewman on TBF Avengers. Their sons flew in Vietnam and Nick III was until recently an F-15 fighter pilot with the USAF and then in the Oregon Air National Guard and became the squadron commander.

Here in one family are 100 years of American military flying: World War One, World War Two, Southeast Asia, the Cold War and the 21st century. Nick told me that when he was training to fly the F-15, the tactics created by his great grandfather were the basis of being an effective and victorious fighter pilot. "Climb fast, keep the sun behind you and hit them just as fast."

LAFAYETTE ESCADRILLE MEMORIAL
APRIL 20, 2016
CHIEF JOHN YELLOWBRID STEELE
OGLALA SIOUX

TOUGHNESS
LEADERSHIP
BRAVERY
COURAGE
PROTECTION

In the documentary film, The Lafayette Escadrille, producers interviewed former USAF Chief of Staff, General Merrill McPeak, who stated that "these men are the very basis of all American combat flying".

The celebration at the memorial had a lineup of dignitaries from the USA and France who spoke. There was a large representation of the United States Air Force and the Armee" de la Air, the French Air Force. The USAF band and choir performed the "La Marseillaise" and the French band and choir performed the "Star Spangled Banner."

Speakers from both countries noted that the alliance between France and the USA is the longest standing alliance, going back in history to our Revolutionary War, well over 200 years.

Another dignitary approached the podium dressed in the traditional Sioux feathered war bonnet. Oglalla Sioux Chief John Yellow Bird Steele had been invited and came from Oklahoma. He spoke to the squadron symbol which was adopted by the unit, an American Indian with a very similar war bonnet. He addressed the controversy of the symbol from a century before was not "politically correct" in the 21st century. He spoke with eloquence and said that his nation was proud to have been the symbol as the values of the volunteers are the same as those of the Sioux warriors; Toughness, Leadership, Bravery, Courage, Protection.

Before the ceremonies concluded the memorial was overflown by the still active Sq. 24 of the French Air Force, their jet fighters flying in the 21st century with the same symbol on the tails as a century before, the Sioux warrior. Shortly after that the USAF thundered over with four Lockheed F-22s.

The ceremony completed, the restored memorial would be managed by the American Battle Monuments Commission, forever.

The circle had been completed.

Nick Rutgers visits with American Airlines captain George Thenault, the great grandson of the commander of the Escadrille.

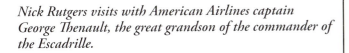

The combined bands of the USAF in Europe and the French air force.

French veterans parade with flags and battle streamers.

French Air Force Mirage 2000 fighters led by a specially marked aircraft commemorating the long-standing alliance between the USA and France, followed very quickly by a flight of F-22s from the same unit with which some of the Lafayette Escadrille pilots flew after the USA entered World War I.

After the ceremonies the descendants of the original thirty-eight pilots gathered in front of the memorial.

Two of the Mirage 2000 French jets which fly and honor the symbol and the legacy of the American pilots, a Sioux Warrior.

Bibliography

Air Force Museum Foundation. United States Air Force Museum. Wright Patterson Air Force Base, Ohio: The Museum, 1993

Anderson, David A. History of the U. S. Air Force. New York: The Military Press, 1981.

Apple, Nick and Gene Gurney. The Air Force Museum. Dayton, OH: Central Printing, 1991.

Beck, Alfred M. With Courage: The U. S. Army Air Forces in World War II. Washington, DC: Air Force History and Museum Program, 1994.

Berger, Carl. The United States Air Force in S. E. Asia. Washington, DC: Office of Air Force History, 1977.

Bowers, Peter M. Boeing B-17 Flying Fortress. Seattle, WA: Museum of Flight, 1985.

Boyne, Walter. The Smithsonian Book of Flight. Washington, DC: Smithsonian Books, 1987.

_____. Beyond the Wild Blue Yonder (Second Edition) A History of the United States Air Force. New York: Thomas Dunne Books, 2007.

Bryan, C. D. B. The National Air & Space Museum. New York: Harry N. Abrams, 1979.

Christy, Joe. American Air Power—The First 75 Years. Pennsylvania: TAB Books, 1982.

Cole, Goldberg, Tucker, and Winnacker. The Department of Defense, 1944-78. Washington, DC: Secretary of Defense Historical Office, 1978.

Controvich, James T. United States Air Force and its Antecedents. Lanham, MD: Scarecrow Press, 2004.
Copp, DeWitt S. A Few Great Captains. Garden City, NY: Doubleday & Co. 1980.
_____. Forged in Fire, Garden City, NY: Doubleday & Co., 1982

Craven, W. F. and J. L. Cate. The Army Air Forces in W. W. II. Washington, DC: Office of Air Force History, 1983.

Daso, Dik Alan. U. S. Air Force: A Complete History. Washington, DC: The Air Force Historical Foundation, 2006.

Dear, I.C.B. and M.R.D. Foot. The Oxford Companion to W.W. II. New York: Oxford University Press, 1995.
Ford, Daniel. Flying Tigers. Washington, DC: Smithsonian Institution Press, 1991.

Furrell. The U.S.A.F. in Korea. Washington, DC: Office of Air Force History
Gilster, Herman L. The Air War in S. E. Asia. Maxwell AFB, AL: Air University Press, 1993.

Goldberg, Alfred. A History of the United States Air Force. Princeton, NJ:Van Nostrand, 1957.

Hart, B. H. Liddell. History of the Second World War. London: Cassell, 1970.

Haulman, Daniel. The High Road to Tokyo Bay. Washington, DC: Center for Air Force History, 1993.

Home Field Advantage. Wright Patterson AFB, OH, Air Force History and Museums Program, 2004.

Hoyt, Edwin P. War in the Pacific. New York: Avon Books, 1991.

Inoguchi, Rikihei and Tadashi NAKAJIMA. The Divine Wind. New York: Bantam Books, 1978.

Jablonski, Edward, Air War. Doubleday, 2979

Josephy, Alvin M. The American Heritage History of Flight. New York: American Heritage, 1962.

Karnow, Stanley. Vietnam. New York: Viking Press, 1983.

Keegan, John. The Second World War. New York: Viking Press, 1990.

Keisel, Kenneth M. Wright Field. Charleston, SC: Arcadia Publishing, 2016.

Kennett, Lee. The First Air War 1914-1918. New York: Free Press, 1991.

Kester, Marissa N. There from the Beginning: Women in the US Air Force. United States: Air University Press, 2021.

Maksay, Kenneth, David Brown, and Christopher Shores, The Guinness History of Air Warfare. Enfield, Middlesex: Guinness, 1976

Manchester, William. American Caesar, Boston: Little, Brown, & Co., 1978.

Mason, Herbert Molloy. The U.S.A.F. – a Turbulent History. New York: Charter, 1976.

McCullough, David. Truman, New York: Simon & Schuster, 1992.

_____. The Wright Brothers. New York, Simon & Schuster, 2015.

Messimer, Dwight R. An Incipient Mutiny. Lincoln, NE: Potomac Books, 2020.

Micheletti, Eric. Air War over the Gulf. London: Windrow & Greene, 1991.

Miller, Roger G. Like a Thunderbolt, Washington, DC: Air Force History and Museums Programs, 2007.

Momyer, William W. Air Power in Three Wars. Washington, DC: Government Printing Office, 1983.

Nalty, Bernard C. Pearl Harbor and the War in the Pacific. New York: Smithmark, 1991.

Nicholls, Jack C. and Warren E. Thompson. Korea: The Air War 1950-53. London: Osprey, 1991.

Overy, R. J. The Air War 1939-45. New York: Scarborough Books, 1982.

Pimlott, John. Strategic Bombing. New York: Gallery Books, 1990.

Price, Alfred. The Bomber in W. W. II. New York: Charles Scribner's Sons, 1979.

Redding, Robert and Bill Yenne. Boeing, Planemaker to the World. New York: Crescent Books, 1983.
Rhodes, Richard. The Making of the Atomic Bomb. New York: Simon & Schuster, 1986.

Schlight, John. A War Too Long: The USAF in S. E. Asia. Air Force History and Museums Programs, 1996.

Sherry, Michael S. The Rise of American Air Power. New Haven, CT: Yale University Press, 1987.

Splendid Vision, Unswerving Purpose. Wright-Patterson AFB, OH: Air Force History and Museums Program, 2002.

Strategic Bombing Survey Teams. U. S. Strategic Bombing Surveys (Summaries). Maxwell Air Force Base, AL: Air University Press, 1987.

Taylor, John W. R. A History of Aerial Warfare. London: Hamlyn 1974.

Weigley, Russell F. Eisenhower's Lieutenants. Bloomington: Indiana University Press, 1981.

Weinberg, Gerhard L. A World at Arms. New York: Cambridge University Press, 1994

Wohl, Robert. A Passion for Wings. New Haven, CT: Yale University Press, 1994.

Wood, Tony and Bill Gunston. Hitler's Luftwaffe. New York, Crescent Books, 1979.

Yenne, Bill. History of the U. S. Air Force. Stamford, CT: Longmeadow Press, 1992.

Index

Note: Page references to photos are to the photos' captions. Page numbers in parentheses indicate intermittent references.

Acknowledgments

Dan and Clint have accumulated a long list of debts for this book and our other collaborations.

Rick Rinehart for his unwavering belief in this 2nd Edition. Brad Ball and Paula Allen for continual support and always new thoughts.

To the late Air Vice Marshal of the RAF, Ron Dick, whose contribution to the first edition of American Eagles served as the point of departure for this volume. His encyclopedic knowledge of the history of flight informed much of the text.

David Ferris, advertising executive and consummate professional, for bringing Dan and Clint together some thirty-five years ago.

Dan also wishes to thank:
My dear friend and mentor Dan Hutcheson. NMUSAF photographer Ty Greenlees, NMUSAF Videographer Ken Larock have been wonderful collaborators throughout this endeavor. Fully supported by the Museum Director Dave Tillotoson and his staff. Air Force Musuem Foundation Mary Bruggeman, Mary Fessler, Alan Armitage, Board Member Emeritus William Harrell

George Mongon, boundless energy and ideas . . . gone too soon.

Charles Carney who provided a unique idea.

My three adult children, who have lived through more than one of these experiences. Nate, Brigitta and Joe and their respective partners; Bailey, Rob, and Liz. Future creative person, Fela Patterson. My mom and dad, Bill and Jane Patterson . . . Dad showed me the way, Tom Patterson.

Cindy Ljungren, my soulmate in every way.

Collaborators and advisors, some from projects published previously which now can be found in used bookstores. Paul Perkins, Donald Nijbore, Kathy Fraser, Jon Denison, Stephen Quick, Nick Cosco, Trish Graboski, Paul Glenshaw, Darroch Greer, Dawne Dewey, Betty Darst, Ross Howell, Cargill Hall, David Tallichet, Clive and Linda Denney, Dave Barry, Bruce Zigler, Jim O'Neil, Tom Horton, Kurt Weidner, George Merva, Jon Gimpel, Larry Smith, Denise Stewart, Amanda Wright Lane, Stephen Wright, Dean Alexander,

Clint also thanks:
Mercer University, my academic home throughout my teaching career, particularly Dean Priscilla Danheiser of the College of Professional Advancement and Fred Bongiovanni, Chairperson of the Department of Liberal Studies. Their leadership and collegiality create an environment for academic excellence in and beyond the classroom.

My parents, Robert and Edith Terry, who taught me the power of words and that education barely begins in the classroom.

Marsha and Ellen Terry, for their love and support. Lt. Colonel Robert Michael Rives, USAF (ret), for his friendship and insight on so many things related to the military in general, and the USAF particularly.

NMUSAF photographer Ty Greenlees and Author/Photographer Dan Patterson

Author Clinton Terry